THE MILWAUKEE MILE

FRONT COVER: A.J. Foyt poses in the victory lane with chief mechanic George Bignotti as he accepts the Leader Card trophy after winning the 1962 Rex May Classic. Foyt and Bignotti, considered one of the all-time great chief mechanics, won numerous championships during their five years as a team. (Courtesy of Mark Wilke of Leader Paper Products.)

COVER BACKGROUND: Wisconsin State Fair Park Speedway is pictured during the early 1920s. The pace car to the left gives the green flag to drivers as they move out, ready to take each other on. The field of the day would have consisted of Chevrolets, Buicks, and a few imported makes as well. The grandstand is packed with spectators who have come to see the driving contraptions that many may only have heard of. (Courtesy of Milwaukee County Historical Society.)

BACK COVER: Modified stock cars are seen at the start of the 1962 race on the quarter-mile dirt track. Two by two, cars lap the track and inch their way ahead of the field. Modifieds had character, and the power to match. They were known for their painted personalities, and fans could not get enough. Favorites included "the Mouse," "the Cat," Etchie "the Flying Grandpa" Biertzer, and Fuzzy "the Hound" Fassbender. The drivers were as colorful as their cars. (Courtesy of Tom Trettin.)

The Milwaukee Mile

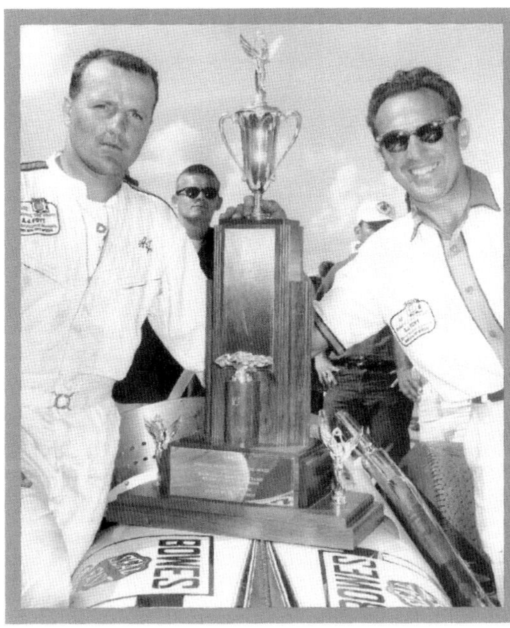

Brenda Magee
with a foreword by Michael Andretti

ARCADIA PUBLISHING

ISBN 978-1-4671-1422-6

Published by Arcadia Publishing
Charleston, South Carolina

Printed in the United States of America

Library of Congress Control Number: 2015930921

For all general information, please contact Arcadia Publishing:
Telephone 843-853-2070
Fax 843-853-0044
E-mail sales@arcadiapublishing.com
For customer service and orders:
Toll-Free 1-888-313-2665

Visit us on the Internet at www.arcadiapublishing.com

To my husband, Gerard, and daughter Devon, I give my heartfelt thanks for seeing this project through with me. Your support, encouragement, and belief in me—at times when I needed it most—have made this all possible. My love and thanks.

CONTENTS

FOREWORD

There is no experience like the feeling you get on race day. The electricity and excitement you feel when you step onto the track is unlike anything else. It runs deep. The drivers feel it. The fans feel it. It is awesome, and I would like as many people as possible to experience it.

My exposure to racing came out of growing up around the track, watching the drivers, cheering for my dad, my hero, Mario Andretti, and I knew I wanted to experience what they did; I wanted to be like my dad. To be a great driver, I had to commit myself wholeheartedly, there was no question. Above all, racing has to remain fun and challenging, and that is one of the things I like about the Milwaukee Mile. The Mile is fun to race, and if you can get your car through traffic, there is nothing like it. But that is just one aspect of the Mile that gives drivers the expectations they are looking for. The legend of the Mile is widely known, but for fans to have a track like this in their own backyard is just amazing. Who would ever expect Milwaukee's to be the oldest track in the world?

Next to Indianapolis, the Mile is the one racetrack that shares the tradition of Indy cars. It is vital to the sport and important for the series. The history, the legends, the experience, and the heritage—these would be terrible things to lose. I could not let that happen. Along with Andretti Sports Marketing, I decided to do what I could to bring Indy car racing back to Milwaukee, make it a successful event that both teams and fans would want to be a part of, and keep it on the schedule for many more years to come.

The Milwaukee Mile has a story to tell, one that is too important to lose.

—Michael Andretti

ACKNOWLEDGMENTS

The Milwaukee Mile has a very long history and an amazing story to tell, and although not comprehensive, this work could not have been accomplished without the help of many talented and knowledgeable people. I would like to recognize the individuals, clubs, groups, and organizations that have made this labor of love possible. I offer my sincerest thanks to the West Allis Historical Society and its members Eileen Clines, Ed Wilkommen, Devan Gracyalny, and Lila Roberts for their help and anecdotes. A big thank-you to Bryan Gapinski for his assistance. And to my go-to authority, Paul Elliott, my heartfelt appreciation for everything.

The Milwaukee Mile has carved a spot in the hearts of many of its fans and drivers, and I would like to thank the following individuals who are preserving motorsports history: John Surges and the Southeastern Wisconsin Short Track Hall of Fame, Jesse Gant and his Wisconsin Bicycle history, the Motorcycle Hall of Fame, and Ralph Hibbard Jr. of the Greenfield Gallery. Many thanks to Jim Liska, Billy Engelhard, Jerry Zimmerman, Jim Biever, Joe Stawicki, Gary Mitidiero of Midwest Vintage Racing, John Patrick of the Selvedge Yard blog, and David Morrill of Deadly Dave's blog.

Many memories were shared by the following race enthusiasts: David Hobbs, Vern Tretow, Nick Hoffman, Tom Poliak, Brian Caruso, George Wells, Malcolm Krause, Ron Thompson, and Jim Sauter Jr. A big thank-you to Russ Lake for capturing the memories, Mary Champion for her editorial contributions, and my most sincere appreciation to Mark Wilke of Leader Paper Products as well as David and Tana Marchese Salvaggio.

And lastly, to the men and women drivers who race for the checkered flag, and to the owners, crews, and promoters, all of you have sacrificed so much to live the dream and give auto sport fans some of the greatest memories they will forever cherish.

Images in this volume appear courtesy of the author's collection (AC), Arnold Nemitz (AN), Devon K. Magee (DKM), Tom Trettin (TT), Tom Poliak (TP), John Surges (JS), Barbara Bradshaw Hart (BBH), the Library of Congress (LoC), Mark Wilke of Leader Paper Products (MWLPP), Mark Dill of www.firstsuperspeedway.com (MD), Mike Bleisner (MB), Terry Thomas (TTa), Milwaukee County Historical Society (MCHS), Neil Tipton—track maps supplied by www.racingcircuits.info (NTRC), Russ Lake and Mary Champion (RL/MC), West Allis Historical Society (WAHS), Wisconsin Historical Society (WHS), Rob Heyen of www.earlyfordregistry.com (RH), Ralph Hibbard Jr., the Greenfield Gallery–Armin Krueger collection (GGAK), Brian Carusso (BC), George Wells (GW), and the Gene Crucean/Bob Sheldon collection. (GC/BS).

INTRODUCTION

There is a story to tell, one that spans over 138 years and, like all good stories, offers chills, spills, suspense, and disappointments. Legends and victories are part of the story as well, as are tragedies and rumors. This is the story of the Milwaukee Mile, and to appreciate all that it is and was, it is necessary to go back to when it was simply referred to as the Wisconsin State Fair Park Speedway.

From its humble beginnings, the track has served one purpose: *speed*. Originally built for harness racing in 1876 by George C. Stevens, a prominent breeder, to test Standardbred horses, the track was the scene of invitation-only contests including Milwaukee's tycoons and their investments. Breeding horses for pleasure and profit was a valued hobby amongst the well-to-do.

Not far from the Stevens farm stood Cold Spring Park, a 60-acre tract used for sporting events, agricultural exhibitions, and harness racing. Eventually outgrowing this site and eyeing a permanent location for the state's agrarian exhibitions, the Wisconsin State Agricultural Society negotiated the purchase of the Stevens farm.

September 12, 1892, marked the first year the Wisconsin State Fair was held at the new West Allis location. Harness racing was king, but not for long. The early 1900s brought several new varieties of competition. Bicycle, auto, and motorcycle races were now kicking up the dust, bringing a new and dangerous excitement to the track.

During the late 1890s and through the early 1900s, bicycle manufacturing hit its peak, making this era the golden years of cycling. A popular mode of transportation also regarded as a healthy activity, cycling prompted the formation of male and female cycle clubs, resulting in competitive teams that raced cross-country, grand prix–style, as well as on dirt tracks. The State Fair Park hosted several years of racing until dirt tracks fell out of favor after velodromes (wooden board tracks for both cycles and autos) sprang up.

Motorized vehicles, in their early stages, were somewhat foreign to the average person. Spectators packed the park's grandstand to watch these spectacles. The summer of 1903 featured the track's first auto race. For 50¢, spectators cheered as William Jones of Chicago raced his way around the dirt oval at a speed of 63.38 miles per hour in only 72 seconds. It is that date—Sunday, September 13, 1903—that has given the Milwaukee Mile cause to celebrate as the oldest continuously operating major speedway in the world. That weekend was truly a weekend of firsts, including the sport's first driver fatality: 23-year-old Frank Day, driving Ford's Yellow Arrow.

The early 1900s were a time of great experimentation, mechanical engineering, and bravery. One of the earliest mechanic/engineers of the day was Barney Oldfield, an automobile test driver for Henry Ford and Tom Cooper. Hooked during test trials, Oldfield turned to racing the vehicles he had a hand in developing. Part showman, part daredevil, Oldfield knew how to win and woo the crowd. His antics and good looks made him a legend, and winning at State Fair Park helped reinforce that legend.

Dreamers and drivers like Oldfield, Ford, and Cooper influenced the development of the four-wheeled machines they believed would change the world for the better. To prove the worthiness of these horseless carriages, inventors and mechanics conducted endurance races on dirt tracks nationwide. On September 20, 1907, Milwaukee had its day. Along with the standard 5-, 10-, and 15-mile races, a 24-hour endurance race was added. All makes and models of the era showed up, including Benz, Pope-Hartford, and Oldsmobile, to claim the prize, but it was the Locomobile, driven by Robert Drach and mechanic Fred Leiser, that endured the 993 miles, averaging 41.4 miles per hour. Not until 1915 would State Fair Park experience its first 100-mile race, with Louis Disbrow crossing the finish line at a speed of 62.5 miles per hour.

Auto race fans filled the grandstand to capacity, but harness racing continued. Like the automobile, these striking animals were bred to win. Names such as Dan Patch and Harvester drew spectators to the track to watch beauty in motion. Since both sports were using the track, updates and modifications were in order; spectator and driver safety was critical. Concrete barriers were installed where once dangerous wood and wire fencing had existed.

World War I touched lives worldwide, including in America. Although the Wisconsin State Fair and harness racing continued during wartime, automobile races were cancelled because of rubber and fuel rationing.

The 1920s certainly were roaring in Milwaukee, as well as in the rest of the country. Innovations both led and influenced the era. Airplanes were introduced at the fair as the future of travel and adventure. Death-defying wing walkers took off from and performed over the racetrack, unfortunately resulting in several accidents and leaving a negative image on the fair. This issue, coupled with several shoddy circuit promoters, pressed the state fair board to pursue a new direction.

After World War I ended, Tudy and Carl Marchese, auto mechanics at a local Ford dealership, were building a dirt race car in their garage during off hours. After several successful stints at the local dirt tracks, the team had reaped enough money to buy a "real race car"—a Miller special—and entered the Indianapolis 500 in 1929. Showing a respectable fourth-place finish, the Marcheses had become hometown heroes and were thought to be the right team to turn the troubled speedway around.

Shortly after, Tudy and Carl's brother Tom Marchese assumed responsibilities as fair promoter. The Sunday sprint car race on July 21 drew the largest crowd of the 1929 season. Gus Shrader won the 50-mile race, but Carl Marchese was close behind in second. Success seemed to follow Tom Marchese, and building on that, he was able to lock in AAA-sanctioned sprint car races for 1933. That same year, "big cars" made their debut at the track. One Monday-night race in particular is remembered: the rained-out Sunday race was cancelled, and Wilbur Shaw convinced Tom Marchese to run the race the following day, resulting in a rain date for that Monday evening, July 17, 1933, with Wilbur Shaw the winner.

By the mid-1930s, midget racing had made its way to the Midwest and was causing a ruckus. Recognizing the popularity of midgets, the state fair board added a cinder track in 1934 and Friday-night midget races. That season, Tony Willman was crowned the track's first midget champ. To benefit the sport and protect drivers and owners, a new sanctioning body—the Wisconsin Racing Association (WRA), now Badger Midget Auto Racing Association—formed in 1935 with Carl Marchese as president.

Impressed with Marchese's success, the state fair board offered Tom Marchese all midget promotional rights in 1938. Both big car and midget racing continued until World War II. During his 38-year tenure, Tom Marchese was responsible for attracting more annual national championship races than any other major track in the United States.

State fair billboards promised "something for everyone," and while most of the excitement was related to track activity, the infield had its own programming: circuses, football, and thrilling grandstand shows. The Green Bay Packers sparred against many of their NFL opponents on the infield. For 18 seasons, 1934–1951, the Packers split games between Milwaukee and Green Bay fields. Their most memorable game was in 1939 when the team hosted the New York Giants for the NFL championship game. In the match dubbed "the Dairy Bowl," the Packers were victorious over the Giants, 27-0.

With the outbreak of World War II, the world stopped, particularly for auto racing. August 24, 1941, marked the last AAA Indy car race (which Rex Mays won) until peacetime. The end of World War II signaled a return to normalcy, and that included race fever. The summer of 1948 marked the first year AAA-sanctioned stock-car races ran at the Wisconsin State Fair Park. Paul Bjork won the first major 100-mile stock-car race driving his 1948 Kaiser. Fans were hooked. No other sport could match the thunder and excitement of racing. But that day in June 1948 was remembered for much more; it was a day that endeared Rex Mays to Milwaukeeans and racing history. On June 6, 1948, Rex Mays risked his own life to save fellow driver Duke Dinsmore after Dinsmore was thrown from his car onto the track. Unfortunately, Mays lost his life in a similar accident a year later on November 9, 1949.

A 150-lap AAA stock-car race drew 33,131 spectators, all on their feet, to watch Myron Fohr from Milwaukee finish with an average speed of over 86 miles per hour. From 1952 through 1970, the State Fair Park promoted modified and full-bodied stock-car and Indianapolis-style champ car races. Both mile and quarter-mile race circuits drew thousands of fans, making Milwaukee one of the most popular and well-paid purse tracks. Postwar racing created a new breed of race drivers, heroes who were approachable and fan friendly, average guys more like their fans.

By mid-century, the race world recognized lost legends, renaming the June event the Rex Mays Classic, which ran from 1950 to 1987. Not everyone who raced at State Fair Park was legendary or remembered by name, but one in particular was Jim Rigsby. Rigsby, an Indy car and sprint driver, added his name to the record books on June 8, 1952, etching a track record of 102.13 miles per hour that stood until 1959. Stepping into a new era, the State Fair Park's track was paved with asphalt in 1954, and the following year, a new road course was created on the infield, generating its own fan base. Weekly contests featured modified race cars, painted in caricatures to capture drivers' personalities. Drivers like Miles Melius, Carl Kulow, Bill Bohn, and Paul Feldner dominated short track. A horrific road race accident in Europe convinced AAA that racing was a detriment to drivers' welfare, and it ceased as a sanctioning body. In its place, the United States Auto Club (USAC) came into being in 1956.

By the 1960s, almost every home had a television, and auto races were broadcast coast to coast, although on a very limited basis, creating new race fans. Television was great, but there was no substitute for the thrill at track side. The summer of 1962 saw rear-engine Indy cars compete for the first time in the Rex Mays Classic. Two years later, A.J. Foyt won the classic in his front-engine champ car; it was his fourth USAC win and was to be the last race for the roadster. However, in 1965, Foyt drove his front-engine dirt car in the Tony Betttenhausen 200 at State Fair Park since his Lotus-Ford arrived too late to qualify. Not one to sit the race out, he readied his car for pavement, qualified for pole position, and brought the fans to their feet, but he eventually finished second. By the end of the 1960s, rear engines were the choice of champions.

More changes came in the late 1960s: the track was repaved, and an enlarged pit lane eliminated the 1.2-mile road course and the quarter-mile oval. Leadership again changed when Tom Marchese sold partial interest in his Wisconsin Auto Racing Inc. to John Kaishian, a local short-track promoter who continued to book quality series as racing grew in popularity.

Stock-car fans packed the grandstand to see their favorite drivers. Predominant drivers of the 1960s and early 1970s included Don White, who set a record for the most wins (14) in State Fair Park history. Rick Mears made his first appearance in Milwaukee for the 1977 USAC stock-car race. The State Fair Park both made and hosted many of racing's legends, including Al Unser Sr. The 1970 Bettenhausen 200 found itself in the record books after Unser finished four laps ahead of the field.

Auto racing had always been a part of the Wisconsin State Fair, but the 1980s saw the elimination of auto racing during fair week because of noise and parking conflicts. Race days were scheduled throughout the season. NASCAR made its way to the track on May 13, 1984, when a new promoter, GO Racing, brought the first NASCAR Busch Sportsman Late Model Series to the speedway. It was won by Sam Ard, while Wisconsin natives Alan Kulwicki and Dick Trickle placed second and third respectively.

The year 1992 saw a new promoter, Carl Haas Racing. Driver and car owner Haas knew racing. Sensing the need for a new image, the State Fair Park Speedway was officially dubbed "the Milwaukee Mile." During the early 1990s, NASCAR returned to the Mile, remaining through 2009. In 1995, The NASCAR Craftsman Truck Series ran its inaugural season of the series; it also exited in 2009.

Following Haas's departure, the state fair board contracted, unsuccessfully, with several new track promoters and confirmed its decision to eliminate IndyCar and NASCAR races in 2010. Nagging financial issues rumored a track closure, while state and local supporters, including Historic Mile LLC, rallied to keep the track open during the pursuit of a new promoter. "Save The Mile" became a plea to save a legend. There would be no victory lap for the Mile unless someone stepped up to help.

And who better than someone who knows the Mile intimately—its every curve and straightaway, and the thrill of a win on this legendary oval? Michael Andretti and Andretti Sports Marketing have brought the Verizon IndyCar Series back to the Mile. Promoting Indy-style racing at the site is serious business for the Andretti Sports Marketing team, and thanks to ABC Supply Co., the race's title sponsor, and with support from Metro Milwaukee Honda Dealers, race fans can experience every emotion of an Indy-style race right in their own backyard.

There is no place like the Milwaukee Mile. It is a hard place to get right, and when you do, it's so rewarding.

—Ryan Hunter-Reay

Everyone goes to Milwaukee after Indy.

—Frank Capua (played by Paul Newman), *Winning*

We always seem to qualify well in Milwaukee in the Team Penske car, and I love racing there with all of the history.

—Helio Castroneves

It's important to me because I've had such great times there as a driver and team owner.

—Michael Andretti

Milwaukee is a real driver's track because it's flat and you have to drive the car hard.

—Will Power

I'm looking forward to going back to the Milwaukee Mile this weekend. The Mile is just one of those tracks where anything can happen, and it's always a great show for the fans, too.

—Charlie Kimball

It's always good to go back to Milwaukee, a place that you really have to drive the car hard and be on your toes 100 percent of the time.

—Tony Kanaan

It's a true driver's track.

—J.R. Hildebrand

1

Playground of the Rich and Famous

1876–1920

From its inception in 1851, the annual Wisconsin State Fair was held in several locations. Increasing attendance and agricultural entries demanded a permanent location. One such location was eyed in West Allis, Wisconsin. Six miles from Milwaukee lay a parcel of land owned by the widow Stevens, whose husband, George, had bred and raced his beloved Standardbreds. To feed his hobby, his private track offered invitation-only events for those who shared his passion. The purchase provided both a permanent annual state fair location and immediate revenue in the form of track receipts. Harness racing was a huge spectator sport at the time, and such names as Goldsmith Maid, Dexter, Dan Patch, and the Harvester, owned by August Uihlein, became household names. Harness racing was king, but not for long. September 1892 marked the first year the Wisconsin State Fair was held at its new West Allis location.

The turn of the 20th century exploded with new technology, influencing everyday life. The bicycle, retooled for performance and safety, made its way to the track and became a means to test man's strength and endurance. Challenged to go faster, ingenious dreamers created two-wheeled "motor-cycles," then four-wheeled horseless carriages. The State Fair hosted its first automobile race on September 11, 1903, and the first motorcycle race in 1905. Riders, wearing little more than shirts and knickers, straddled cycles branded with names like Indian, Jefferson, and Harley Davidson. Early motorcycle races fielded independent riders, but eventually champions signed onto factory teams, creating legends on two wheels.

Spectators packed the grandstand to see the likes of Barney Oldfield set a track record in 1910 with his Blitzen Benz, clocking over 70 miles per hour down the track. His friend and competitor Ralph DePalma won the inaugural State Fair Park championship in 1911. Both men frequently tested each other in 10-, 15-, and 25-mile heats. Ever the engineer, Oldfield showcased his Golden Submarine. Built by Harry Miller and Fred Offenhauser, the vehicle was completely enclosed, a safety feature Oldfield considered the wave of the future.

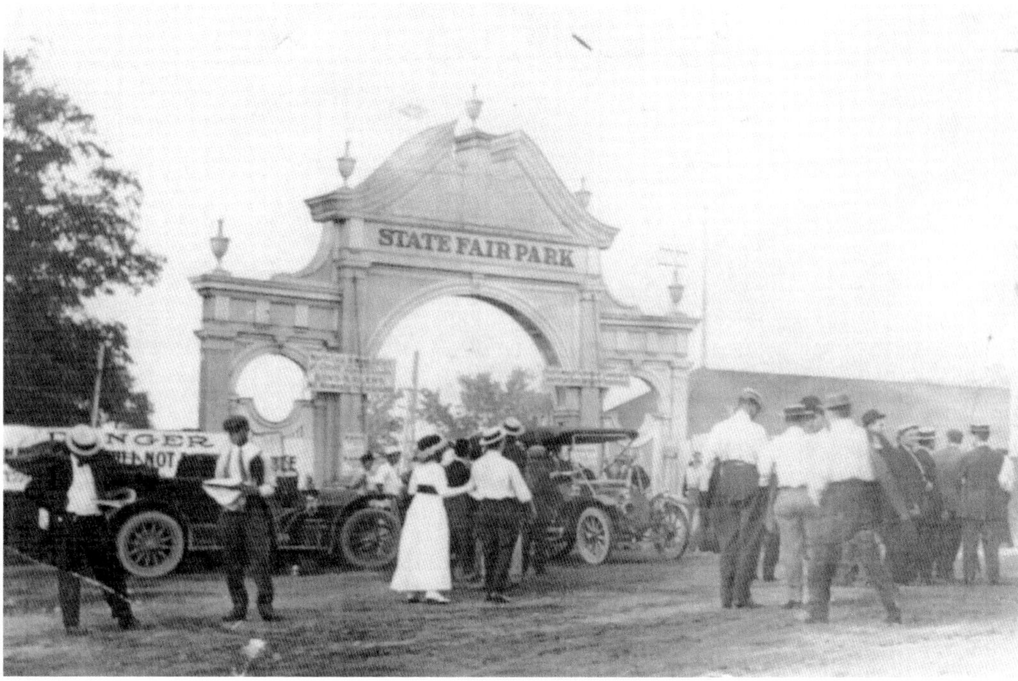

Sponsored by the State Agricultural Society, the first annual Wisconsin State Fair was held in Janesville, Wisconsin, in 1851, then rotated to different regions of the state, each season exceeding attendance goals. As fair attendance grew, the State Agricultural Society searched for a permanent location. September 12, 1892, marked the first year of the Wisconsin State Fair in its permanent home, located in West Allis, Wisconsin. (AC.)

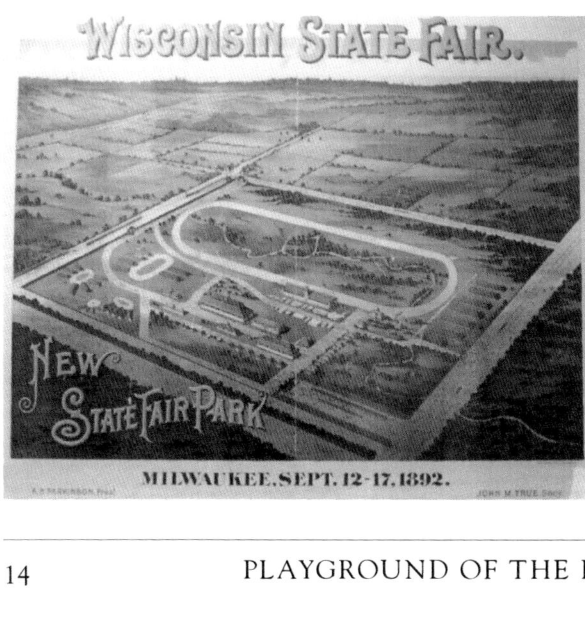

This is an artist's rendering of the proposed new Wisconsin State Fair in West Allis. The purchase of the George Stevens farm and harness track gave the fair a permanent location. This image depicts the park's development around the existing track. Six horse barns, enough to accommodate 100 horses, were erected at the first turn. The Cold Spring Creek is seen meandering throughout the track site, creating several engineering issues. (WAHS.)

In 1892, Wisconsinites were interested in the development of the "new mile trotting track" at the Wisconsin State Fair Park. This detailed sketch of the track's regulation pattern appeared in the September 3, 1892, *Wisconsin Farmer*. Designed to avoid abrupt transitions from straight stretches to turns and back again, the track, the first of its kind, promised the fastest times while allowing for an uninterrupted view by spectators and judges alike from start to finish. (WAHS.)

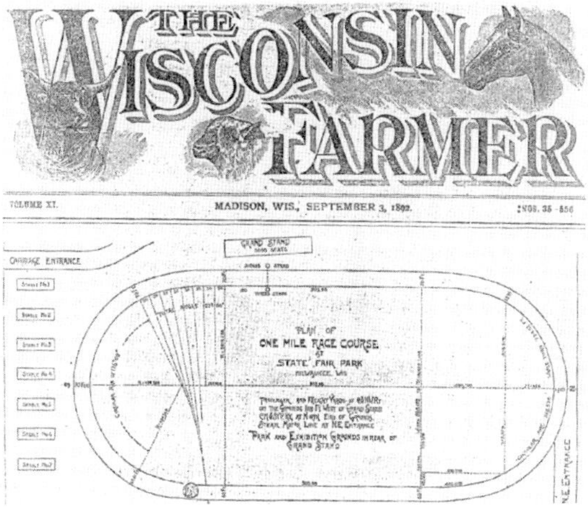

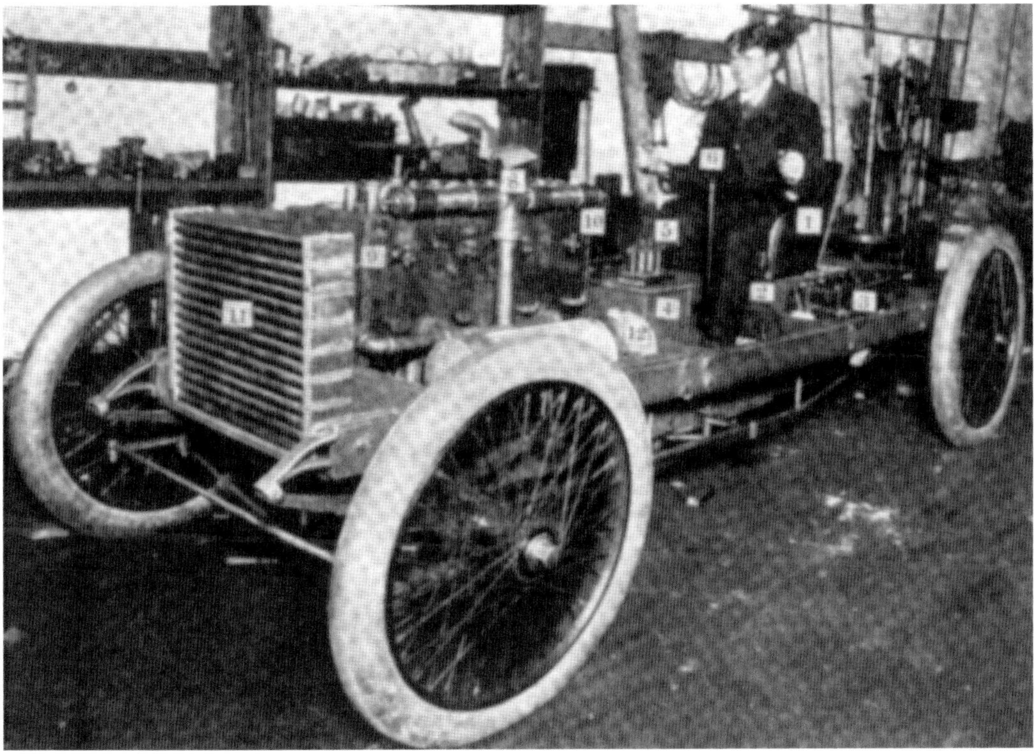

No need to check under the hood with this racer, everything is in plain sight with this perfect racing machine. Manufactured by Henry Ford and Tom Cooper, the bare chassis previewed in 1902 illustrates the sheer size of the vehicle. Barney Oldfield, Ford's driver, pitted the racer against American and European models. Usually victorious, each win validated the attributes of Ford's production vehicle. (LoC.)

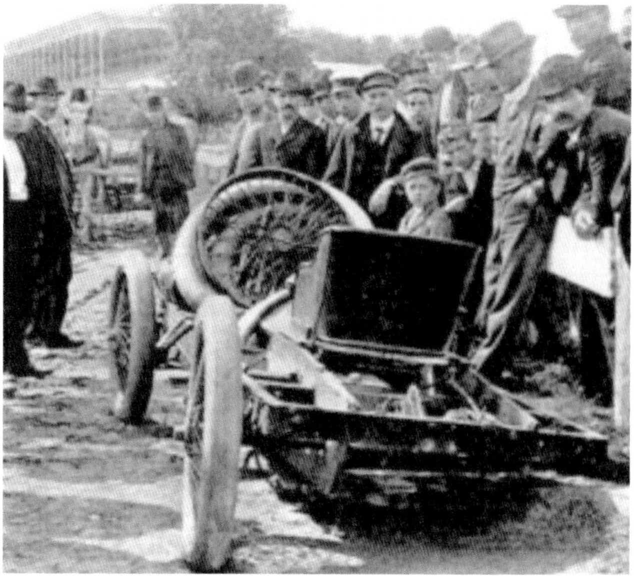

The first race at State Fair Park was in 1903. The track's first tragedy occurred on the same day, taking the life of 23-year-old Frank Day. Day was racing Ford's Arrow; although Tom Cooper owned the automobile, Ford retained promotional rights to the vehicle. After the accident, Ford purchased the vehicle, shipped it to Detroit, rebuilt it, and won a land-speed record two years later. (RH.)

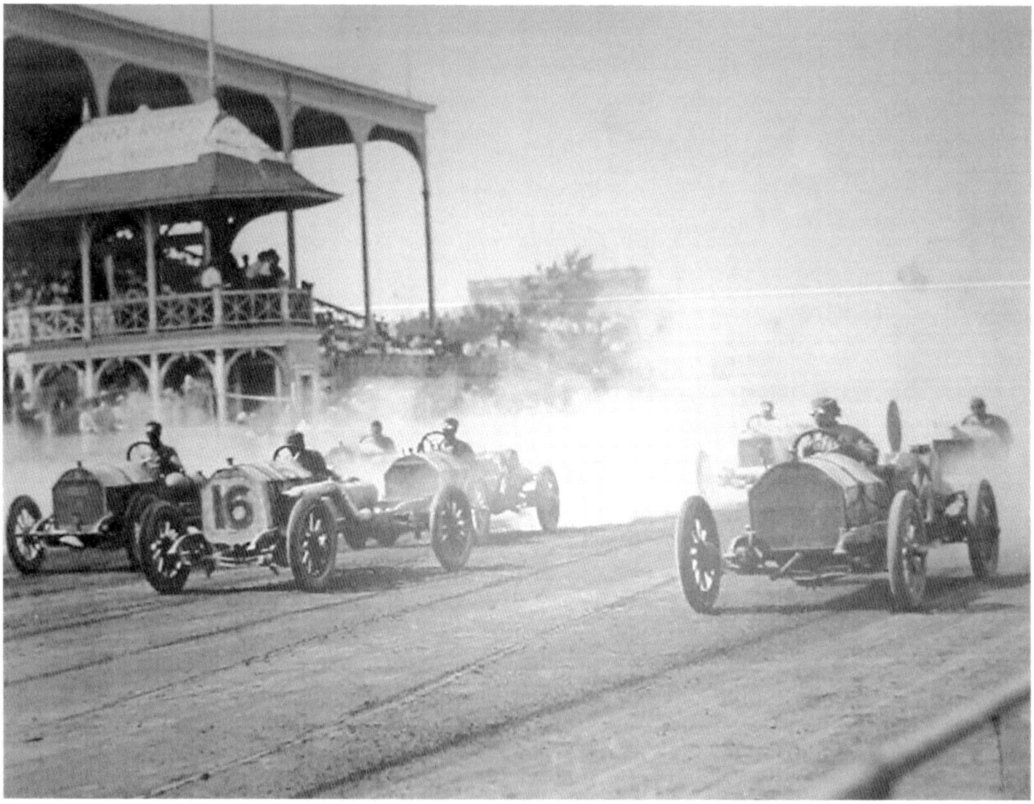

This 1908 photograph is of a 24-hour, 993-mile endurance race at Wisconsin State Fair Park won by Robert Drach and mechanic Fred Leiser, driving Old 16. In 1908, Old 16 was the first American-designed and -built automobile to win the Vanderbilt Cup. Spectators filled the grandstand to see "the car that raced the world and won." It was a matter of American pride. (TMS.)

State fairs were the epicenters of innovation, hometown pride, and oddities. One such spectacle gawkers could not resist in 1902 was a train wreck. Presented by "Head On" Joe Connolly, the event drew thousands. Lengths of track were laid out, and at the signal, two train engines thundered toward each other, crashing head-on in a ball of fire as the crowd cheered. (WSHS.)

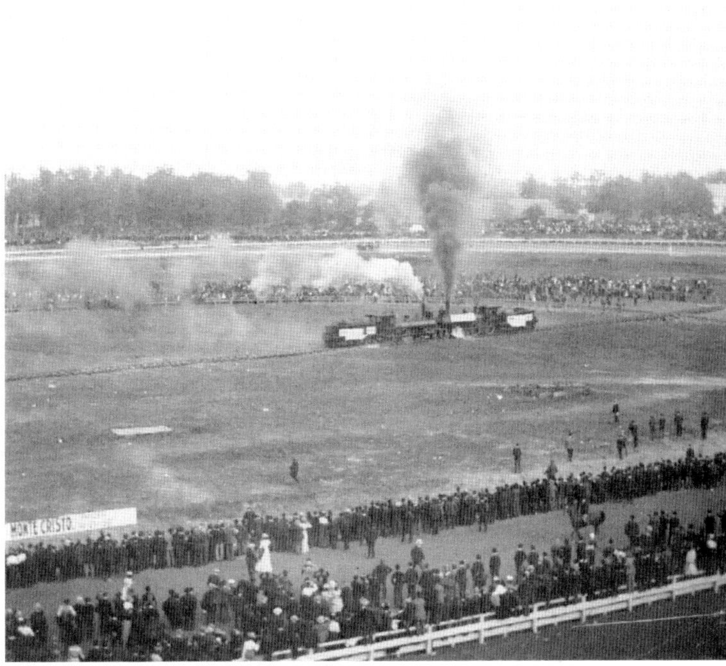

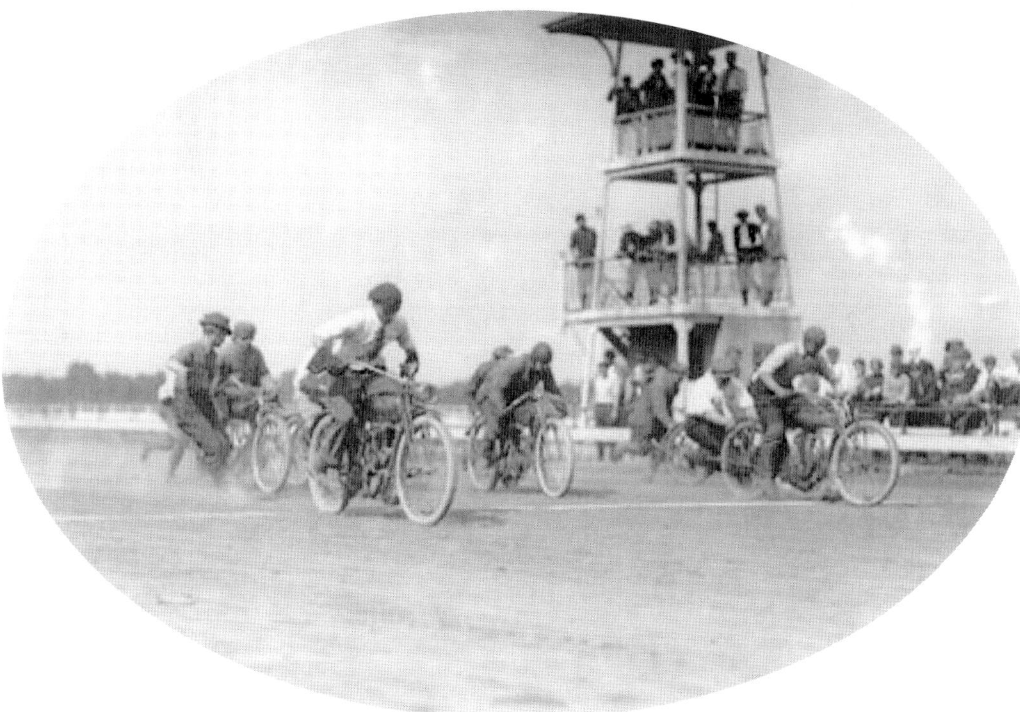

This c. 1909 photograph of a motorcycle race at the state fairgrounds depicts a field of men riding what resemble bicycles with motors. The field of the day would include J.A. Prestwich (JAP), Harley Davidson, Indian, and many more. Predecessors of today's models, these early motorcycles tested the endurance of both the machine and rider. (MCHS.)

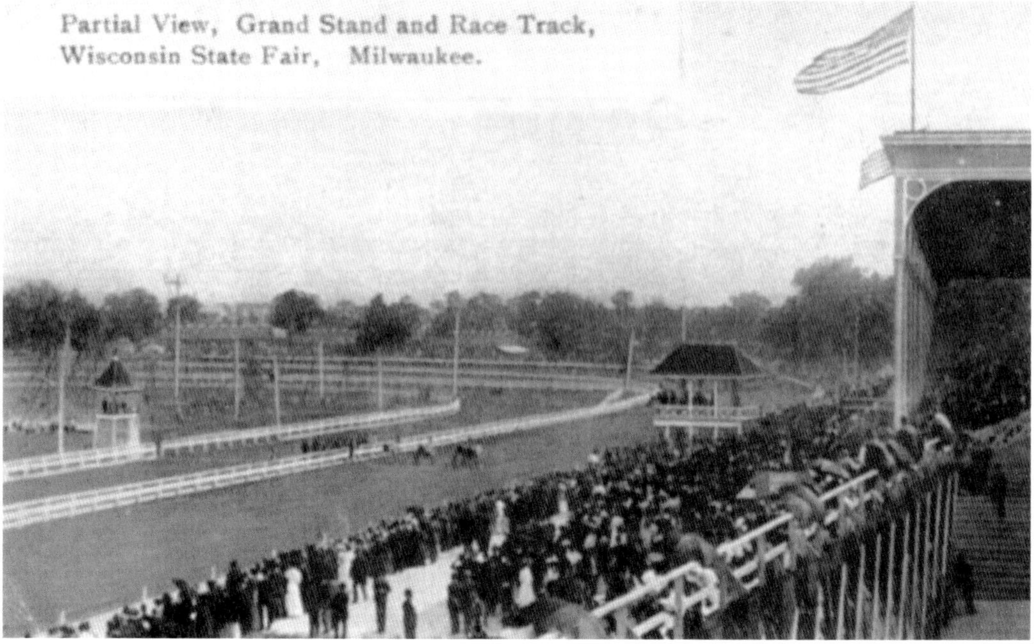

Taken from the grandstand and looking south, this 1910 Wisconsin State Fair postcard photograph depicts three trotters on the straightaway, entering the first turn. The state fairgrounds were built around the track, a wise decision since the track had been a moneymaker since day one. (WAHS.)

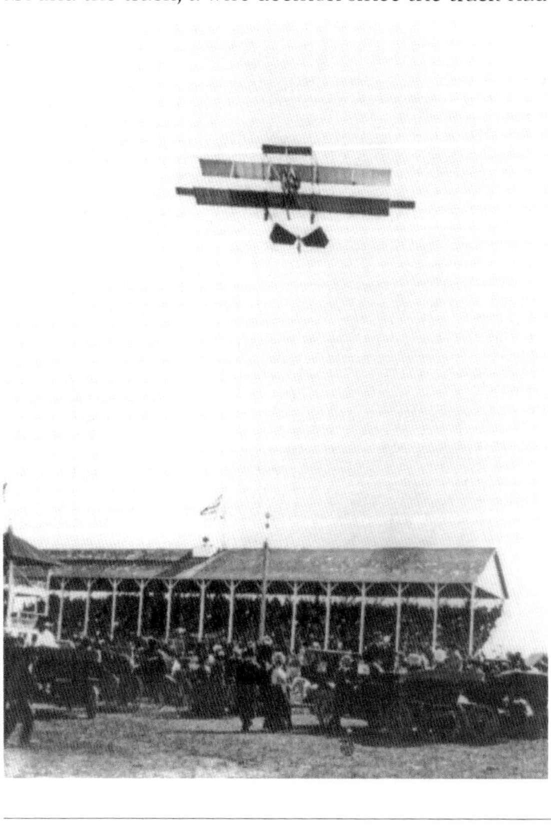

Lincoln Beachey knew how to thrill an audience. Constantly challenging limits, Beachey joined the exhibition team of aviation pioneer Glenn Curtis. During the June 1911 State Fair, Beachey took off from the park's track to perform his death-defying stunts. Climbing to the highest point ever reached over Wisconsin soil—10,000 feet—Beachey rolled his biplane into a dive, pulling up at the last possible moment to the delight of the cheering crowd. (WAHS.)

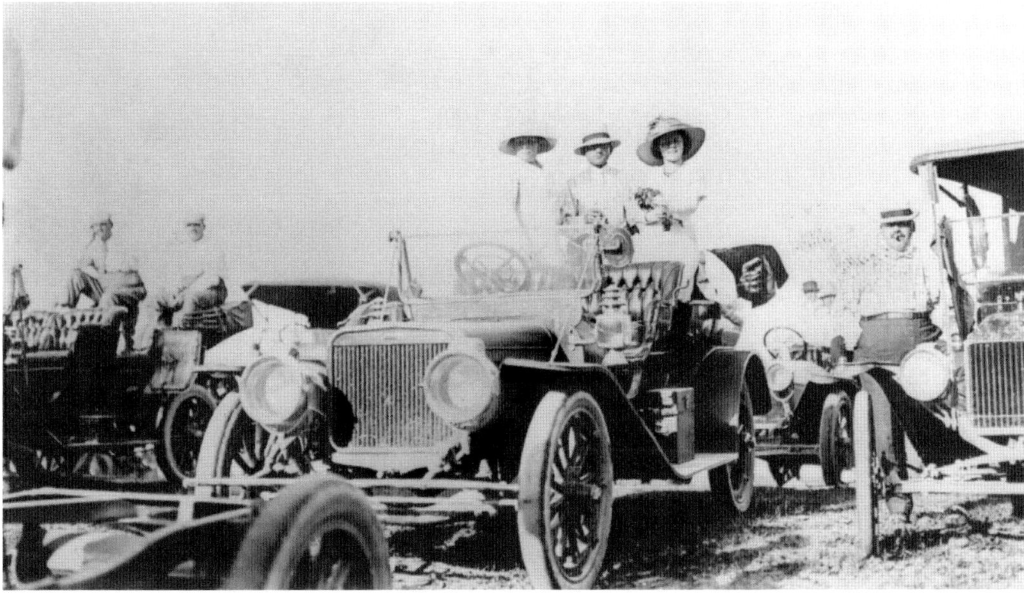

This early 1910 photograph catches spectators on the infield watching an auto race. Depending on several factors, either before or after the race, spectators were permitted to drive on the track, tracing the ruts of their favorite drivers and experiencing the thrill of a race. (WSHS.)

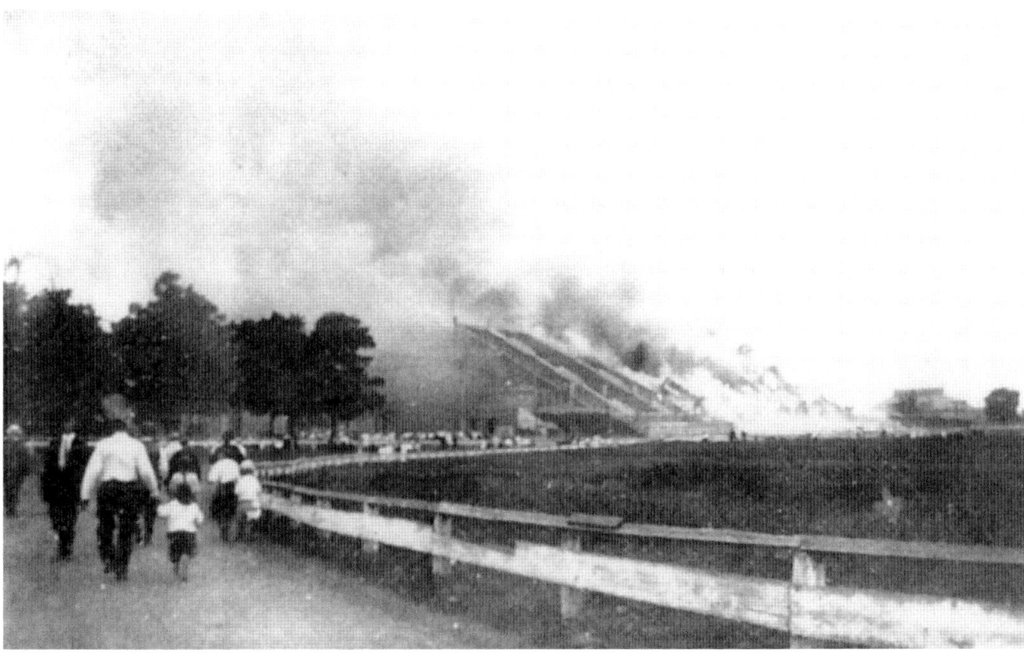

The summer of 1914 was devastating for the state fair, with a tornado and fire destroying the grandstand and many buildings. Rebuilding was questioned but was accomplished on time the following year. Billowing smoke carried by the wind blackened the sky, prompting panic amongst the fairgoers. As always, disaster draws gawkers, and this photograph shows adults and children heading toward the fire instead of trying to escape. (WAHS.)

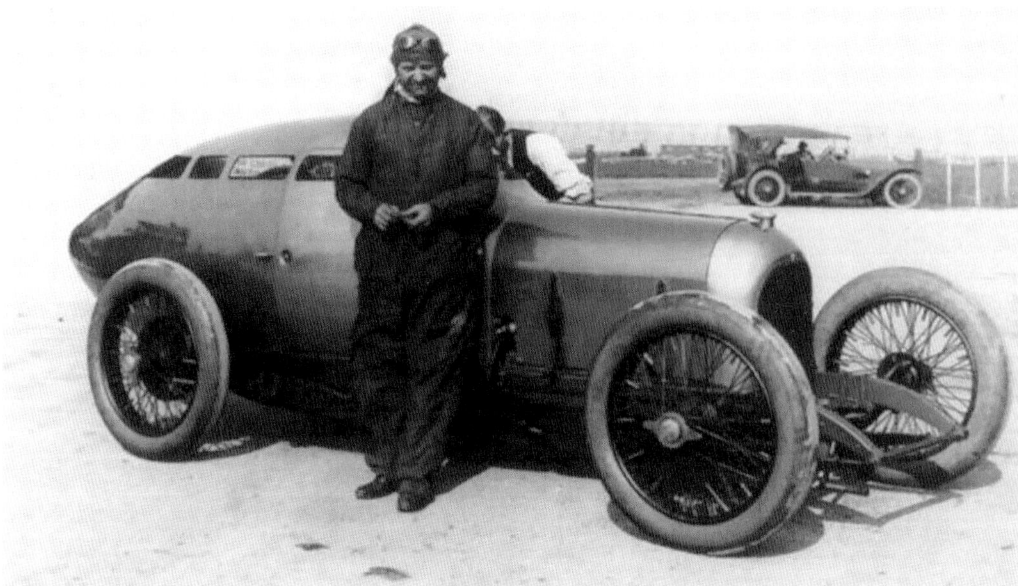

Pictured in 1917 is Barney Oldfield with his Golden Submarine. An innovative pioneer, Oldfield focused on racing safety. After the death of a friend, Oldfield partnered with Miller and Offenhauser to design a vehicle with unrestricted visibility and safety. The streamlined aluminum body incorporated a roll cage. To showcase the vehicle, Oldfield competed nationally in matched races against his friend and nemesis Ralph DePalma. (MD.)

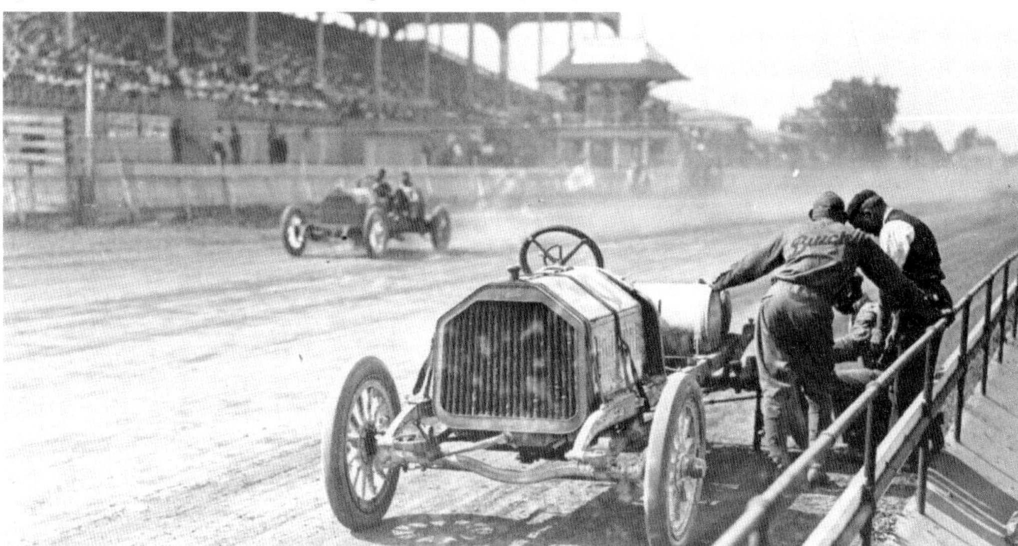

This early 1920s image of a driver at the rail shows that repairs were done directly on the track since there was no pit yet. At this point in racing, two-man teams—a driver and a mechanic, as required—rode together. The mechanic's job consisted of directional guidance for passing (like a backseat driver), spotting, tire repair/replacement, and any other necessities. This driver, seen with leather helmet and Buick jacket, drove on the Buick factory team. (WHS.)

Harness racing continued to draw large crowds well into mid-century; through both World Wars I and II and the Depression, race fans continued to turn out to cheer on their favorite four-legged athletes. The state fair track was a successful circuit stop, inviting the best drivers and horses, and purse sizes continued to be some of the best in the country. (MCHS.)

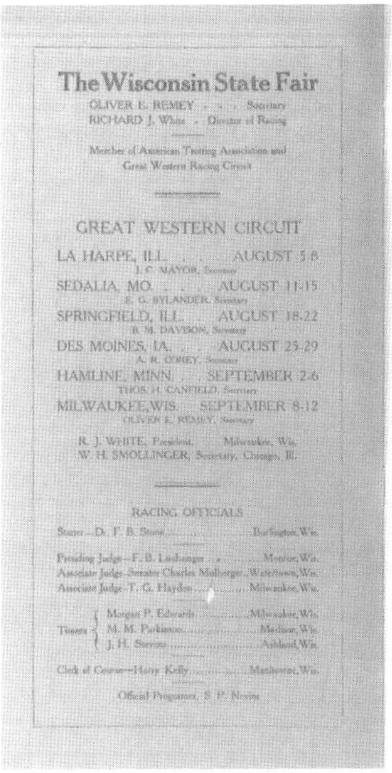

The Wisconsin State Fair

OLIVER E. REMEY . . . Secretary
RICHARD J. White - Director of Racing

Member of American Trotting Association and Great Western Racing Circuit

GREAT WESTERN CIRCUIT

LA HARPE, ILL. . . . AUGUST 5-8
J. C. MAYOR, Secretary
SEDALIA, MO. . . . AUGUST 11-15
E. G. BYLANDER, Secretary
SPRINGFIELD, ILL. . . AUGUST 18-22
B. M. DAVISON, Secretary
DES MOINES, IA. . . AUGUST 25-29
A. R. COREY, Secretary
HAMLINE, MINN. . . SEPTEMBER 2-6
THOS. H. CANFIELD, Secretary
MILWAUKEE, WIS. SEPTEMBER 8-12
OLIVER E. REMEY, Secretary

R. J. WHITE, President, Milwaukee, Wis.
W. H. SMOLLINGER, Secretary, Chicago, Ill.

RACING OFFICIALS

Starter—D. F. B. Stone .... Burlington, Wis.

Presiding Judge—F. B. Luchsinger .... Monroe, Wis.
Associate Judge–Senator Charles Mulberger .. Watertown, Wis.
Associate Judge–T. G. Hayden .... Milwaukee, Wis.

Timers { Morgan P. Edwards .... Milwaukee, Wis.
M. M. Parkinson .... Madison, Wis.
J. H. Stevens .... Ashland, Wis.

Clerk of Course—Harry Kelly .... Manitowoc, Wis.

Official Programer, S. P. Nevins

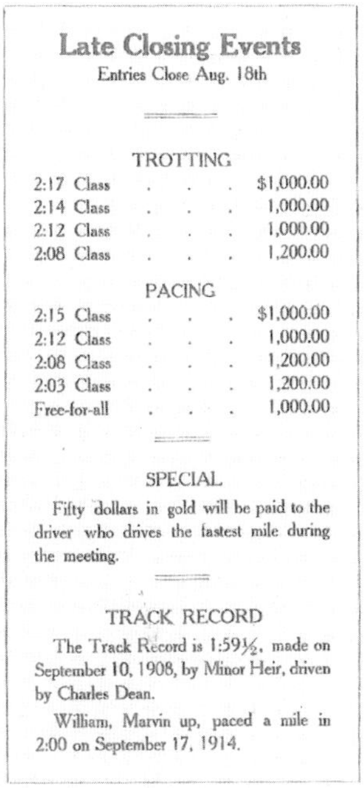

Late Closing Events

Entries Close Aug. 18th

TROTTING

2:17 Class	$1,000.00
2:14 Class	1,000.00
2:12 Class	1,000.00
2:08 Class	1,200.00

PACING

2:15 Class	$1,000.00
2:12 Class	1,000.00
2:08 Class	1,200.00
2:03 Class	1,200.00
Free-for-all	1,000.00

SPECIAL

Fifty dollars in gold will be paid to the driver who drives the fastest mile during the meeting.

TRACK RECORD

The Track Record is 1:59½, made on September 10, 1908, by Minor Heir, driven by Charles Dean.

William, Marvin up, paced a mile in 2:00 on September 17, 1914.

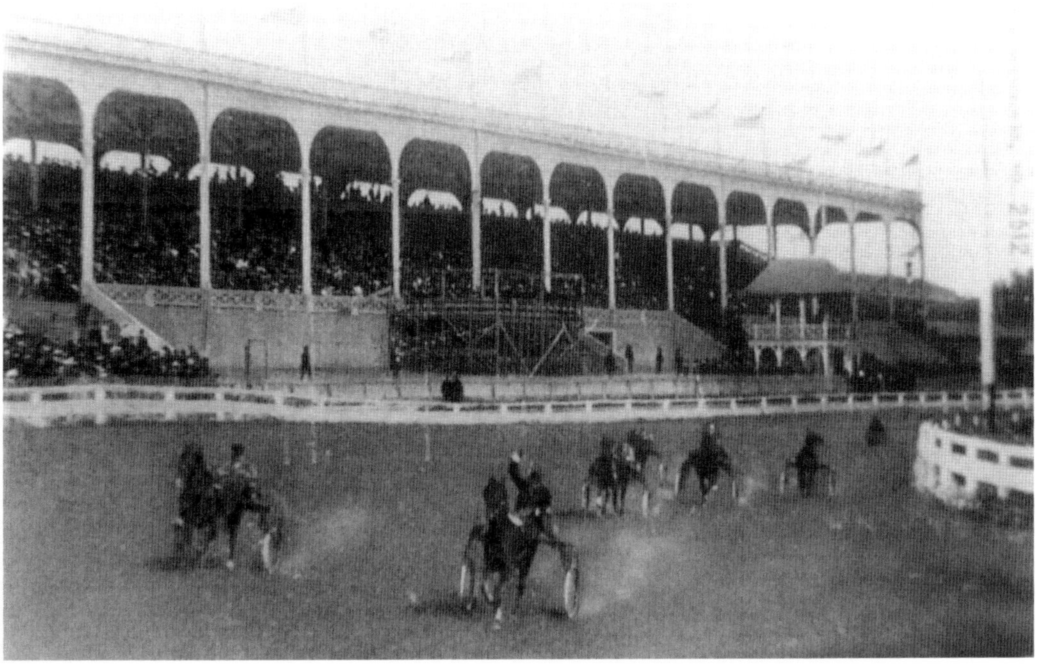

This is an early 1920s image of trotters rounding the first turn on the "Trotters Track." Deliberately built to allow both spectators and judges full sight from first sound of the gun to the first nose to cross the wire, State Fair Park must have been a spectator's favorite, given the packed grandstand. (MCHS.)

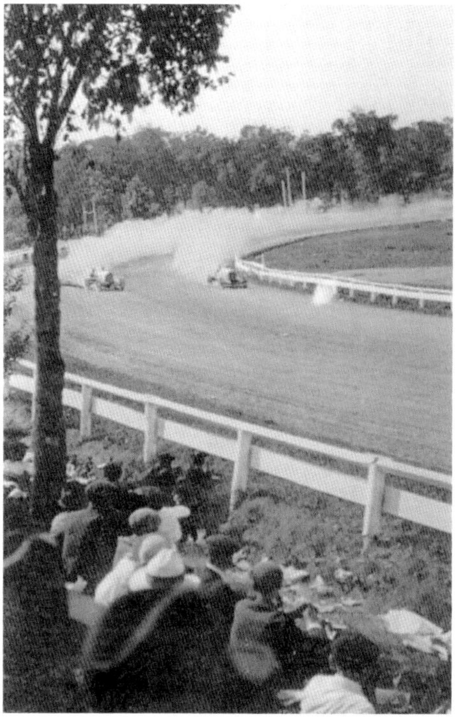

Sitting in the "cheap seats," spectators have a great view of two cars rounding a turn. With the choking dust kicked up, it is hard to tell if the two drivers in this c. 1919 photograph—one in a Deusenberg, the other a Hudson—are last or neck-and-neck for first. (MCHS.)

This early 1920s photograph catches the start of a race as the pace car leads the way. Cadillac, Benz, Miller, Buick, Dodge, and Ford, the same factory names of today, manufactured for the track with the purpose of convincing fans to become consumers. Note the precarious position of the personnel on the track—photographers, spectators, officials—they all show little regard for their own safety. (JSC.)

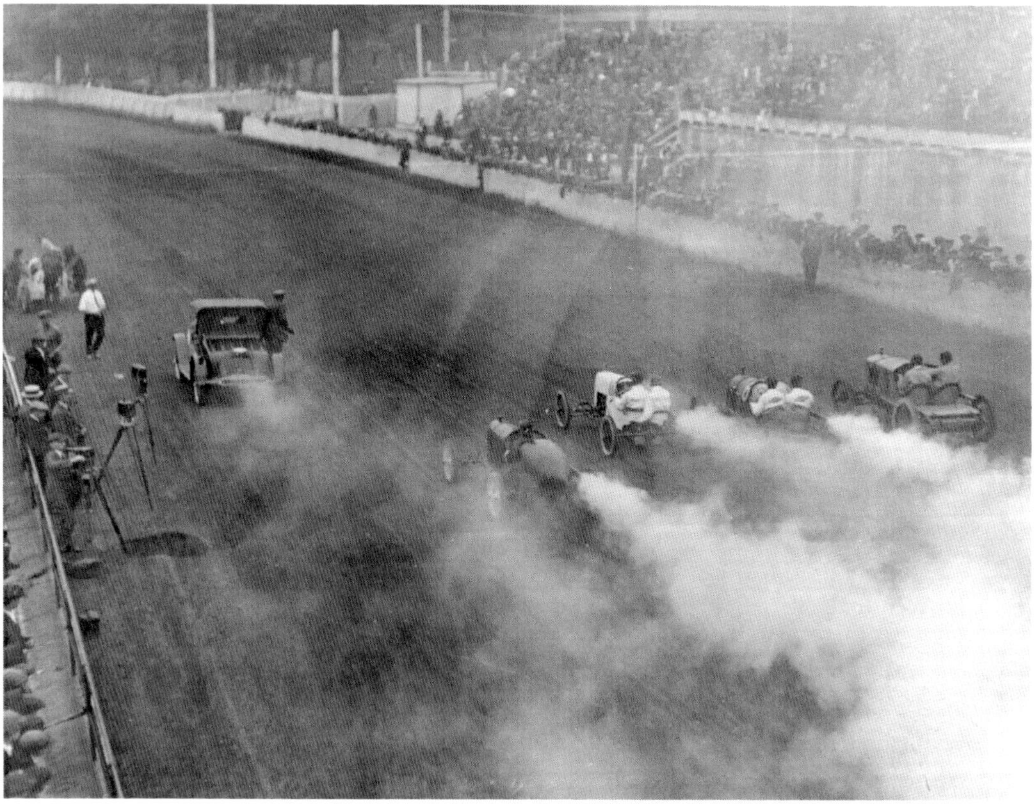

2

State Fair Park Becomes a Proving Ground

1921–1930

The Roaring Twenties were exactly that—roaring—leaving no aspect of life untouched. The decade was also known as the Golden Age of Sports. World War I was over, prosperity was growing, and Americans were into sports of all types. Technology took center stage, improving and influencing competitive sports; faster was the game. Promoters struggled with the issues technology brought to the track: speed and danger. Speed did not always center on the track, and jaw-dropping aviation spectacles frequented the infield, promoting the future of air travel.

Racing, in particular, was everything the 1920s was: fast, thrilling, dangerous, fashionable, and full of beautiful people. All of this could be found at the State Fair Park Speedway. With multiple sports using the track, officials recognized the need for better safety precautions. A new grandstand addition in 1925, closer to the action, provided additional seating but prompted the installation of safety fencing around the course. Two years later, additional concrete barriers replaced flimsy, dangerous obstacles. By the mid-1920s, several fair and track misfortunes had contributed to poor ticket sales—the state fair needed a boost. As it does sometimes, opportunity appeared right around the corner in the form of Milwaukee's hometown heroes, Carl, Tudy, and Tom Marchese. Carl had been the 1929 Indy 500 Rookie of the Year; they had all the clout needed to turn things around.

The state fair board wasted no time in approving Tom Marchese as general manager and Carl as his right-hand man. To fill the seats, Tom needed a plan. With the expectation that crowds would turn out to cheer on local boys, the call for drivers spread quickly, and a handsome cash purse attracted the best—and ensured their return year after year.

Sprint and champ cars ruled the track during the 1930s, and thousands of fans filled the stands for six races during the summer. Gus Schrader, Wilbur Shaw, Frank Brisko, Johnny Sawyer, and others brought fans to their feet as they roared down the track.

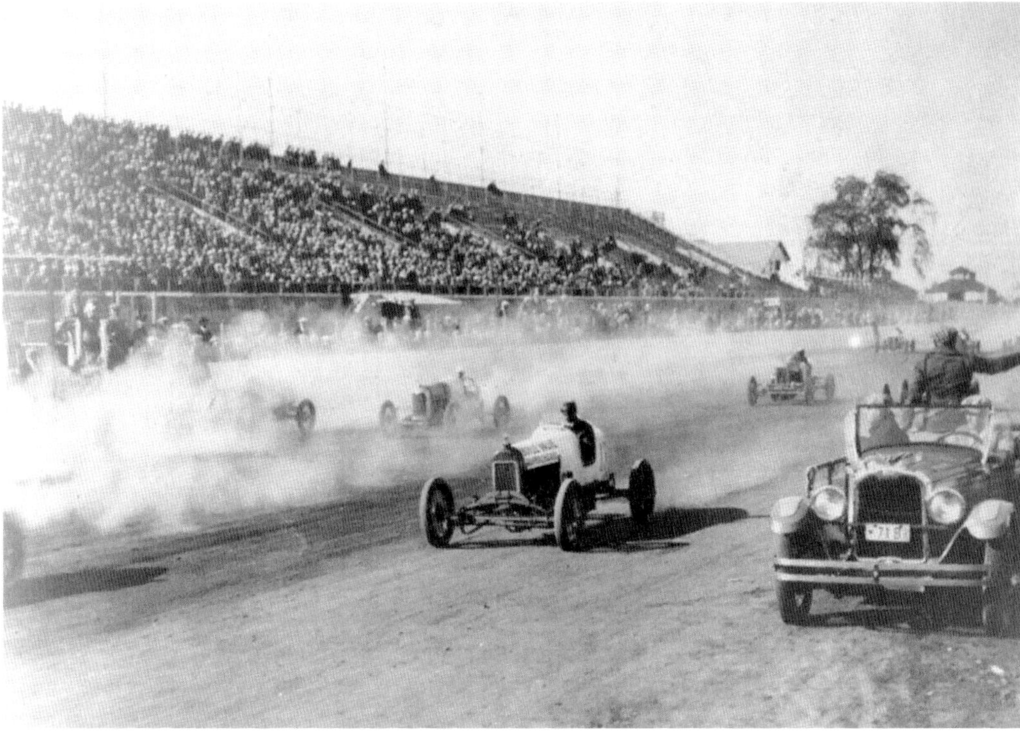

Taken on September 26, 1926, at the 150-mile race, this photograph shows drivers up to speed at the end of their parade lap, led by the pace car, ready to start the race. Although sanctioned by AAA at this time, few records are available of State Fair race results. Judging by the crowded stands, racing was already a popular pastime. (TMS.)

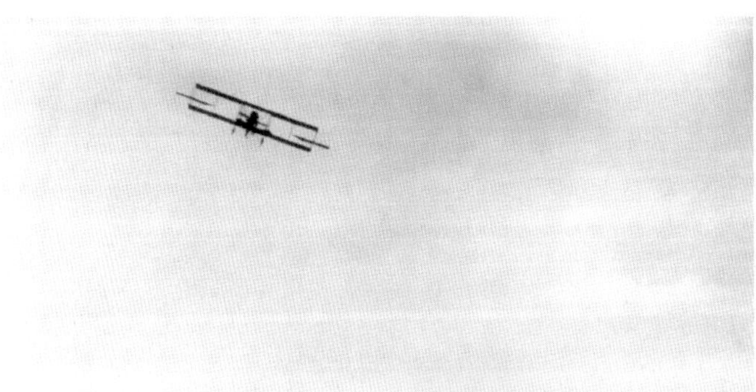

May 29, 1921, was a dark day for the state fair, one of many to follow. This image captures the beginning of what should have been an easy exploit. Stunt man Al Wilson was to descend from the plane, piloted by Dallas Spears, on a rope ladder and overtake the auto, driven by Lou Disbrow. Unfortunately, the ladder caught the automobile's exhaust pipe and caused the plane to nosedive into the grandstand, injuring 16 spectators. (TMS.)

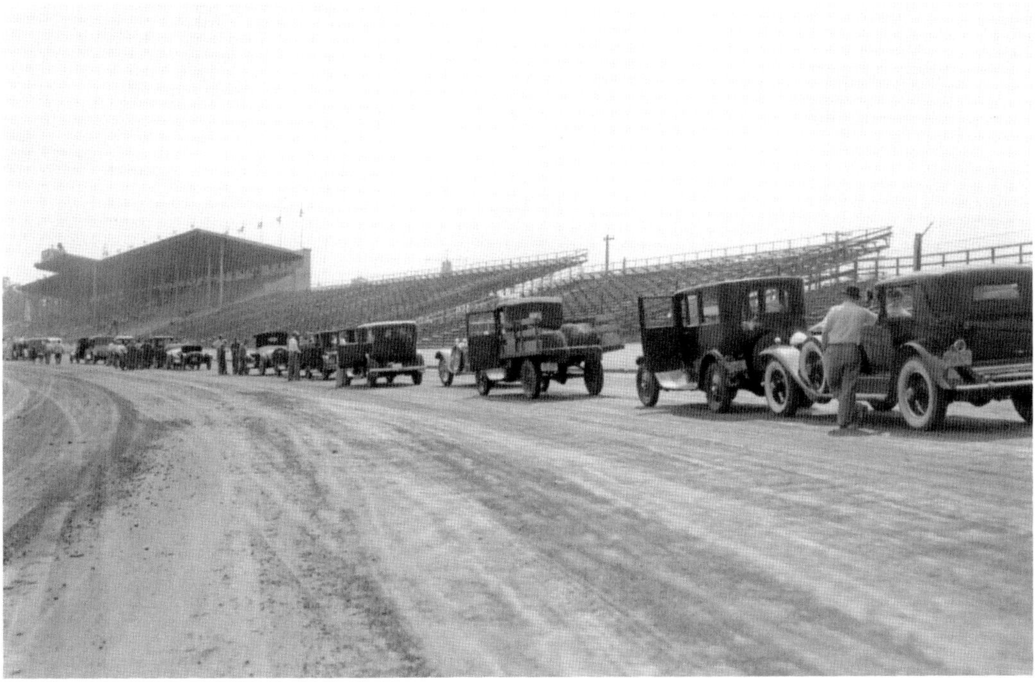

This 1930s photograph, taken from turn four, shows drivers and autos lined up and ready for time trials. The vehicles include an array of sedans, coupes, and trucks. (GGAK.)

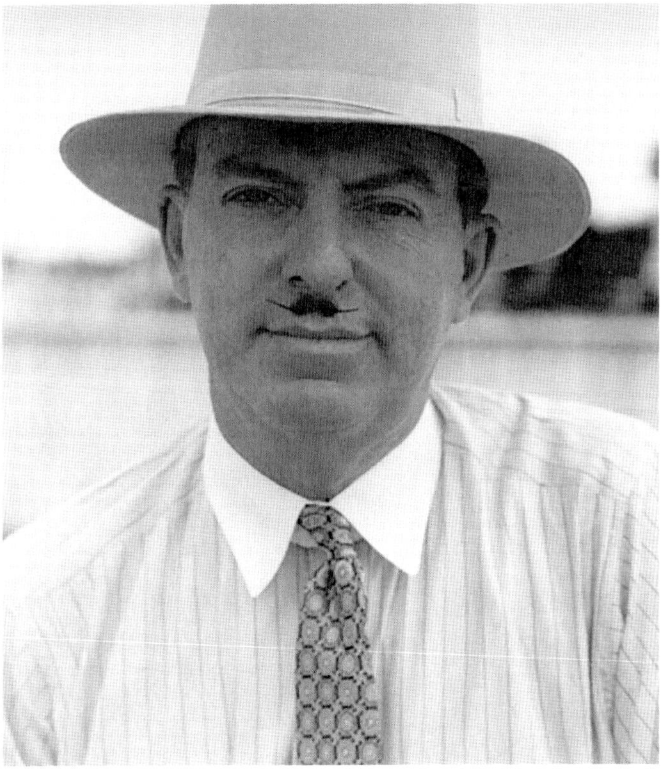

One of the most creative and brilliant designers and builders of race cars between 1910 and his death in 1943, Harry Miller's passion for metalwork and machinery fueled his imagination. His Master Carburetor dominated not only racing but also aeronautics, marine, and passenger vehicles. Regrettably, the Depression led him to lose it all. Fortunately, his astute chief machinist, Fred Offenhause, picked up the pieces and, as they say, the rest is history. (LoC.)

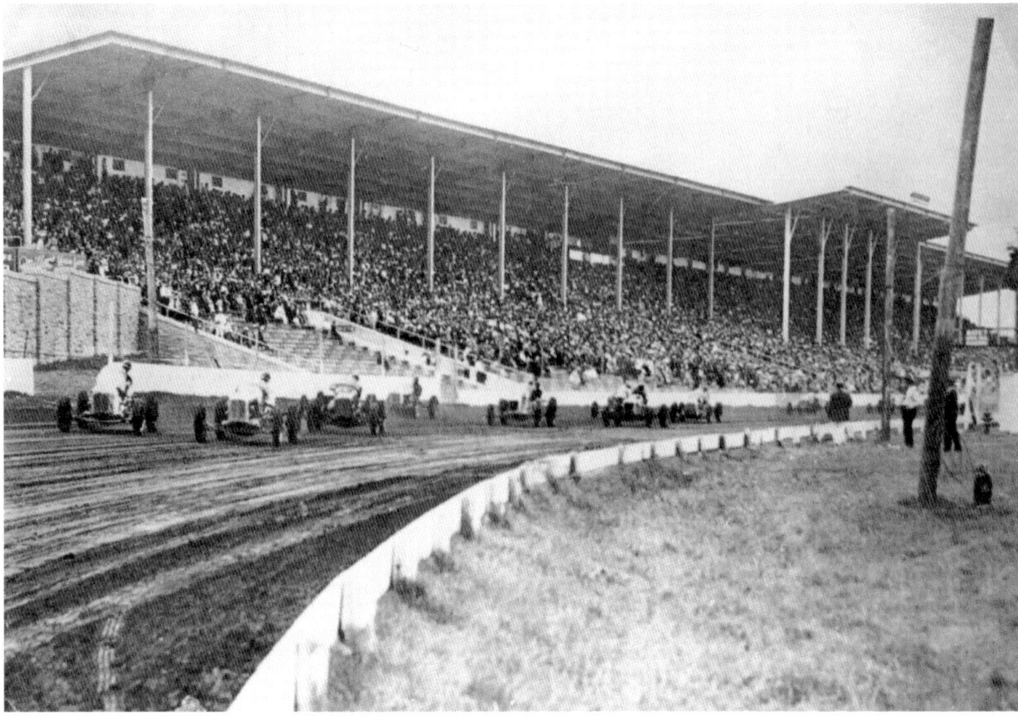

Snapped from the infield, this c. 1920 photograph of race cars zipping down the straightaway into turn one illustrates the lack of proper safety measures for drivers. The dirt track perimeter barrier, a short white fence, offered little protection for either spectators or drivers. As the sport evolved, officials both required and promoted safety precautions for everyone. (GGAK.)

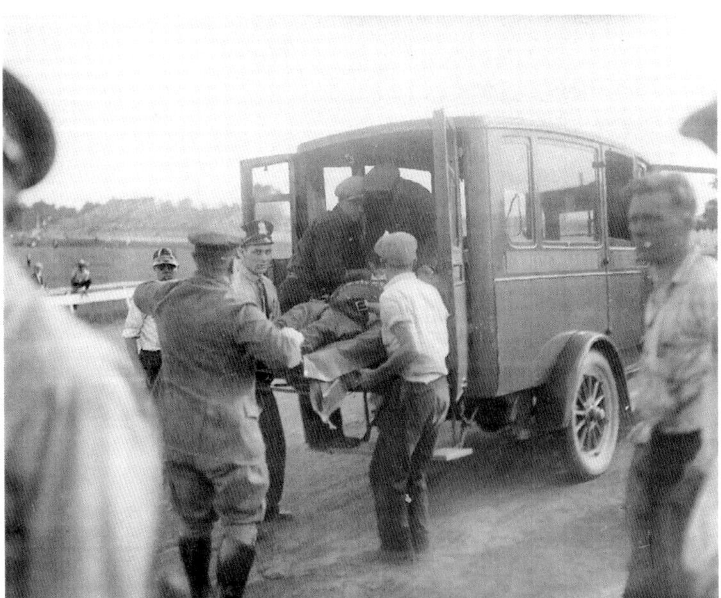

Danger was an inherent aspect of life in the fast lane; drivers and riders understood and accepted this reality. Here, an unidentified injured motorcycle rider is eased into a B&W ambulance, a 1921 Nash, to be transported to the nearest hospital for medical treatment. Ray Minturn and Herb Drager, West Allis police officers, assist the response team. (WAHS.)

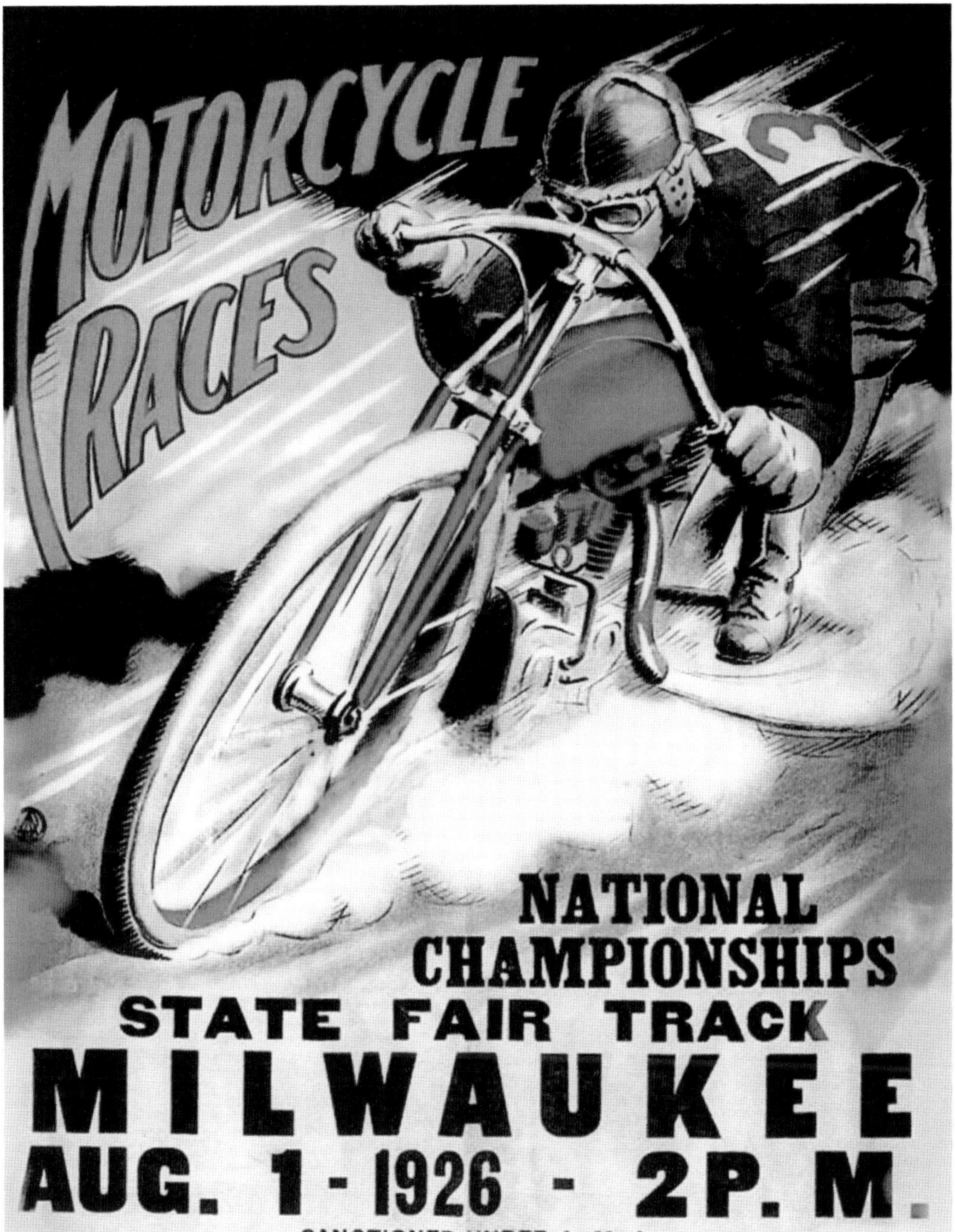

Motorcycle racing was an exciting sport that drew large crowds to the track. What started out as friendly competitions between individual racers soon became opportunities for manufacturers to duke it out. Top competitors were scouted by manufacturers to race for company teams. Generous salaries, all equipment, and preferential treatment contributed to the star quality of the riders. Top contenders were Harley Davidson, Indian, and John Alfred Prestwich (JAP). (AC.)

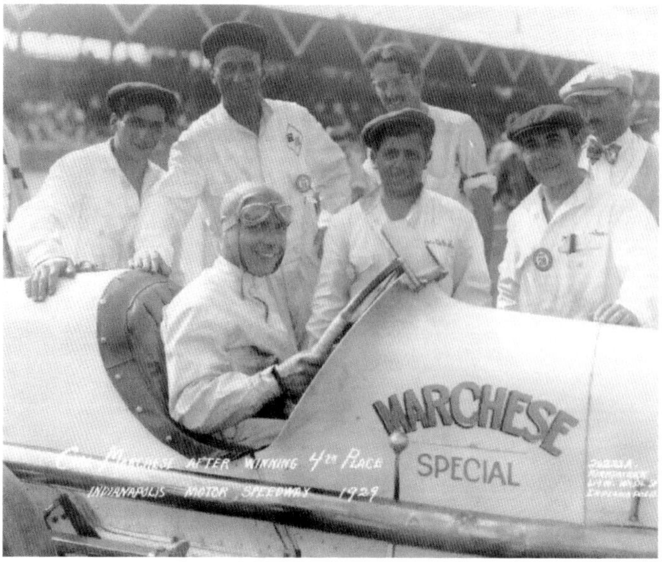

Taken after the 1929 Indy 500 race, this photograph captures the pride and energy of the Marchese brothers' team. From left to right are Tudy, Carl (driving), and Tom Marchese, surrounded by their pit crew. Placing fourth was enough to propel the Marchese brothers into the limelight as Milwaukee heroes. That same year, Tom Marchese accepted the position as promoter for the State Fair Park Speedway. Milwaukee's future was on the right track. (TMS.)

CHAMPION SERIES

1930 GREEN BAY PACKERS 1930

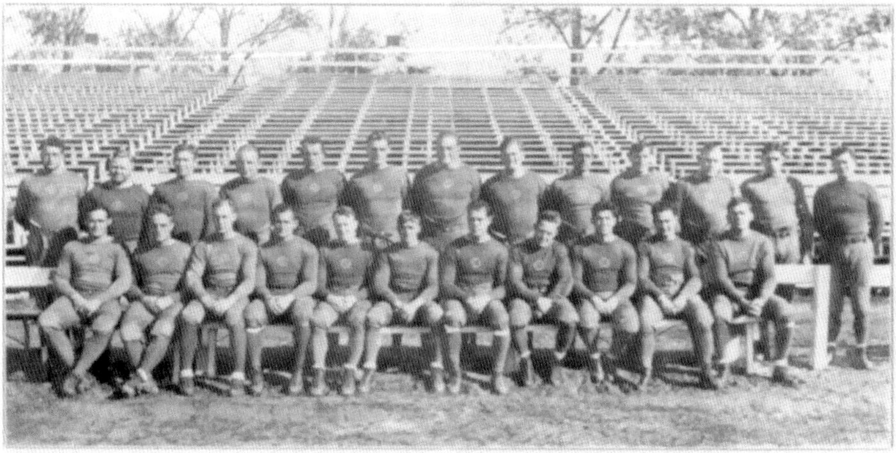

Top Row—left to right—Darling, Woodin, Molenda, Perry, Nash, Dilweg, Hubbard, Sleight, Lewellen, Blood, Earpe, Michalske, Coach Lambeau.
Bottom Row—Bowdoin, Radick, Englemann, McCrary, Dunn, Zuidmulder, Zuver, Fitzgibbon, Herber, O'Donnell, Lidberg.

The 1930 season proved to be a great one for the Green Bay Packers. With a 10-3-1 record, they clinched their second straight NFL championship, topping the Portsmouth (Ohio) Spartans (later the Detroit Lions). Although the Packers' home field remained in Green Bay, the team's popularity provided an opportunity to seek out larger venues, increasing the fan base and revenue. (AC.)

3

Midgets, Sprints, and Field Goals

1931–1949

With great excitement, Midget Auto Racing arrived in Wisconsin in July of 1935. Carl Marchese formed the Wisconsin Racing Association (WRA) to sanction midget racing in Wisconsin. To avoid confusion with Wisconsin Auto Racing, the track promotion name, Wisconsin Racing Association changed its name to Badger Midget Auto Racing Association in 1937. Eight decades later, Badger is the oldest active open-wheel racing organization in the country. Promoters and fans were anxious to bring Milwaukee back to national prominence and in 1930, State Fair Park Speedway saw the return of big car racing and packed the stands. Tony Willman made his mark at the speedway, and the 1930s was his decade. Whether driving midget or sprint car, he was beloved by fans.

At the same time, the Green Bay Packers were in the limelight. To attract a larger following, the Packers played half their home games on the infield at State Fair Park and the remainder in Green Bay. The 1939 season brought the New York Giants to West Allis for the NFL championship game, which was billed as the "Dairy Bowl" and saw the Packers beat the Giants 27-0.

The early 1940s saw the world change, and Americans pitched in to help their allies. Conservation programs were adopted. Rubber and metal, essential to racing, were rationed. The summer of 1941 saw the last 100-mile big car race, won by Rex Mays, until peacetime.

Drivers, mechanics, and backyard gearheads refined their skills gained in the motor pool or at airplane factories. The end of the war brought new passions, and all Americans were ready to live a postwar life. Opening their toolboxes and scouting salvage yards for projects, America's youth hauled their prizes to the nearest track to blow off steam. Cut-down coupes raced the short track, giving fans what they came for. Although midget racing had been active before the war, a new appetite for these powerhouses spawned greater interest. A new quarter-mile dirt track replaced the infield cinder track in 1946. On August 22, 1948, State Fair Park held its first stock-car race, a 100-mile, AAA-sanctioned event won by Paul Bjork.

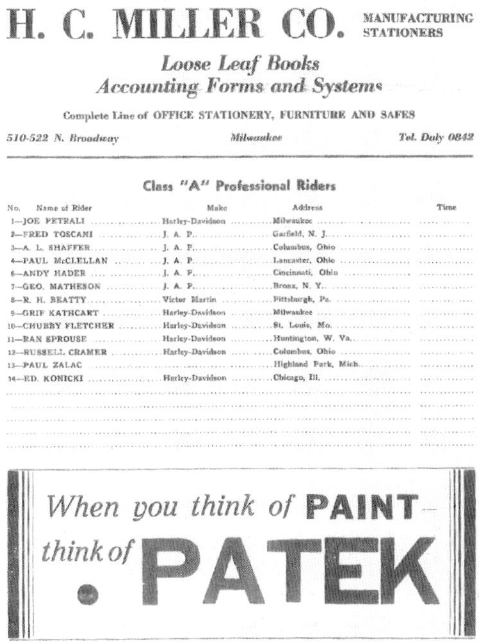

H. C. MILLER CO. MANUFACTURING STATIONERS

Loose Leaf Books

Accounting Forms and Systems

Complete Line of OFFICE STATIONERY, FURNITURE AND SAFES

510-522 N. Broadway *Milwaukee* *Tel. Daly 0842*

Class "A" Professional Riders

No. Name of Rider	Make	Address	Time
1—JOE PETRALI	Harley-Davidson	Milwaukee	
2—FRED TOSCANI	J. A. P.	Garfield, N. J.	
3—A. L. SHAFFER	J. A. P.	Columbus, Ohio	
4—PAUL McCLELLAN	J. A. P.	Lancaster, Ohio	
6—ANDY HADER	J. A. P.	Cincinnati, Ohio	
7—GEO. MATHESON	J. A. P.	Bronx, N. Y.	
8—R. H. BEATTY	Victor Martin	Pittsburgh, Pa.	
9—GRIF KATHCART	Harley-Davidson	Milwaukee	
10—CHUBBY FLETCHER	Harley-Davidson	St. Louis, Mo.	
11—RAN SPROUSE	Harley-Davidson	Huntington, W. Va.	
12—RUSSELL CRAMER	Harley-Davidson	Columbus, Ohio	
13—PAUL ZALAC		Highland Park, Mich.	
14—ED. KONICKI	Harley-Davidson	Chicago, Ill.	

When you think of **PAINT**—

think of **PATEK**

State Fair Park continued to bring exciting talent to the track, and motorcycle races were one of the biggest draws. This rider profile page from a 1930s program lists riders for the day's race. This particular race, like most, featured professional, or Class A riders. Contracted factory-sponsored competitors, "A" riders' compensation included all equipment, gear, paid expenses, and a salary, all of which contributed to star-quality riders. (JS.)

Auto racing has been and always will be a dangerous sport, and not just for drivers. From the earliest races, spectators, team members, and track personnel have lost their lives and suffered disabilities. The photographer in this image is taking his life in his hands to get the perfect shot. With just a short fence between him and the track, luck must have been on his side. (GGAK.)

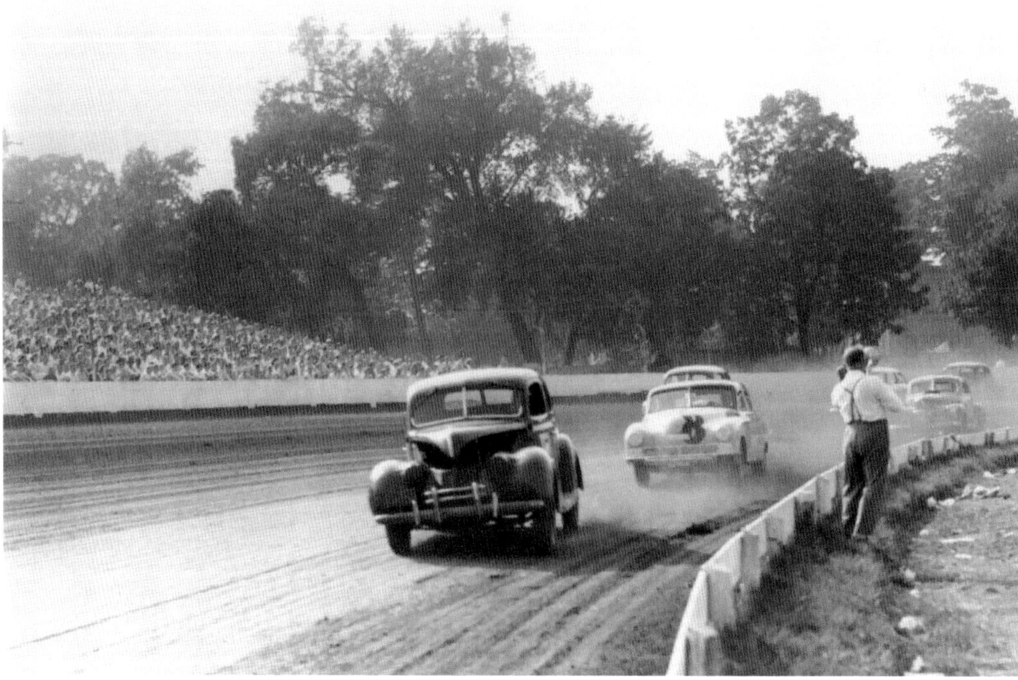

GREEN BAY PACKERS

1939 World Champions
National Football League

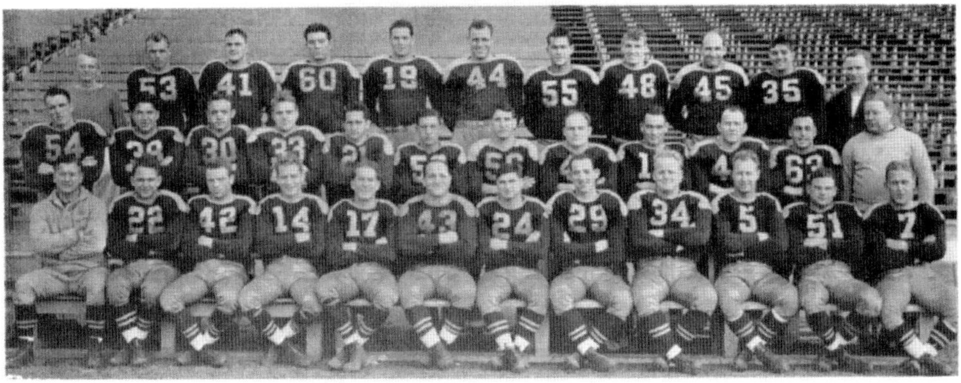

Front Row, left to right: Head Coach Curly Lambeau, Gantenbein, Uram, Hutson, Isbell, Goldenberg, Laws, Charley Brock, Engebretsen, Bruder, Lawrence, Jankowski. *Second Row:* Craig, Herber, Hinkle, Weisgerber, Tinsley, Buhler, Greenfield, Letlow, Lee Mulleneaux, Lee, Zarnas, Coach Red Smith. *Back Row:* Trainer Woodward, Svendsen, Kell, Schultz, Carl Mulleneaux, Ray, Moore, Jacunski, Smith, Balazs, Jorgensen.

Eager to find an additional home field, the Green Bay Packers negotiated with the state fair to lease the track's infield and play half of their home games in West Allis. From 1934 to 1951, the infield hosted many teams, but the most notable match was the 1939 game against the New York Giants, known as the "Dairy Bowl." The Packers secured another NFL championship title, dominating the Giants 27-0. (AC.)

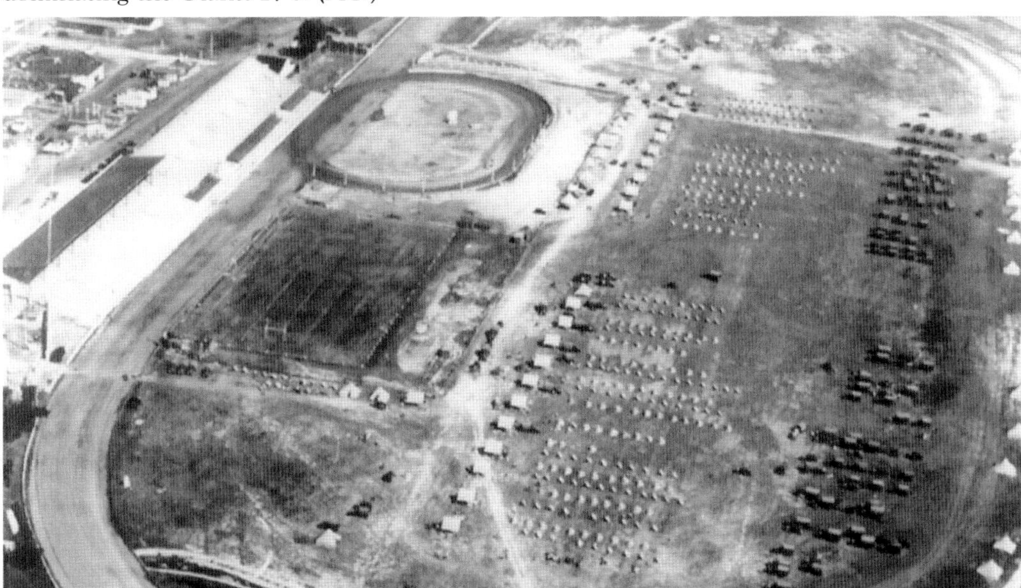

Considered the Green Bay Packers' second home field, the infield is pictured here during the early 1940s. Positioned directly in front of the grandstand, the field was laid out north to south. Locker rooms were built under the grandstand. The goalposts are clearly visible. The image also shows a military training encampment of the Wisconsin National Guard. (JS.)

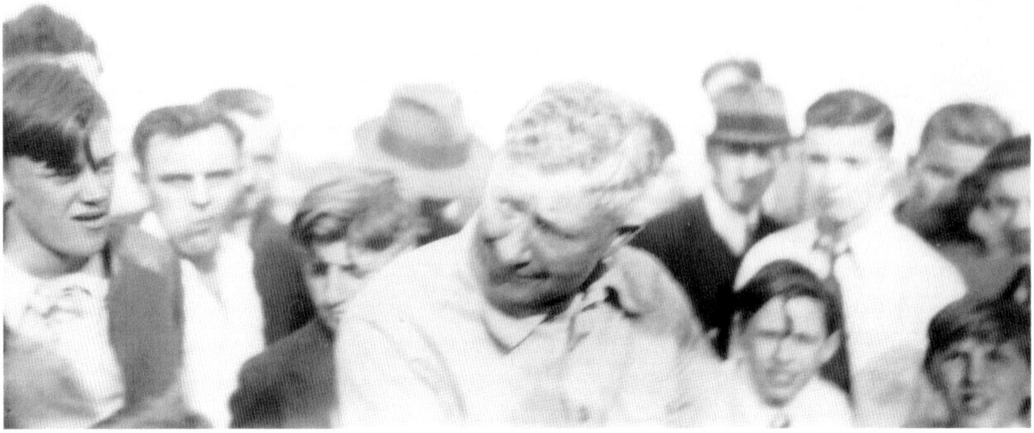

Chet Gardner, known as "King of the money drivers," had claimed the Midwest AAA Sprint Car championship in 1932. He considered himself just a regular guy; he owned his own car and personally trailered it between tracks. Shouldering the entire cost of racing himself kept his focus on one thing: track purses. Although he was popular, a cheering crowd's roar was lost in the dust of the track. (GGAK.)

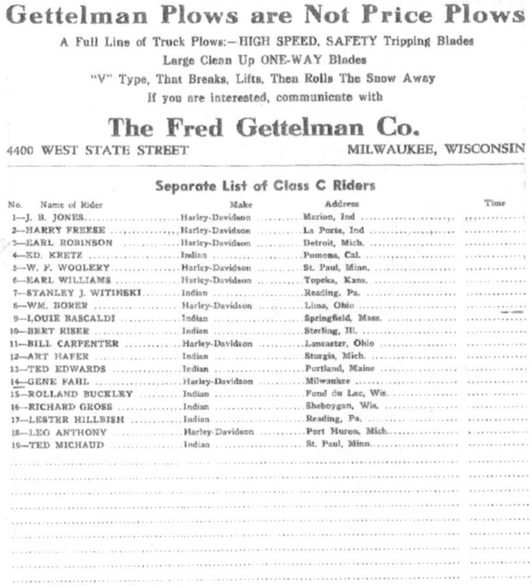

Gettelman Plows are Not Price Plows

A Full Line of Truck Plows:—HIGH SPEED, SAFETY Tripping Blades
Large Clean Up ONE-WAY Blades
"V" Type, That Breaks, Lifts, Then Rolls The Snow Away
If you are interested, communicate with

The Fred Gettelman Co.
4400 WEST STATE STREET MILWAUKEE, WISCONSIN

Separate List of Class C Riders

No.	Name of Rider	Make	Address	Time
1	J. B. JONES	Harley-Davidson	Marion, Ind	
2	HARRY FREESE	Harley-Davidson	La Porte, Ind	
3	EARL ROBINSON	Harley-Davidson	Detroit, Mich.	
4	ED. KRETZ	Indian	Pomona, Cal.	
5	W. F. WOOLERY	Harley-Davidson	St. Paul, Minn.	
6	EARL WILLIAMS	Harley-Davidson	Topeka, Kans.	
7	STANLEY J. WITINSKI	Indian	Reading, Pa.	
8	WM. BORER	Harley-Davidson	Lima, Ohio	
9	LOUIE BASCALDI	Indian	Springfield, Mass.	
10	BERT RISER	Indian	Sterling, Ill.	
11	BILL CARPENTER	Harley-Davidson	Lancaster, Ohio	
12	ART HAFER	Indian	Sturgis, Mich.	
13	TED EDWARDS	Indian	Portland, Maine	
14	GENE FAHL	Harley-Davidson	Milwaukee	
15	ROLLAND BUCKLEY	Indian	Fond du Lac, Wis.	
16	RICHARD GROSS	Indian	Sheboygan, Wis.	
17	LESTER HILLBISH	Indian	Reading, Pa.	
18	LEO ANTHONY	Harley-Davidson	Port Huron, Mich.	
19	TED MICHAUD	Indian	St. Paul, Minn.	

RED RIBBON BRAND FOOD PRODUCTS
J. & M. STEINER, Inc.
WHOLESALE GROCERS
525 W. McKINLEY AVE. MILWAUKEE, WIS.

During the Depression, factories cut back on the high-end, competitive, Class A motorcycles. As a result, in 1937, the AMA introduced Class C, featuring less-expensive, street-legal motorcycles, in an effort to make motorcycle racing more affordable. Prior to World War II, Class C competition helped fuel intense competition between Indian and Harley Davidson, America's top two major manufacturers at the time. (JS.)

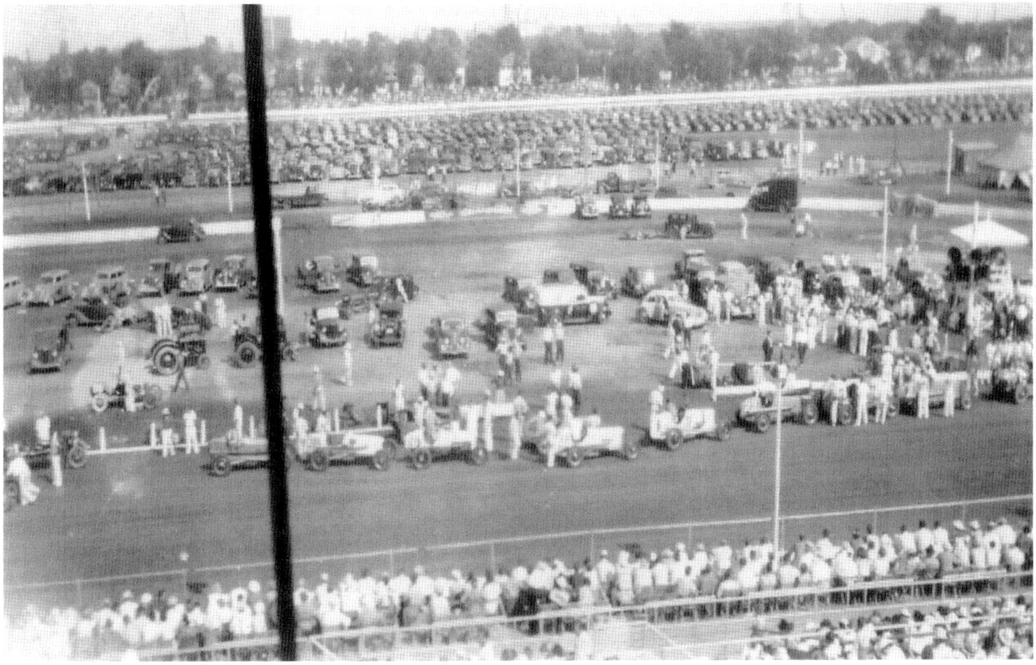

Waiting is always the hardest part. During this 1936 AAA-sanctioned sprint car competition, drivers stage in the pits, waiting for time trials. The field was large that day, but a few drivers seen here include Frank Fohr, No. 70; Wilbur Shaw, No. 12; Joe Thorne, No. 22; Bill Cummings, No. 1; and Frank Beeder, No. 4. Logged into history that day was Tony Willman in first place, followed by George Conner in second and Bill Cumming in third. (GGAK.)

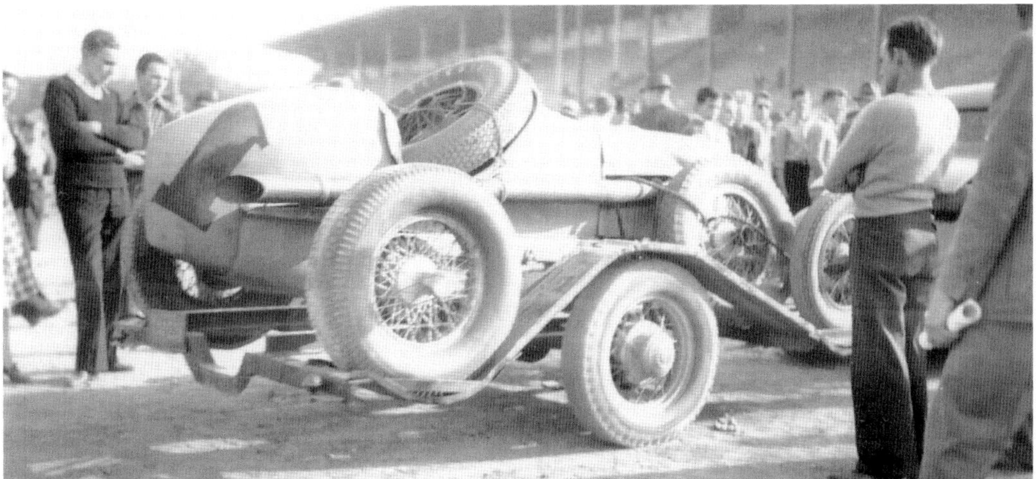

Ed Teter raced both automobiles and motorcycles, earning a reputation as a veteran stunt driver and daredevil. Several close calls earned him the nickname "Lucky." Encouraged by sold-out crowds, Teter organized the Lucky Teter Hell Drivers in 1938 (shown is Lucky Teter Spl. No. 1) and went on the road. Teter and his drivers thrilled crowds across the country with their death-defying precision driving. (GGAK.)

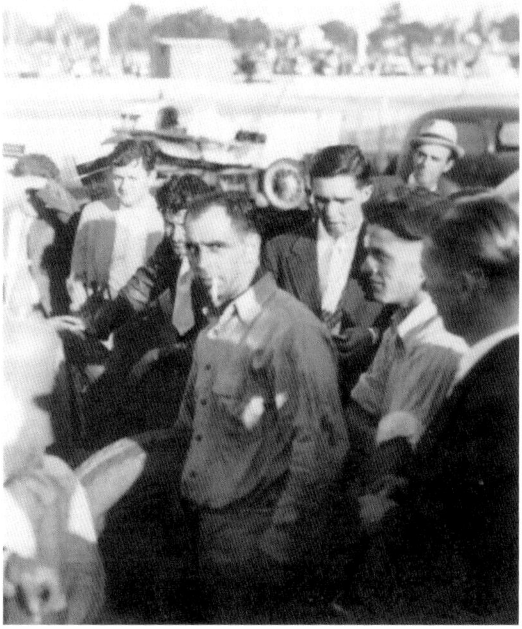

South Milwaukee native Tony Willman, quiet and soft-spoken off the track, was relentless on the track. A nationally recognized driver, Willman did it all, whether Indy, sprint, or midget. Success came easy, and when he finally reached financial independence, he chose to race for the thrills and for his fans. Here, Willman is surrounded by fans in 1936 after his first AAA Sprint Car win at State Fair Park. (GGAK.)

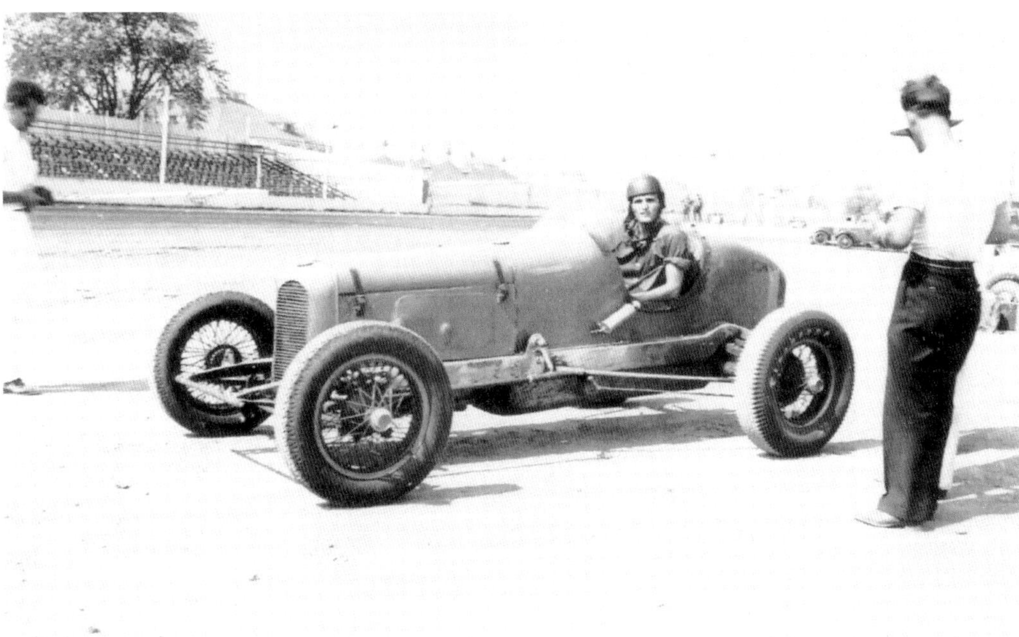

Dashing, charming, and well respected, Rex Mays readies for the August, 29, 1937, AAA Championship Race, in which he finished first. Both Indy and sprint car successes earned Mays two AAA championships. His heroic effort to save a fellow driver in a track accident at Milwaukee in 1948 prompted officials to rename the June race in his honor. The Rex Mays Classic ran from 1950 to 1987. (GGAK.)

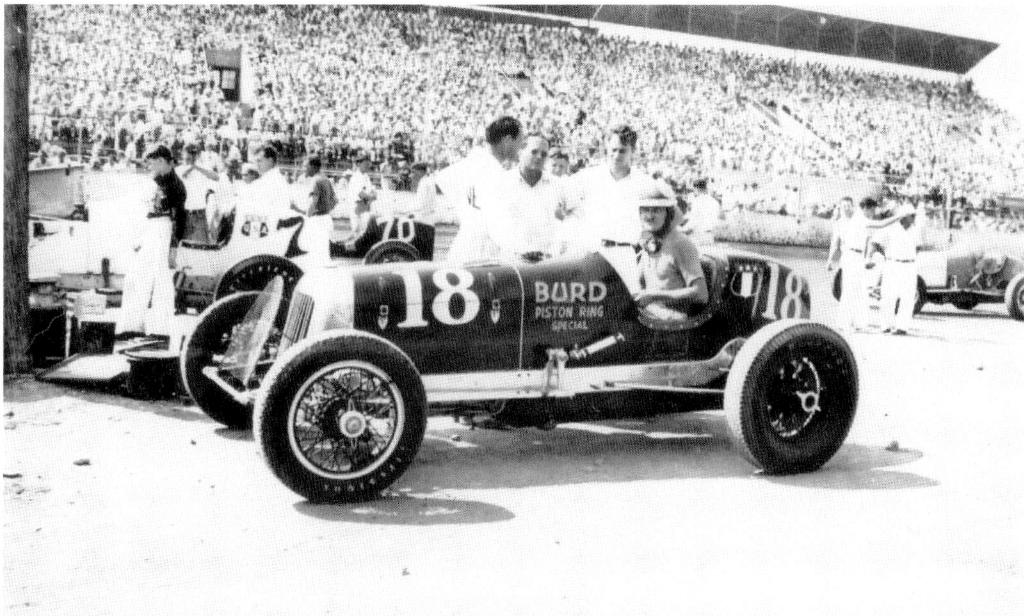

"Wild" Bill Cummings rolled into the state fair track and prepped his Burd Piston Ring Spl., No. 18, for the 1937 Indy car 100 race. As a driver familiar with firsts—he was one of several participants to drive the first Daytona—he ended this day second to Rex Mays after 96 laps. A scoring error ended the race at 96 laps instead of the usual 100, causing something of an uproar. (GGAK.)

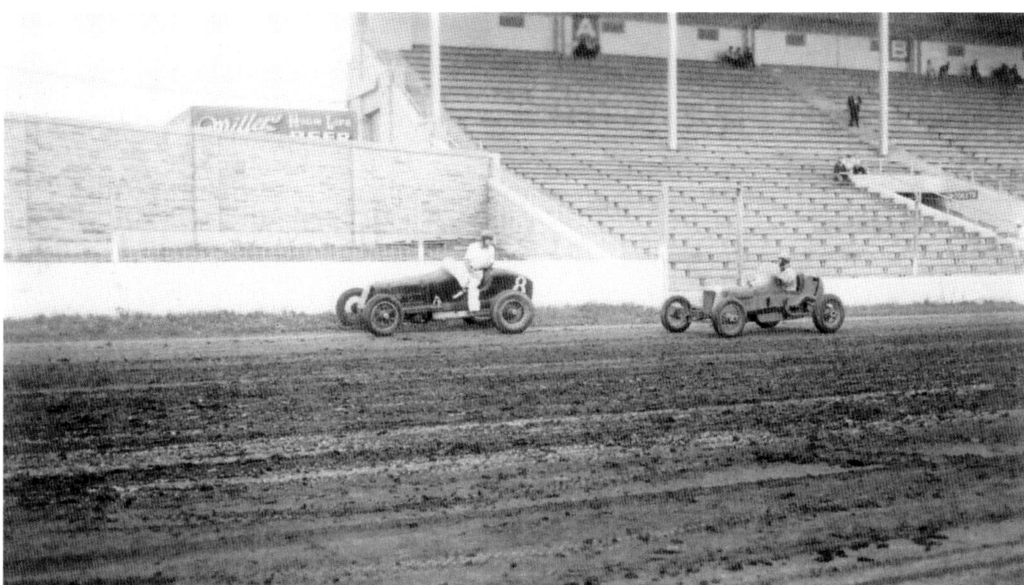

On August 25, 1938, during warmup for a 25-mile AAA sprint car race, Rex May, No. 8, and Tony Willman pause on the track for a bit of a chat. One can only wonder what that conversation entailed, but the caption for this images reads, "Do you want a tow?" That day, Mays won the race in 18:29, and again, Willman was behind. (GGAK.)

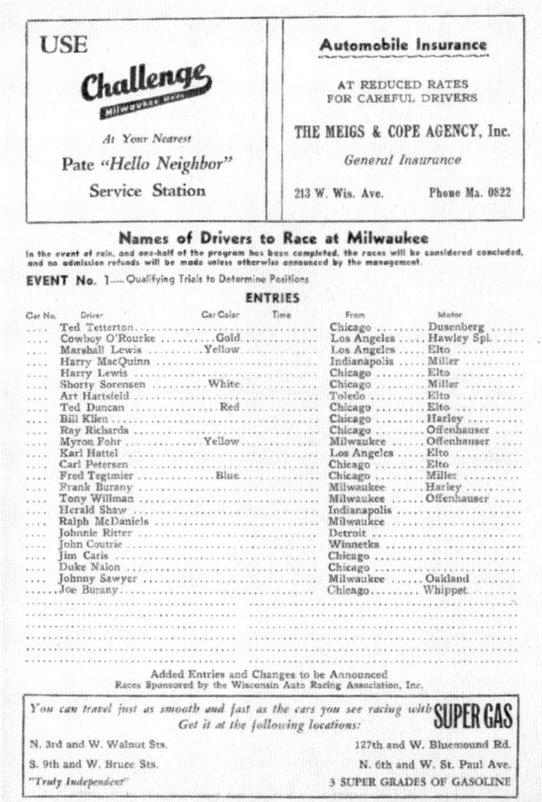

USE

Challenge

At Your Nearest

Pate "Hello Neighbor"

Service Station

Automobile Insurance

AT REDUCED RATES FOR CAREFUL DRIVERS

THE MEIGS & COPE AGENCY, Inc.

General Insurance

213 W. Wis. Ave. Phone Ma. 0822

Names of Drivers to Race at Milwaukee

In the event of rain, and one-half of the program has been completed, the races will be considered concluded, and no admission refunds will be made unless otherwise announced by the management.

EVENT No. 1—Qualifying Trials to Determine Positions

ENTRIES

Car No.	Driver	Car Color	Time	From	Motor
....	Ted Tetterton			Chicago	Dusenberg
....	Cowboy O'Rourke	Gold		Los Angeles	Hawley Spl.
....	Marshall Lewis	Yellow		Los Angeles	Elto
....	Harry MacQuinn			Indianapolis	Miller
....	Harry Lewis			Chicago	Elto
....	Shorty Sorensen	White		Chicago	Miller
....	Art Hartsfeld			Toledo	Elto
....	Ted Duncan	Red		Chicago	Elto
....	Bill Klien			Chicago	Harley
....	Ray Richards			Chicago	Offenhauser
....	Myron Fohr	Yellow		Milwaukee	Offenhauser
....	Karl Hattel			Los Angeles	Elto
....	Carl Petersen			Chicago	Elto
....	Fred Tegtmier	Blue		Chicago	Miller
....	Frank Burany			Milwaukee	Harley
....	Tony Willman			Milwaukee	Offenhauser
....	Herald Shaw			Indianapolis	
....	Ralph McDaniels			Milwaukee	
....	Johnnie Ritter			Detroit	
....	John Coutrie			Winnetka	
....	Jim Caris			Chicago	
....	Duke Nalon			Chicago	
....	Johnny Sawyer			Milwaukee	Oakland
......	Joe Burany			Chicago	Whippet

Added Entries and Changes to be Announced
Races Sponsored by the Wisconsin Auto Racing Association, Inc.

You can travel just as smooth and fast as the cars you see racing with SUPER GAS
Get it at the following locations:

N. 3rd and W. Walnut Sts. 127th and W. Bluemound Rd.

S. 9th and W. Bruce Sts. N. 6th and W. St. Paul Ave.

"Truly Independent" 3 SUPER GRADES OF GASOLINE

This 1938 driver roster reads as a who's-who of midget racing. From the earliest days of auto racing, State Fair Park Speedway was a well-known and respected track on the national circuit. Although this roster mainly features Midwest drivers, the track's notoriety drew drivers from as far away as California. (JS.)

Ray Richards (left) and Bob Wilke, team owner, prepare for the June 20, 1941, midget season opener. Richards, a native of Chicago, was a popular Milwaukee driver. He drove the Midwest circuit from 1934 to 1952 and held both the national indoor and outdoor midget race car championship titles. (GGAK.)

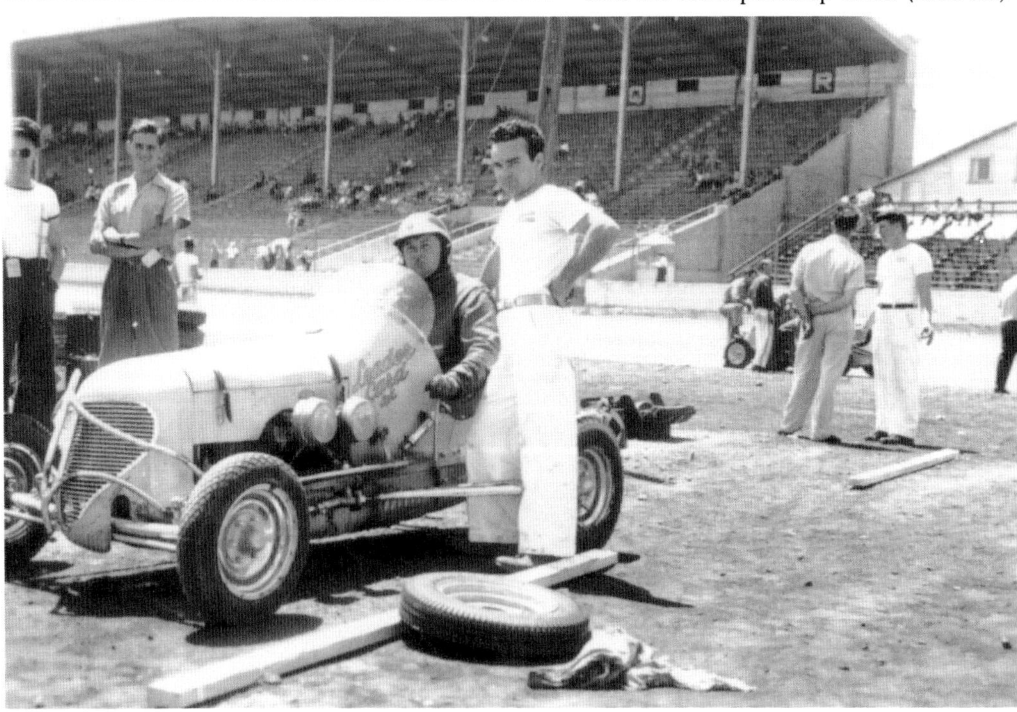

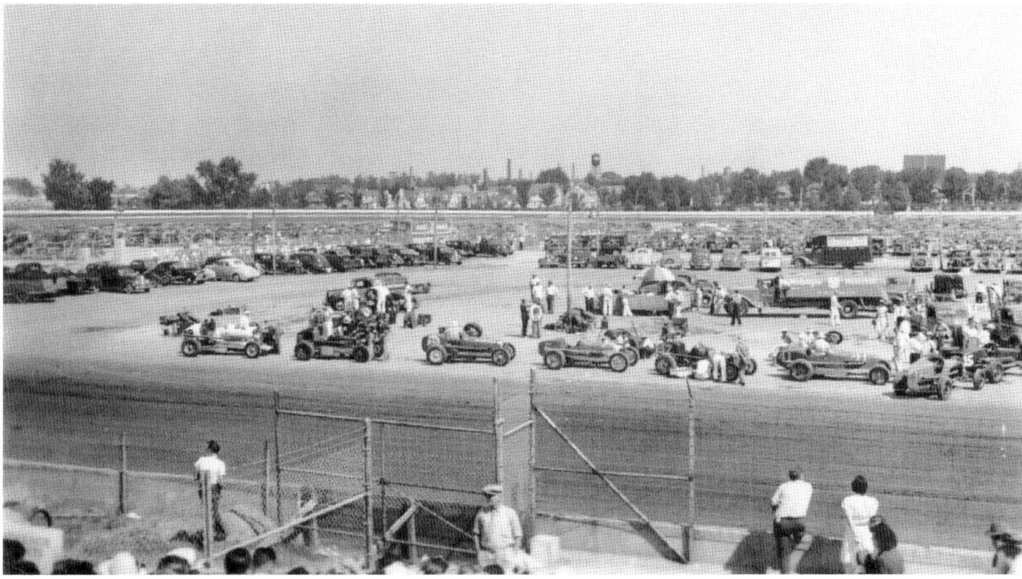

This picture of the August 1939 AAA Indy car race, taken from the grandstand, shows Indy cars in the pit area waiting for their turn to race against the clock. Shown are Shorty Cantlon, No. 47; Rex Mays, No. 15; Babe Stapp, No. 2 (third place); George Barringer, No. 41 (second); and Lewis Durant, No. 28 (winner). (GGAK.)

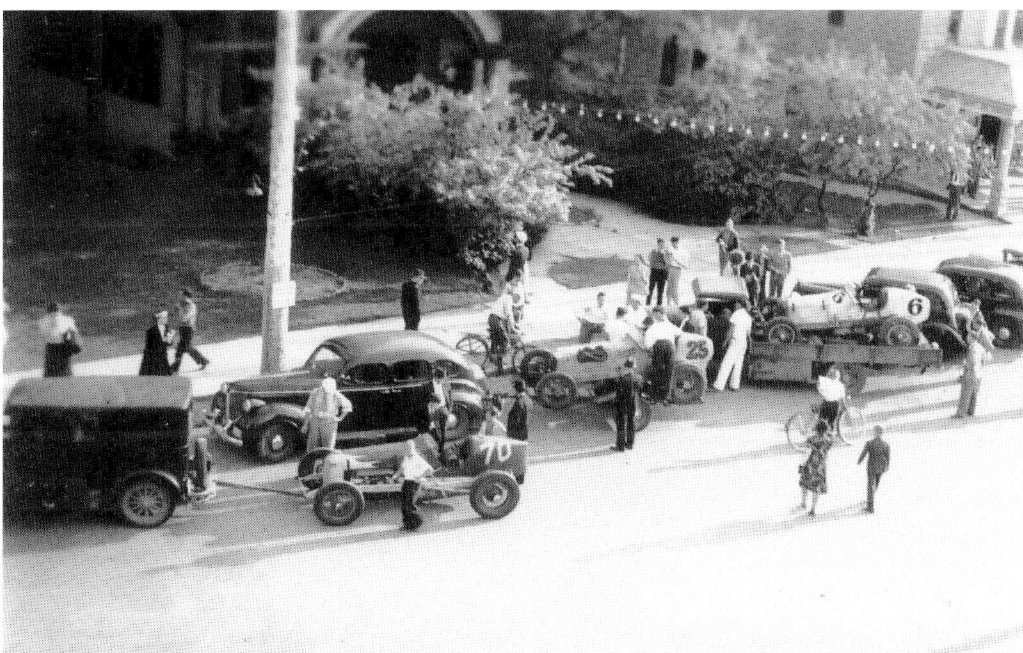

After the stands are empty and the autos trailered, there is nothing left to do but collect one's winnings, as these drivers are lined up to do. Assembled in front of the administration building, drivers wait for their payoff from the day's races. Shown are Myron Fohr, Chrysler No. 70; Duke Nalon, Dryer No. 25; and Weirich No. 6, driven by Jimmy Snyder. (GGAK.)

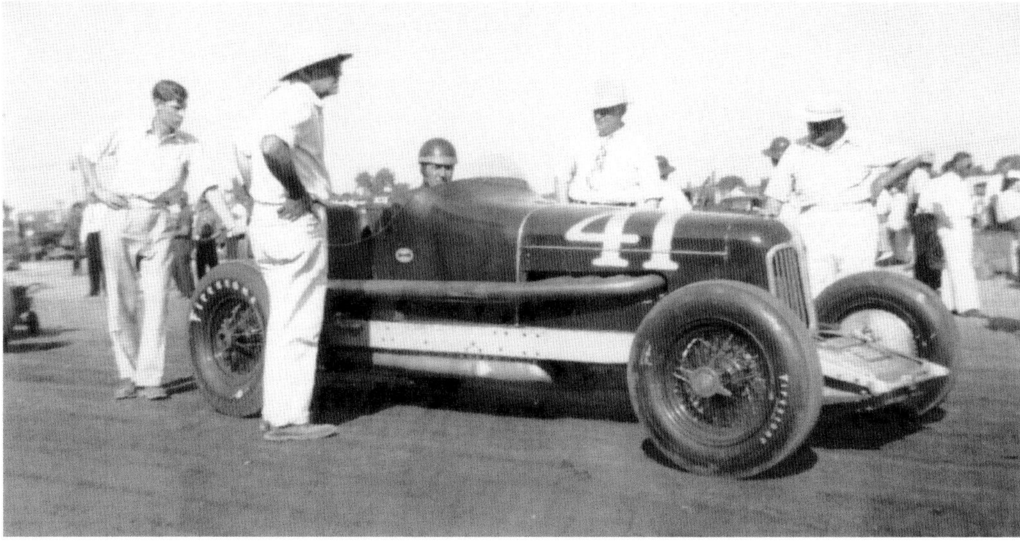

George Barringer, driving No. 41, a Weil/Miller for Bill White, was a consistent and well-liked driver. His appearance at the August 1939 AAA 100-mile race at the State Fair Park placed him at a respectable second place to Babe Stapp. Reflecting the volatility of the sport, Barringer, like so many of his colleagues, perished in a race at Lakewood Speedway on September 2, 1946. (GGAK.)

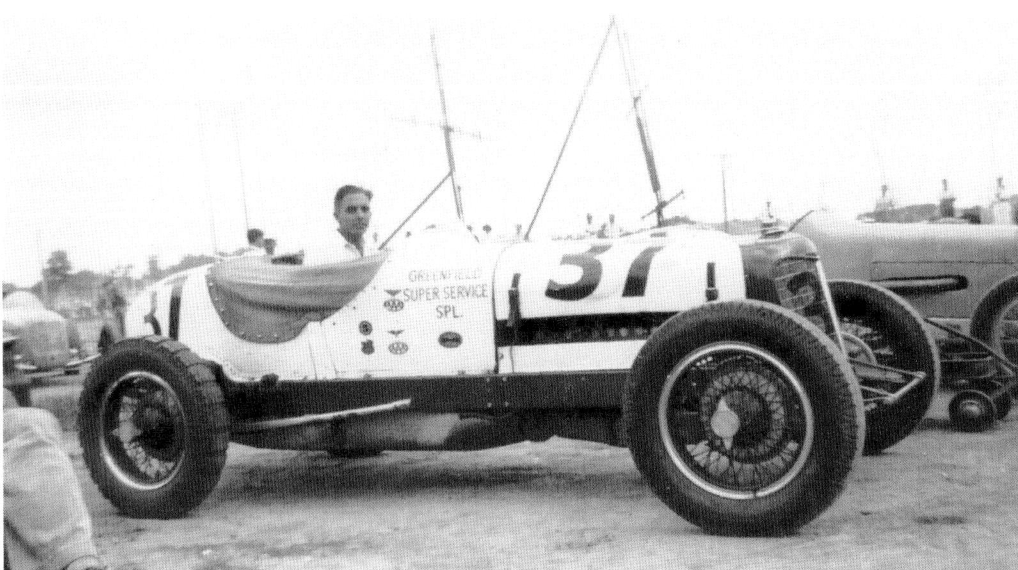

Hal Robson so loved racing he convinced his mother to let him race as a minor. From midgets to sprints, he ran mile tracks to gain the experience he needed for the Indy races. At the August 1939 AAA 100 race, Robson drove his Studebaker, the Greenfield Super Service Special No. 37. Starting in 17th place, Robson fought his way to end the race in 7th. (GGAK.)

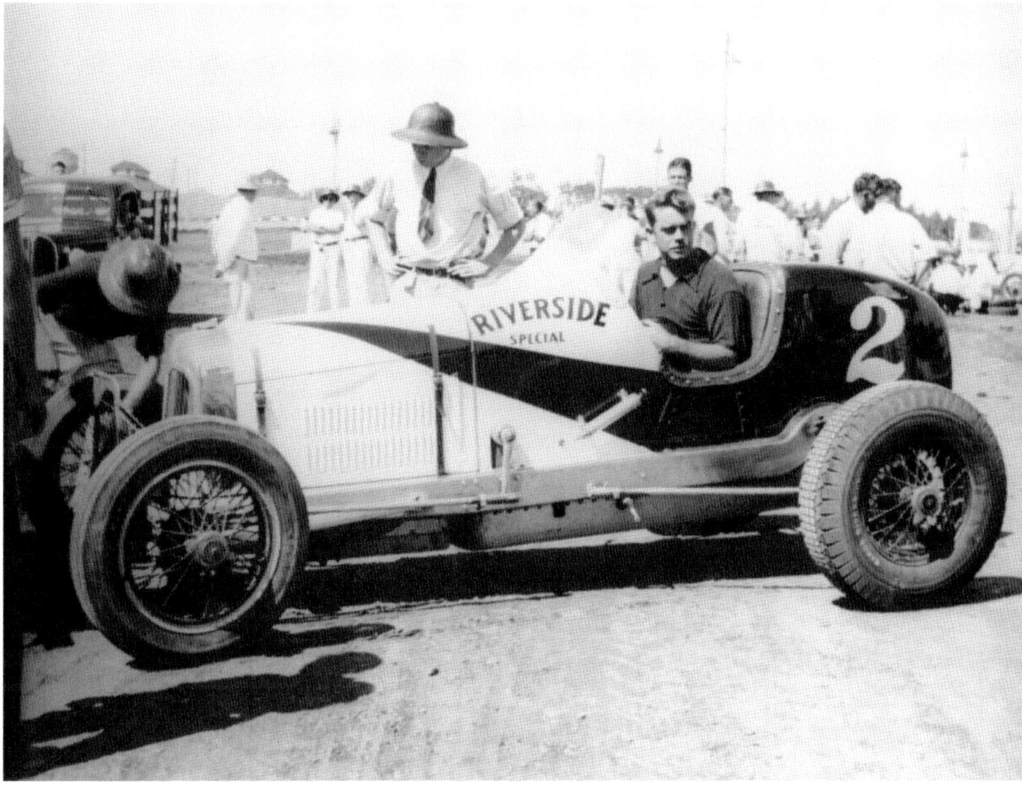

Racing legends might argue it is the driver's skill that makes winners, while others suggest it is the car. Ted Horn, the three-time AAA national champion (1946–1948), might agree it is the car. Horn's No. 2 Riverside had a sordid past as Wilbur Shaw's No. 48 Gilmore and Sam Palmer's No. 9 Gilmore Lion Cub, but the addition of Horn's signature seemed to change its luck. His turnaround year, 1938, added enough points to earn him the Midwestern AAA championship. (GGAK.)

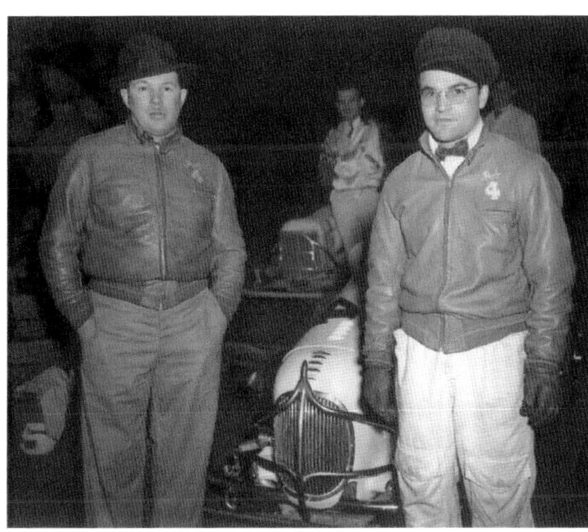

As a young man, Bob Wilke developed his passion for racing while tinkering in the Marchese brothers' garage during the 1920s. He eventually developed the Leader Card racing team. Driver Ray Richards (left) and car owner Wilke stand together around 1939 near a Leader Card Special midget. Competing from the mid-1930s to the early 1950s, Richards earned back-to-back (1937 and 1938) titles under the Badger Midget Auto Racing Association (BMARA). (MWLPP.)

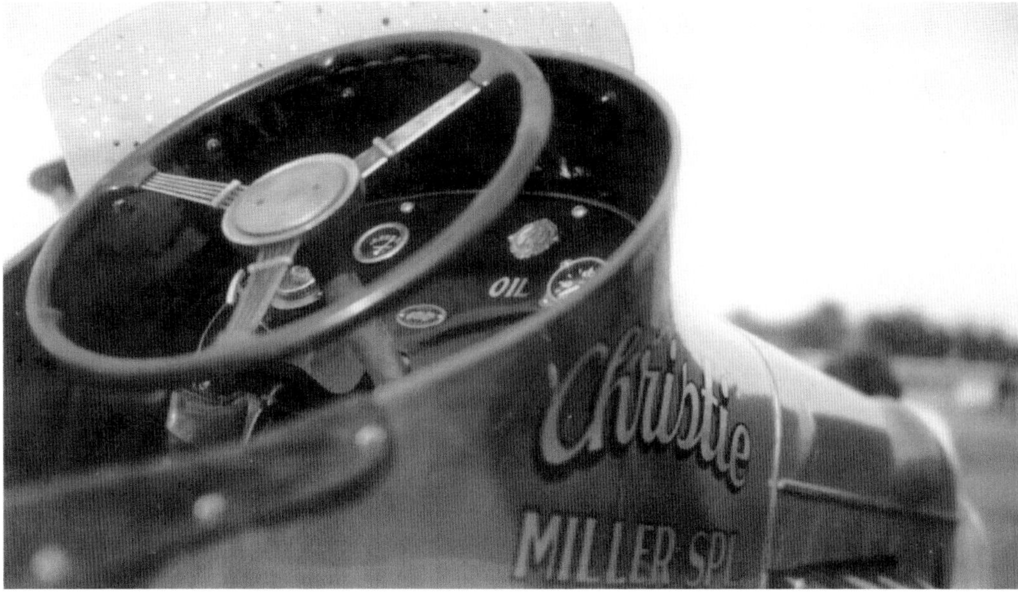

Here is a glimpse into the cockpit of George Connor's Christie Miller Spl. No. 44, which finished sixth in the June 4, 1939, AAA sprint car race. Stealing a peek is about as close as most fans would ever get to a race car. There is not much to see—a short windshield to protect the driver from flying track debris, and the instrument cluster, front and center. It is simple, with little distraction. (GGAK.)

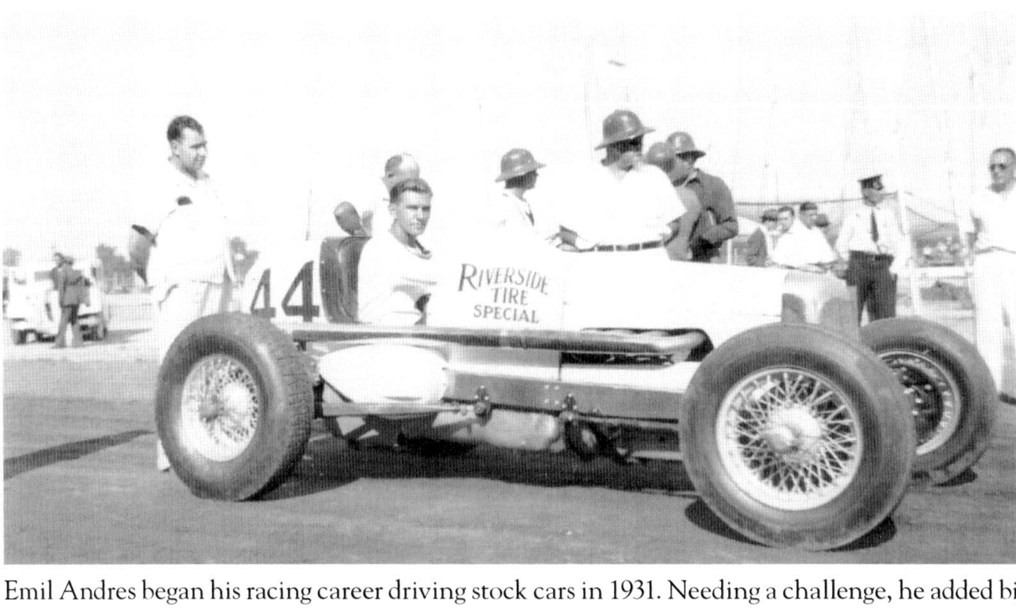

Emil Andres began his racing career driving stock cars in 1931. Needing a challenge, he added big cars the following year, and midgets the year after. Always looking for opportunities, Andres shifted to the Riverside Tire Special sprint car. Success followed; Andres won the AAA Midwest sprint car title in 1940. Seen here before the June 1939 sprint car race, he lapped 25 of the scheduled 30 that day because of rain. (GGAK.)

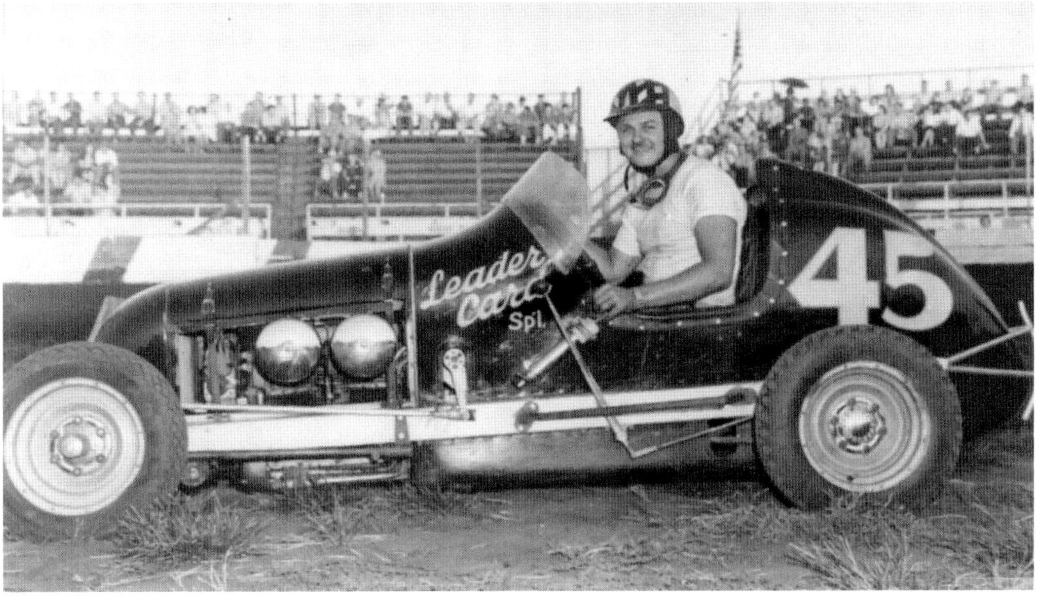

Although Eddy Kracek began his career with stock cars, midgets were his love. Considered one of the top midget drivers in the Midwest, he raced frequently at Milwaukee and dominated many of the tracks where he competed. His tenacity, wins, and love for the sport earned him the title of Nebraska Midget Champion. Taken in 1941, this photograph shows Kracek driving the Leader Card Special for the Wilke team. (MWLPP.)

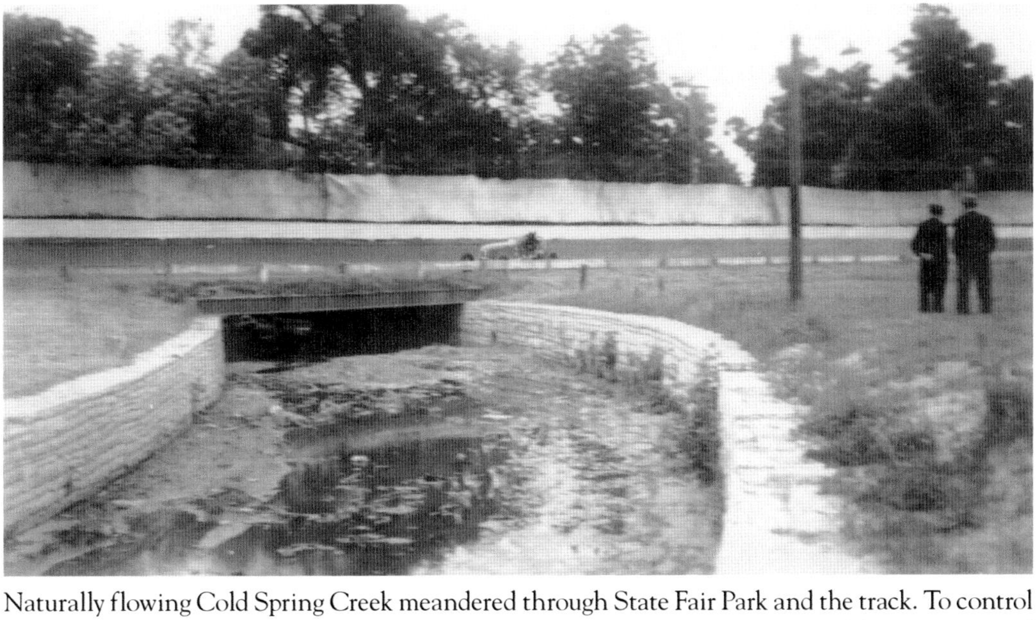

Naturally flowing Cold Spring Creek meandered through State Fair Park and the track. To control its flow, the stream's banks were bricked. Directed under the racetrack, Cold Spring created structural issues, seepage, and leaks over time, as well as a vehicle hazard. Track improvements diverted the creek through underground piping. In the background of this 1940s image, Emil Andres, No. 3, is seen entering the first turn. (GGAK.)

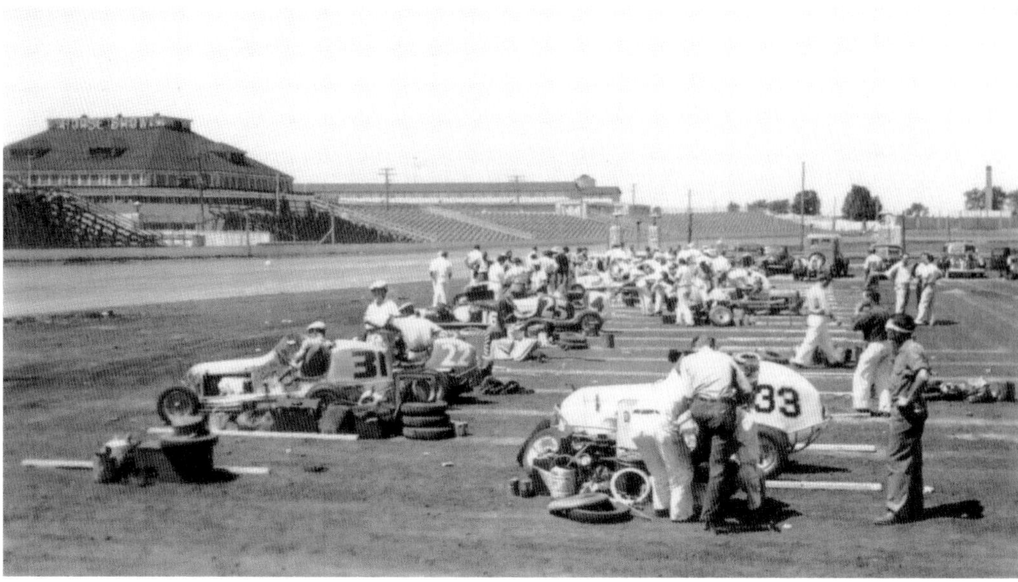

Drivers, cars, and crew members take their designated spots in the pits for this 100-mile AAA Indy car race in 1941. It is all business as crews work diligently to ready their cars for the day's race, with little time for conversation with the other teams—there would be plenty of time after the race for jokes and guarded advice. (GGAK.)

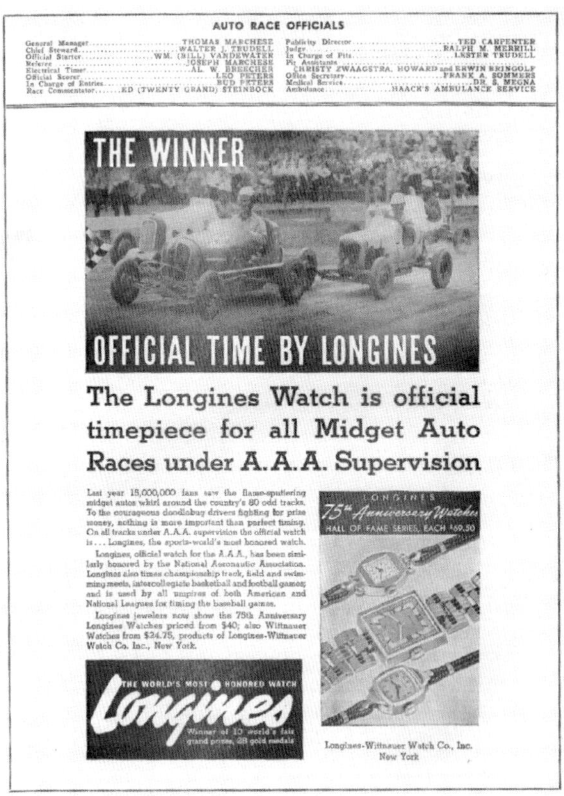

AUTO RACE OFFICIALS

General Manager	THOMAS MARCHESE	Publicity Director	TED CARPENTER
Chief Steward	WALTER J. TRUDELL	Judge	RALPH M. MERRILL
Official Starter	WM. (BILL) VANDEWATER	In Charge of Pits	LESTER TRUDELL
Referee	JOSEPH MARCHESE	Pit Assistants	CHRISTY ZWAAGSTRA, HOWARD and ERWIN BRINGOLF
Electrical Timer	AL. W. BRECHER	Office Secretary	FRANK A. SOMMERS
Official Scorer	LEO PETERS	Medical Service	DR. S. MEGNA
In Charge of Entries	BUD PETERS	Ambulance	HAACK'S AMBULANCE SERVICE
Race Commentator	ED (TWENTY GRAND) STEINBOCK		

THE WINNER

OFFICIAL TIME BY LONGINES

The Longines Watch is official timepiece for all Midget Auto Races under A.A.A. Supervision

Last year 15,000,000 fans saw the flame-sputtering midget autos whirl around the country's 80 odd tracks. To the courageous doodlebug drivers fighting for prize money, nothing is more important than perfect timing. On all tracks under A.A.A. supervision the official watch is . . . Longines, the sports-world's most honored watch.

Longines, official watch for the A.A.A., has been similarly honored by the National Aeronautic Association. Longines also times championship track, field and swimming meets, intercollegiate basketball and football games; and is used by all umpires of both American and National Leagues for timing the baseball games.

Longines jewelers now show the 75th Anniversary Longines Watches priced from $40; also Wittnauer Watches from $24.75, products of Longines-Wittnauer Watch Co. Inc., New York.

THE WORLD'S MOST HONORED WATCH
Longines
Winner of 10 world's fair grand prizes, 28 gold medals

Longines-Wittnauer Watch Co., Inc.
New York

An official partner and timekeeper in numerous prestigious events around the world since 1832, Longines was and still is one of the most respected partners in the world of motorsports, specifically ones that require participants to *cross* a finish line, rather than *touch* at finish. From the beginning, the company's advanced technology has measured time down to its smallest segments. (JS.)

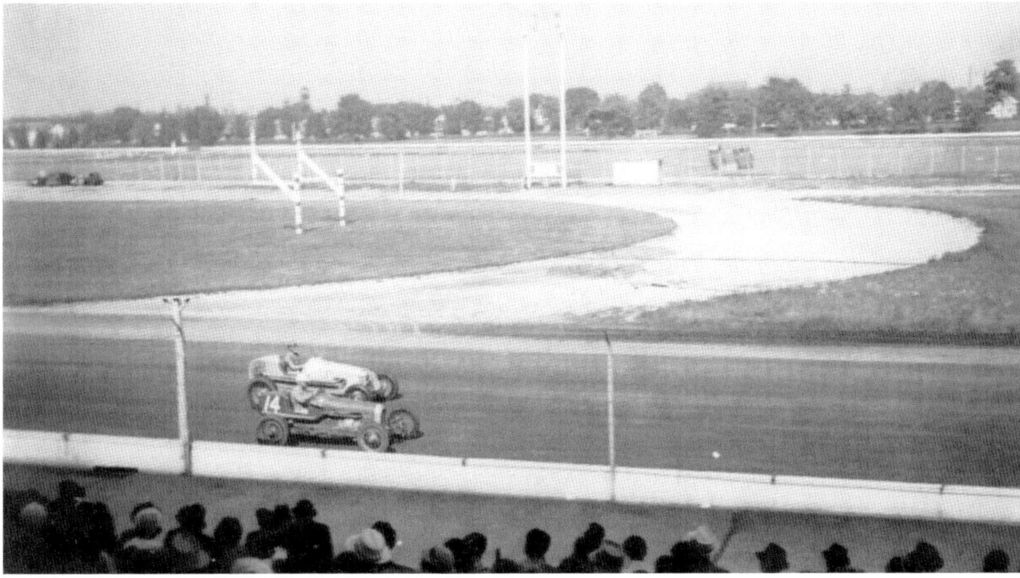

This 1941 photograph shows Rex Mays, No. 2, and Paul Russo, No. 14, pulling out of the fourth turn and down the straightaway, with Russo holding a slight lead. The AAA sprint car race that day, won by Duke Nalon, was called after 25 laps because of rain. Behind the straightaway, goalposts are visible on the Green Bay Packers' football field. Today, the finish line is painted where the 50-yard line once was. (GGAK.)

Billy Huber, pictured around 1945, loved to race, the faster the better. A fearless, spunky crowd-pleaser, Huber, like his father, Alan, became a factory rider—Billy for Harley Davidson, Alan for Indian. Both father and son competed in Class A competitions, specifically held to test the field of motorcycle rivalries. As factory riders, they received the newest prototype vehicles available, gear, all expenses, and a cut of the purse. (WSH.)

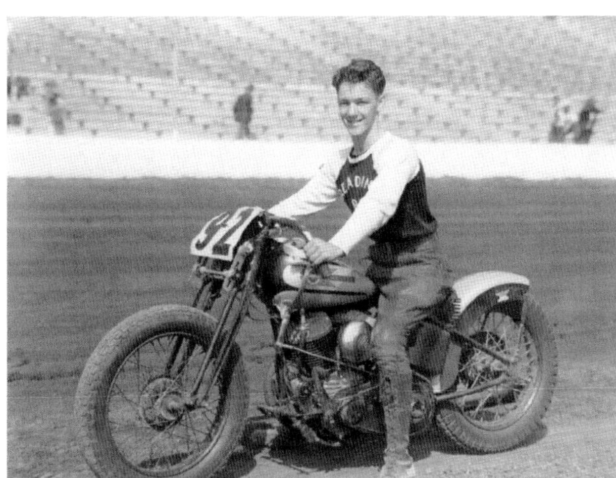

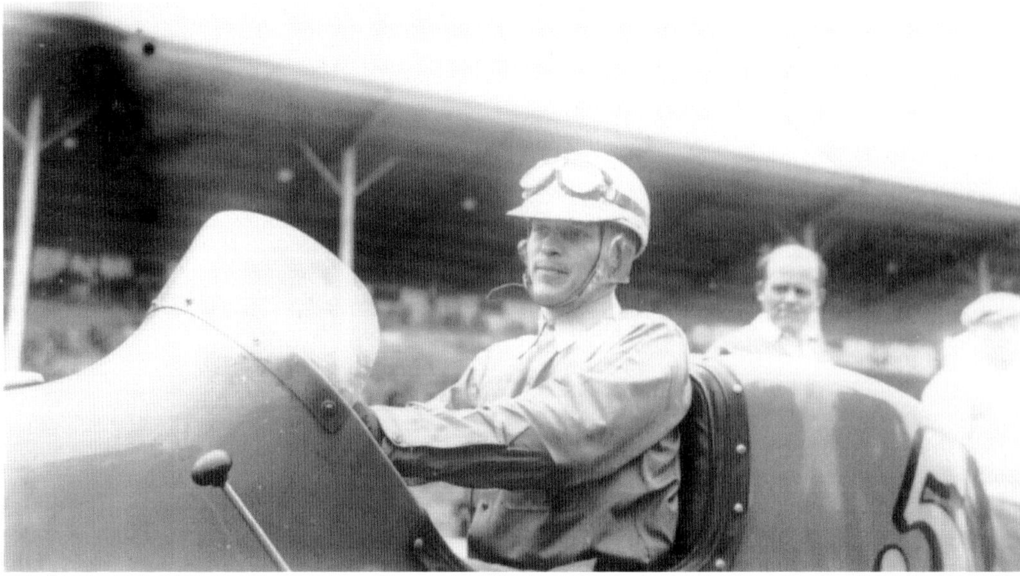

Driving No. 5, Tony Bettenhausen, known as "the Tinley Park Express," was a frequent favorite at State Fair Park, driving midgets and Indy cars. Bettenhausen drove with vigor and passion, which transferred to wins at the speedway in 1942, 1946, and 1947. This photograph was taken minutes before the June 1941 AAA sprint race. (GGAK.)

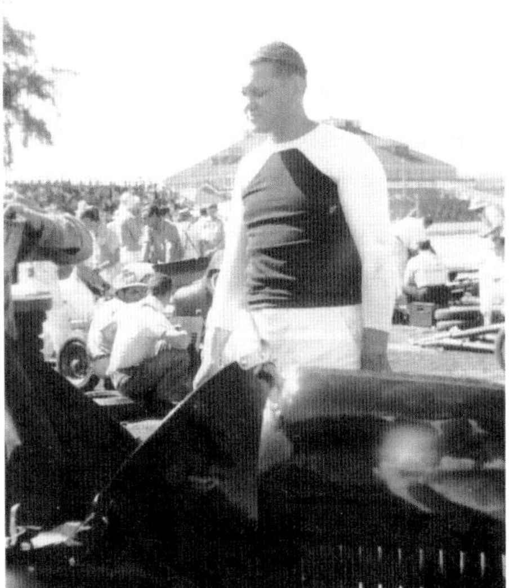

Wally Zale, affectionately known as "the Human Cyclone" and one of seven members of the "Chicago Gang" of midget racers, was a force to be reckoned with. Known to push the envelope, Zale is considered one of midget racing's pioneers. Driving during the golden era of midget racing (early 1930s–1940s), Zale is credited with 178 feature victories, including 65 triumphs in the 1936 season alone. (GGAK.)

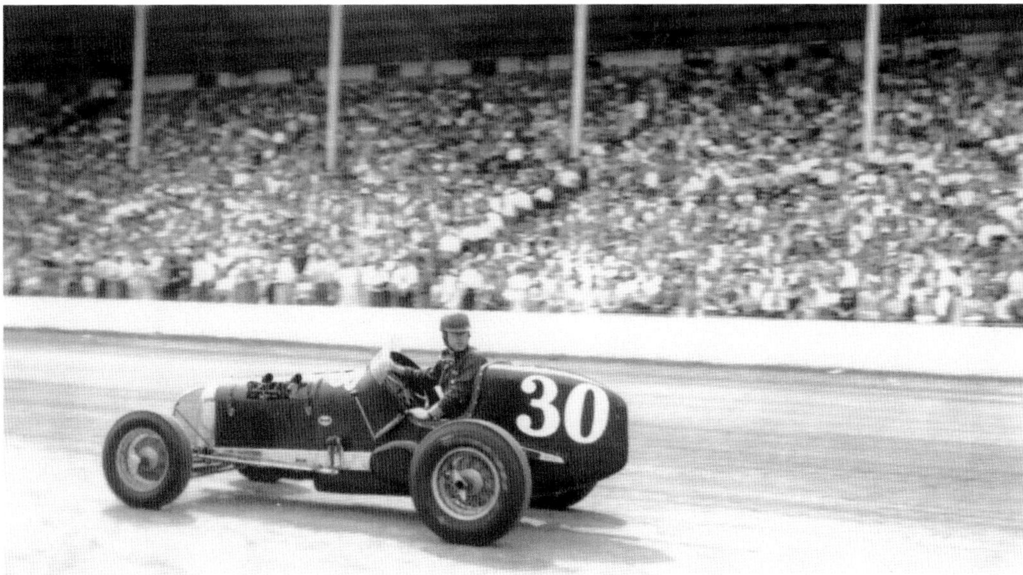

Frank "Wildman" McGurk made a living racing cars until World War II. His orders sent him to the Packard Motor company factory to build aircraft motors. Proficient in motor repair, he opened his own auto shop, eventually shifting to manufacturing speed equipment and engine components. Taken during the 1941 AAA Indy car race, this photograph shows McGurk backing up to the pits, dispelling any idea that No. 30 was missing rear gears. (GGAK.)

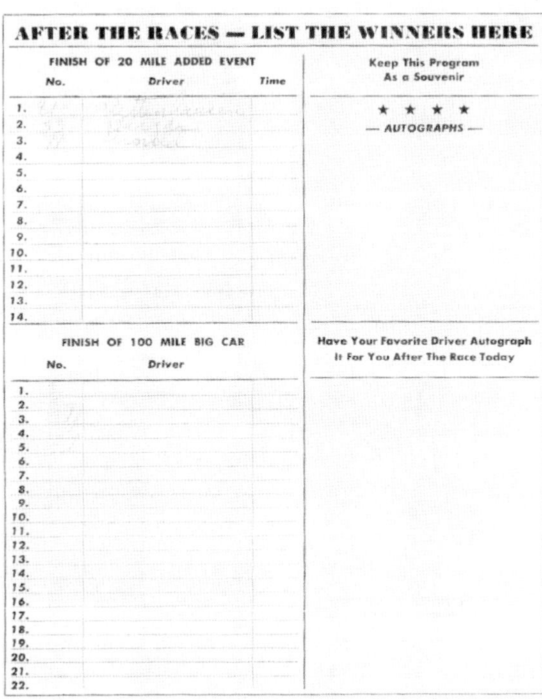

AFTER THE RACES — LIST THE WINNERS HERE

FINISH OF 20 MILE ADDED EVENT

No.	Driver	Time
1.		
2.		
3.		
4.		
5.		
6.		
7.		
8.		
9.		
10.		
11.		
12.		
13.		
14.		

Keep This Program
As a Souvenir

★ ★ ★ ★

— AUTOGRAPHS —

FINISH OF 100 MILE BIG CAR

No.	Driver
1.	
2.	
3.	
4.	
5.	
6.	
7.	
8.	
9.	
10.	
11.	
12.	
13.	
14.	
15.	
16.	
17.	
18.	
19.	
20.	
21.	
22.	

Have Your Favorite Driver Autograph
It For You After The Race Today

Page Twenty-four

Cultivating a fan base is essential to the health of any sport, but especially in auto sports. Race fans frequently have more opportunities to meet their heroes up close and personal, chat, and get an autograph. This inside page from a 1940s race program allows the fan to become a part of the race, eyeing the drivers, logging race results, and collecting autographs. (JS.)

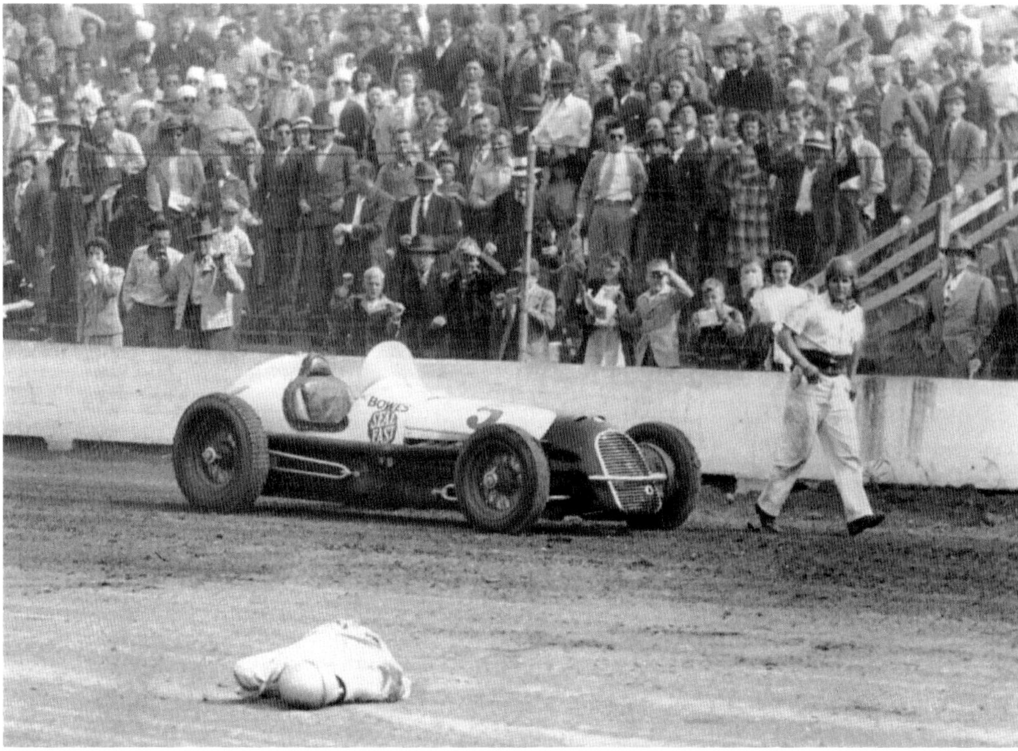

Actions speak louder than words, and on June 6, 1948, Rex Mays not only demonstrated his compassion but also his bravery when fellow driver Duke Dinsmore crashed into the outside wall and was thrown onto the track. Quick-thinking Mays spun his racer into the outside wall to avoid Dinsmore and, risking his own life, proceeded to direct traffic around the unconscious Dinsmore until help arrived. (GC/Bob Sheldon Collection.)

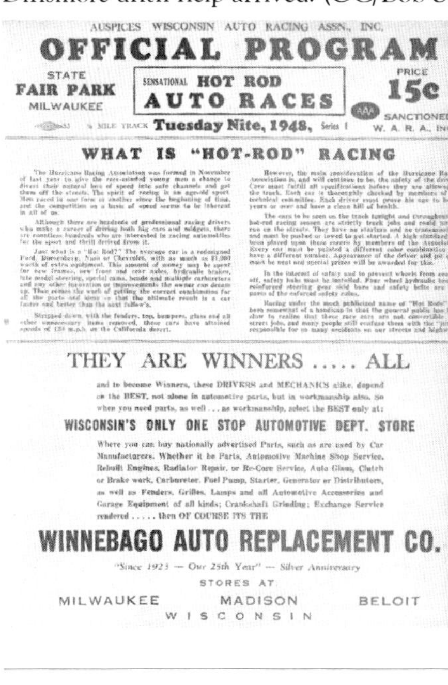

AUSPICES WISCONSIN AUTO RACING ASSN., INC.

OFFICIAL PROGRAM

STATE FAIR PARK MILWAUKEE

SENSATIONAL HOT ROD AUTO RACES

PRICE 15c

SANCTIONED W. A. R. A., INC

½ MILE TRACK Tuesday Nite, 1948, Series 1

WHAT IS "HOT-ROD" RACING

THEY ARE WINNERS ..... ALL

and to become Winners, these DRIVERS and MECHANICS alike, depend on the BEST, not alone in automotive parts, but in workmanship also. So when you need parts, as well . . . as workmanship, select the BEST only at:

WISCONSIN'S ONLY ONE STOP AUTOMOTIVE DEPT. STORE

Where you can buy nationally advertised Parts, such as are used by Car Manufacturers. Whether it be Parts, Automotive Machine Shop Service, Rebuilt Engines, Radiator Repair, or Re-Core Service, Auto Glass, Clutch or Brake work, Carburetor, Fuel Pump, Starter, Generator or Distributors, as well as Fenders, Grilles, Lamps and all Automotive Accessories and Garage Equipment of all kinds; Crankshaft Grinding; Exchange Service rendered ..... then OF COURSE ITS THE

WINNEBAGO AUTO REPLACEMENT CO.

"Since 1923 — Our 25th Year" — Silver Anniversary

STORES AT

MILWAUKEE MADISON BELOIT

WISCONSIN

The front page from the 1948 hot-rod program reads like a want ad encouraging folks to race safely. The Hurricane Racing Association, organized by Andy Granatelli, promoted hot rod and stock-car races in the Midwest that combined racing opportunities for new drivers with crowd-pleasing theatrics. Combining demolition derby with oval racing was the hook. Some events included rollovers and end-over-end crashes. (JS.)

4

Four Tracks Are Better Than One

1950–1968

Racing is a big part of the nostalgia associated with the 1950s. Some consider it the greatest decade of American racing. It was an era before true sponsorships and television's influence on sports, when racing was about the driver.

The 1950s honored those who lost their lives doing what they loved. In June 1950, the 100-mile race became the Rex Mays Classic. Racing offered entrepreneurs an investment outlet; however, few saw a positive return. Some of the champion owners whose teams drove the State Fair Park track included Al Dean, Carl and Tudy Marchese, J.C. Agajanian, Bob Steinman, Bob Wilke, and Carl Kiekhaefer.

To the delight of drivers and fans, the dirt track no longer posed a hazard once paved in 1954. Harness racing moved to the inside half mile. Powerhouse drivers like Norm Nelson, Parnelli Jones, Don White, Bobby Unser, Jim Hurtubise, Joe Leonard, and others frequented the track.

The infield saw its own action, hosting weekly modified races. Drivers and their caricature-splattered cars rounded the dirt quarter mile to cheering crowds. Fan favorites included Miles "the Mouse" Melius, Kenny "Tweety Bird" Tlougan, Billy Johnson, Etchie "the Flying Grandpa" Biertzer, Paul Feldner, and Al Schill.

Summer brought a variety of action, including modified and sportsman racing every Thursday night on the quarter mile, four USAC stock-car races, two champ car races, and road racing on the 2.0 infield road course.

Technology again revolutionized racing with a new engine design. Once considered the greatest racing engine, the "Offy" dominated open-wheel racing for almost 50 years. Through 1963, most race cars ran with front engines designed by Fred Offenhauser. But when a rear-engine Lotus-Ford drove to victory in 1963, everything changed. Two years later, A.J. Foyt proved that front engines did not give up so easily. Prepping his dirt car for pavement (his Indy car showed up too late to qualify), Foyt was able to win the pole and finish second. A fan favorite at State Fair Park, Foyt won his first USAC stock-car race at the park.

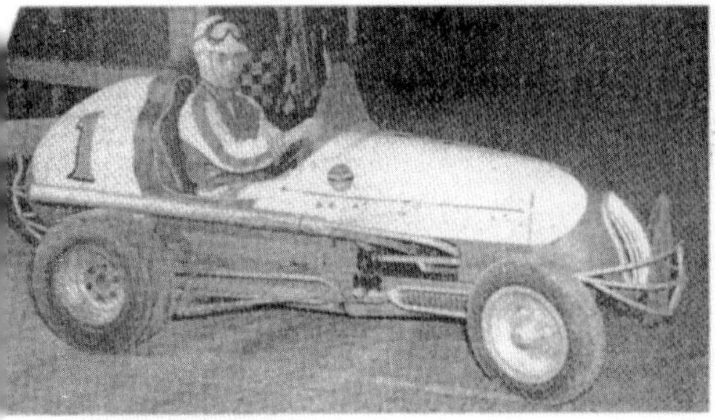

MILES MELIUS — WEST BEND
Won FIRST PLACE in 1950 with 642 Points

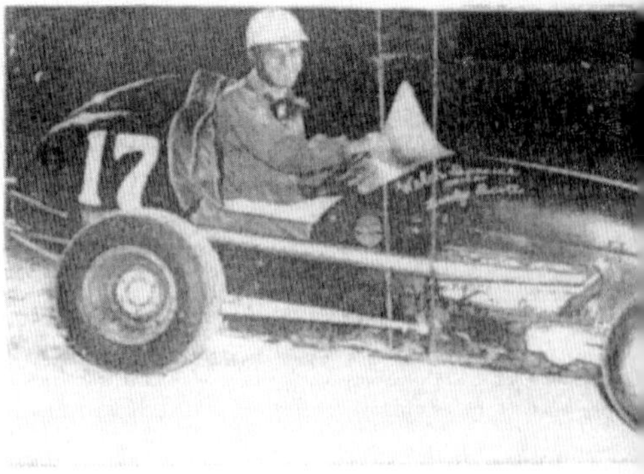

LANDY SCOTT — MILWAUKEE
Won SECOND PLACE in 1950 with 606 P

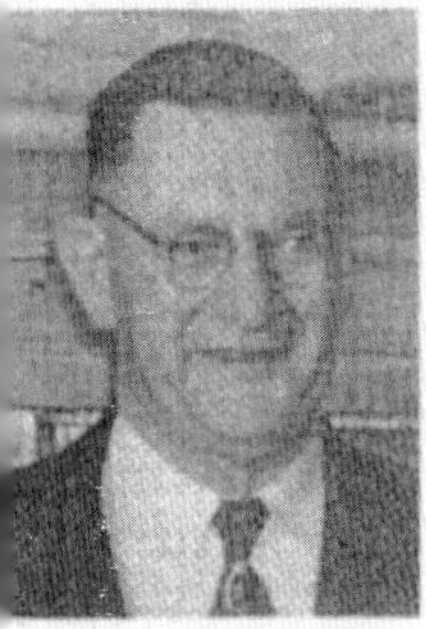

A. T. BREECHER
President

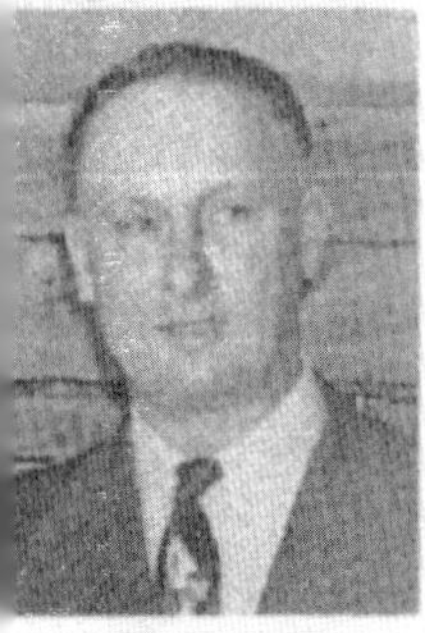

ART PATZKE
Vice President

ALVIN FREDENBURG — MADISON — FIFTH PLACE
503 Points in 1950

Duane Alberts — 7th Place — 466 Points	Gordon Frie — 10th Place — 347 Points	Ed Kichefski —
Miko Ladvinka — 8th Place — 448 Points	Howard Bradshaw—11th Pl.—343 Points	Don Patzke — 1
Wallace Patzke — 9th Place — 399 Points	Frank Connor — 12th Place — 315 Points	Duane Hanson —

Badger Midget Auto

THE BADGER MIDGET RACING ASSOCIATION is the oldest Midget Racing Assn. in the United States today. It was organized in the fall of 1936 beginning as the Wisconsin Midget Racing Association and then changed to the Badger Midget Racing Association in 1937.

It was composed of Midget race car drivers and Midget race car owners, contest and track officials and other personnel taking an active part in Midget Auto Racing. The officers and members felt they should incorporate. Then on February 9th, 1942, they incorporated and have been known as the Badger Midget Racing Association, Inc. since.

The first President of the old association, Carl Marchese is one of the very prominent car owners in the country today.

The acti
on half-mile t
weekly progra
Plymouth, De
programs at t

The Ba
officers for 19
1950.

5425 West Lo

Photos courtesy of Arme

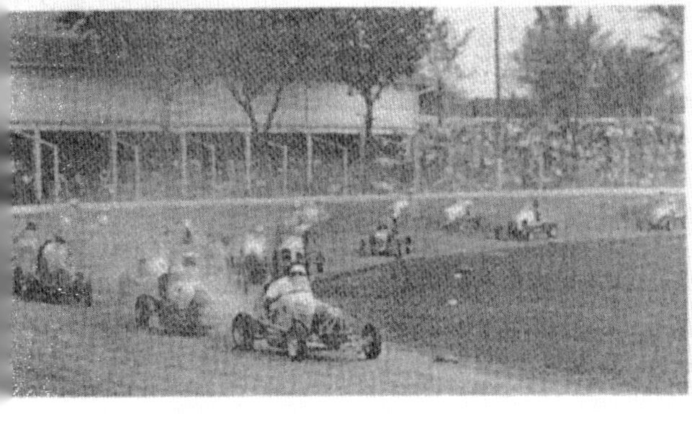

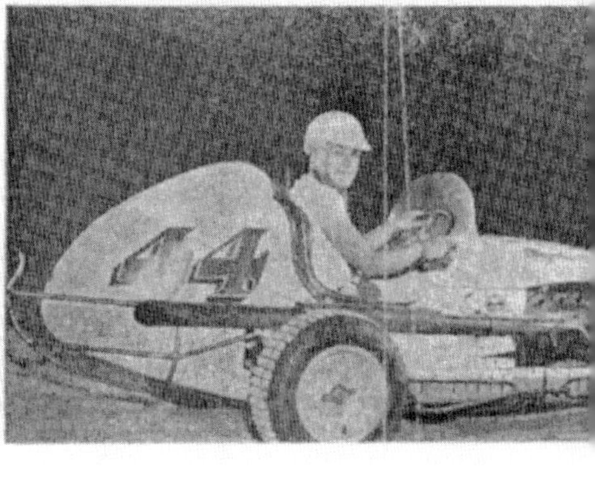

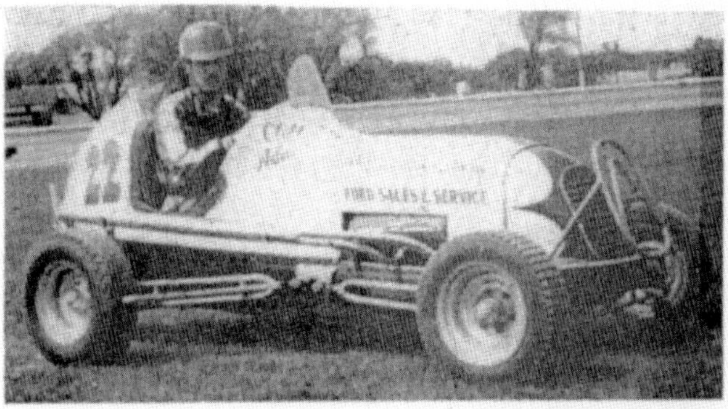

CLIFF ADAMS — CHICAGO
Won THIRD PLACE in 1950 with 534 Points

L HUNTER — RACINE — SIXTH PLACE
496 Points in 1950

)9 Points	F. Deininger — 16th Place — 216 Points
)1 Points	Earl Simmons — 17th Place — 206 Points
53 Points	Don Fischer — 18th Place — 194 Points

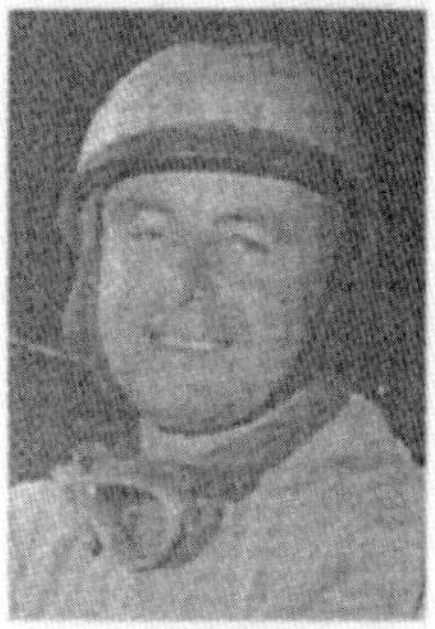

JOE BURANY
Secretary

cing Assn.

sociation consist of putting on racing shows fairs all over the State of Wisconsin plus acks such as, — Sun Prairie, Wis.; Slinger, rburg, Wisconsin, and having competed in ate Fair Park track.

cing Association proudly present their ns for points gained during the season of

ondence to — JOE BURANY
aukee, Wis. — Phone Hilltop 5-3216

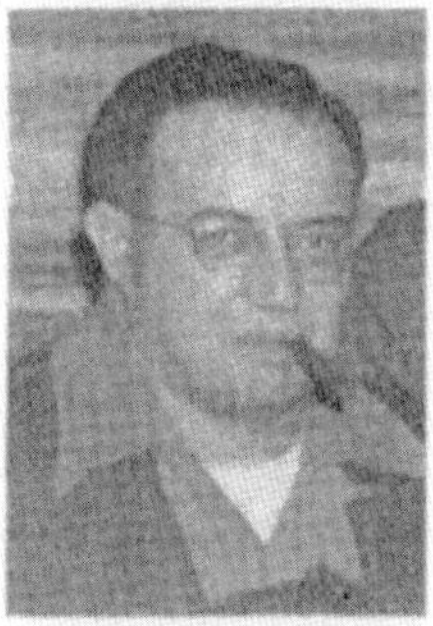

FRED KUTNER
Treasurer

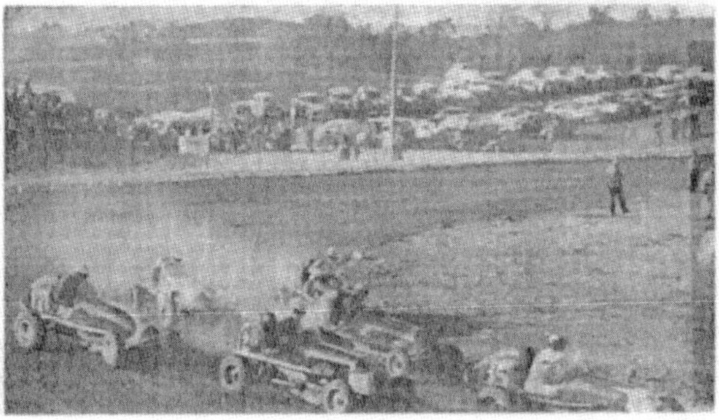

This 1951 Badger Midget Auto Racing Association poster depicts point champions and 1951 board members. Organized in 1935 by Carl Marchese for the betterment of the sport, drivers, and owners, the organization—first known as the Wisconsin Racing Association (WRA)—later changed its name to avoid confusion with the track's promotional organization, Wisconsin Auto Racing Association Inc., owned by Tom Marchese. (BBH.)

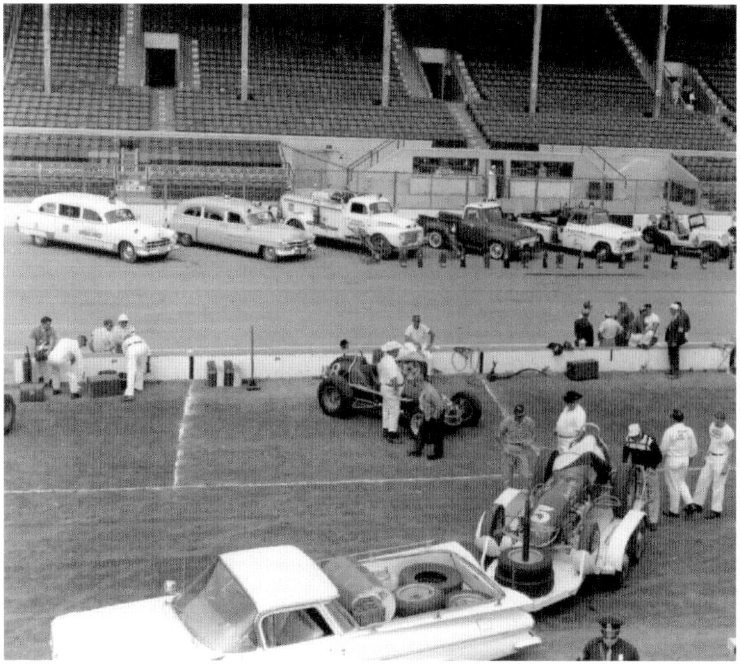

In this mid-1950s image, track personnel and teams prepare for the day's race. In an emergency, when seconds count and medical help is of the essence, drivers and crews could depend on the State Fair Park's emergency safety responders. Sponsored by Tom Marchese and Wisconsin Auto Racing (WAR), ambulances, fire trucks, and other emergency vehicles stand at the ready. (TMS.)

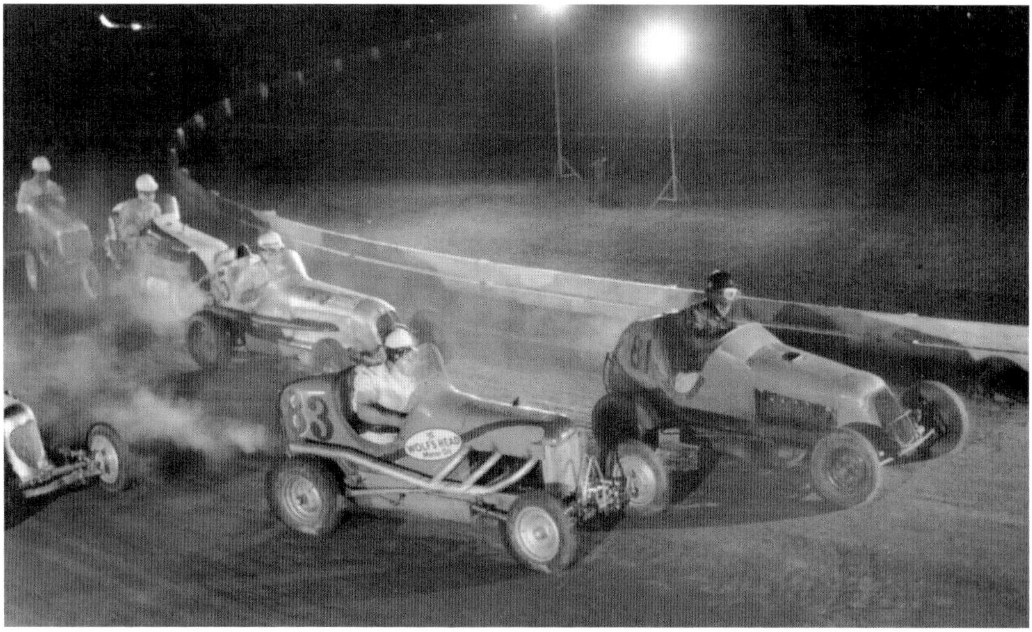

Racing under lights definitely brings a new feel to the event, both for the drivers and the fans. For both, senses are affected differently: the noise, the dust, the darkness, and glare of lights—not to mention the drop in track temperature—making it a different race. Taking advantage of races and potential points, drivers in this c. 1950 race at State Fair Park fight to the finish. (TMS.)

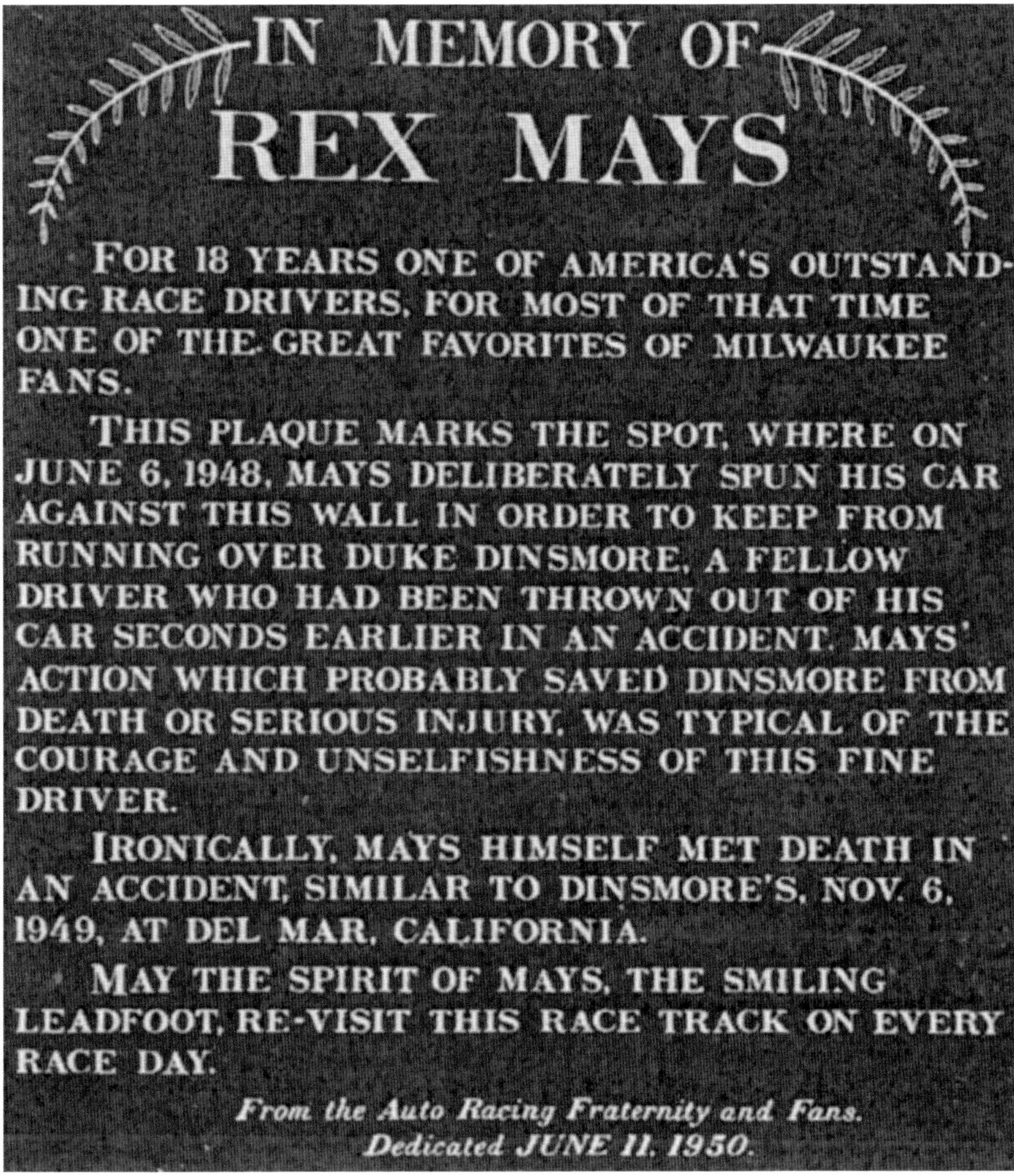

Originally placed on the south turn wall of the accident scene, this plaque honors the bravery and selfless actions of Rex Mays. So highly respected was Mays that Tom Marchese proclaimed the plaque's placement in 1950 so his heroic deeds would forever be remembered. After track improvements, the plaque was moved to the entryway of the newly constructed Milton Peck Media Center. (JS.)

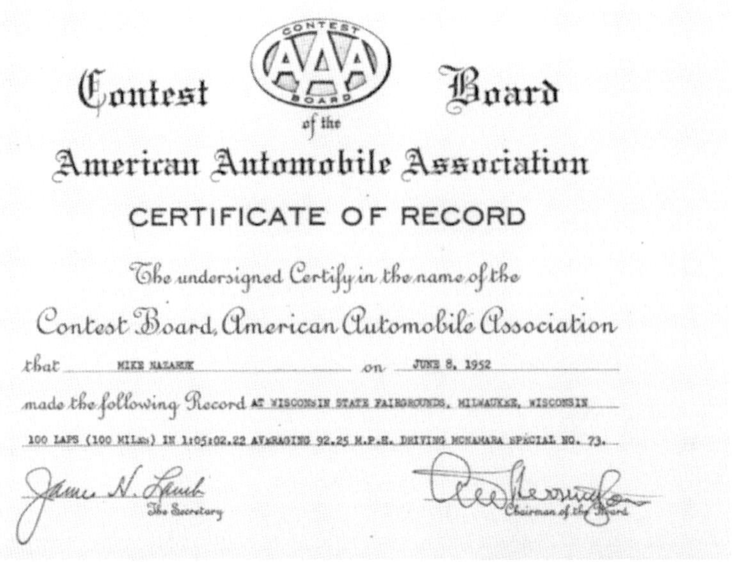

Contest Board
of the
American Automobile Association

CERTIFICATE OF RECORD

The undersigned Certify in the name of the
Contest Board, American Automobile Association
that MIKE NAZARUK on JUNE 8, 1952
made the following Record AT WISCONSIN STATE FAIRGROUNDS, MILWAUKEE, WISCONSIN
100 LAPS (100 MILES) IN 1:05:02.22 AVERAGING 92.25 M.P.H. DRIVING MCNAMARA SPECIAL NO. 73.

The Secretary

Chairman of the Board

This certificate was awarded to Mike Nazaruk for setting a record during his win at the June 8, 1952, AAA Indy car race. Winning for team McNamara, Nazaruk received the certificate, a trophy, and his split of the purse, $4,563. Not bad for a day's work in 1952. (BC.)

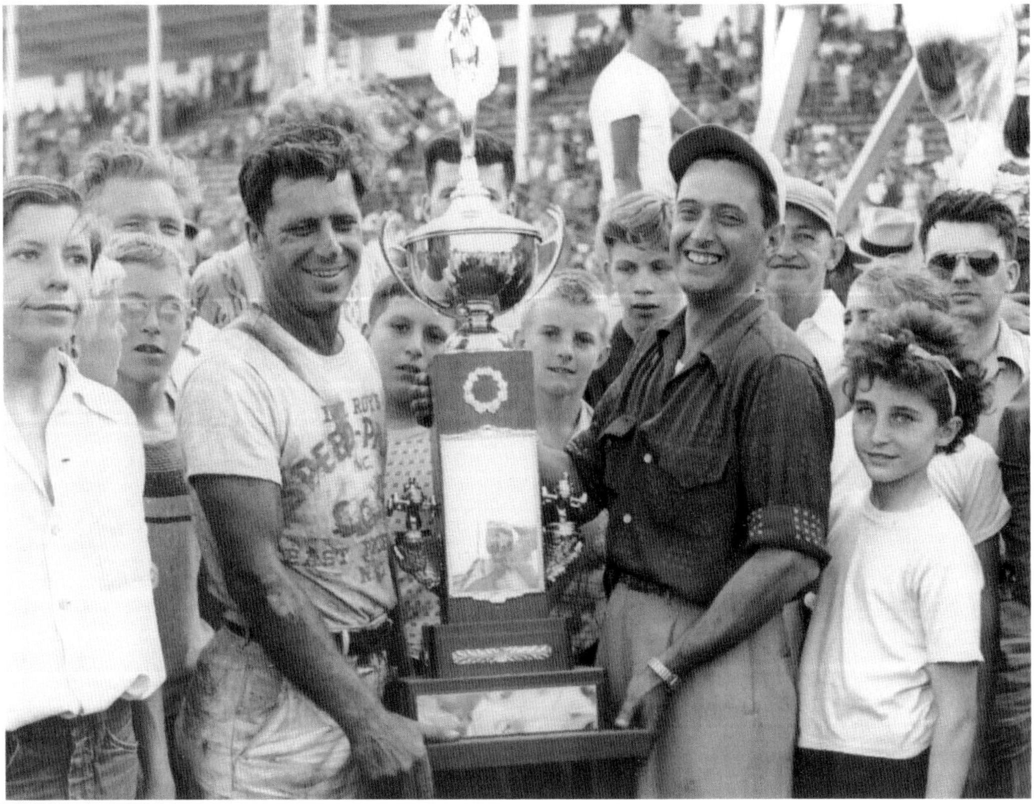

Some might wonder why racers risk their necks—this is why. Mike Nazaruk (left) and Lee Elkins could not be happier with the day's results. Winning the June 1952 Indy car race brought big smiles to both of them. Elkins, a self-made millionaire and owner of McNamar Motor Express, won big with Nazaruk (his favorite driver) in the early 1950s. (BC.)

William "Bill" Vandewater, pictured around 1954, began his career in Indiana officiating AAA races in 1933. Midget races drew Vandewater to Milwaukee, and in 1933, he started his first 100-mile championship race. Always dressed in a sport coat and slacks, he was dubbed "the fashion plate starter." His trademark stance, "the Ascot-Crossover" (standing mid-track before a full field of cars), must have been very dramatic. (JS.)

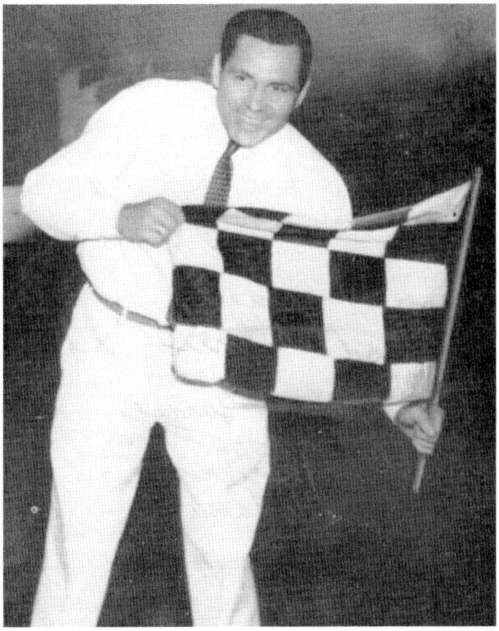

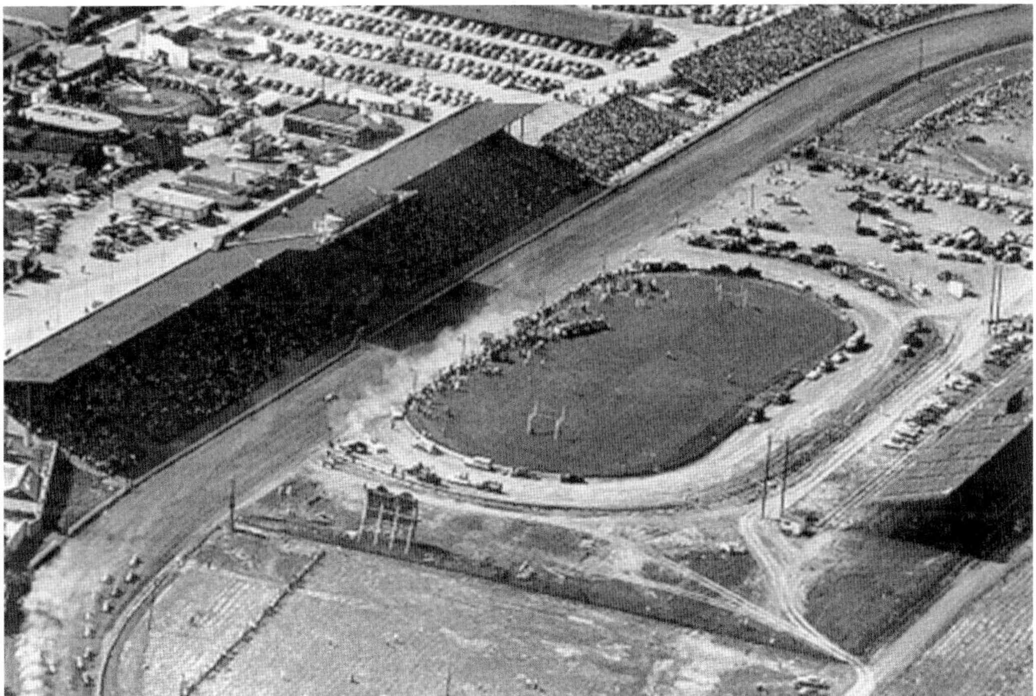

The Green Bay Packers' field is detailed in this c. 1951 aerial photograph. Goalposts are visible, as is the added bleacher section east of the field. While used by the Packers from 1934 until 1951, the field was also home to the Milwaukee Chiefs of the American Football League from 1940 through 1941. The field at the time was Wisconsin's largest stadium, drawing good crowds on game day. (JS.)

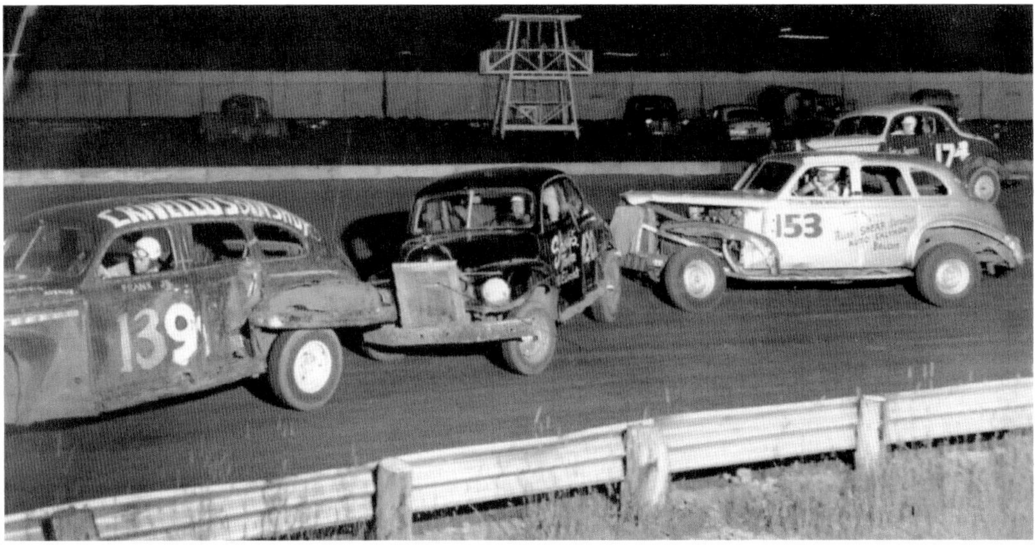

Thursday nights drew large crowds for stock-car races at the quarter-mile track during the 1950s. Fans followed and cheered for their favorites with passion. Race night was good family fun, featuring many local drivers as well as some regional drivers. Frequently, stock-car drivers gained valuable educational experiences before moving on to Indy cars or midgets. Often, drivers divided their time between several races for the purse and the fun.

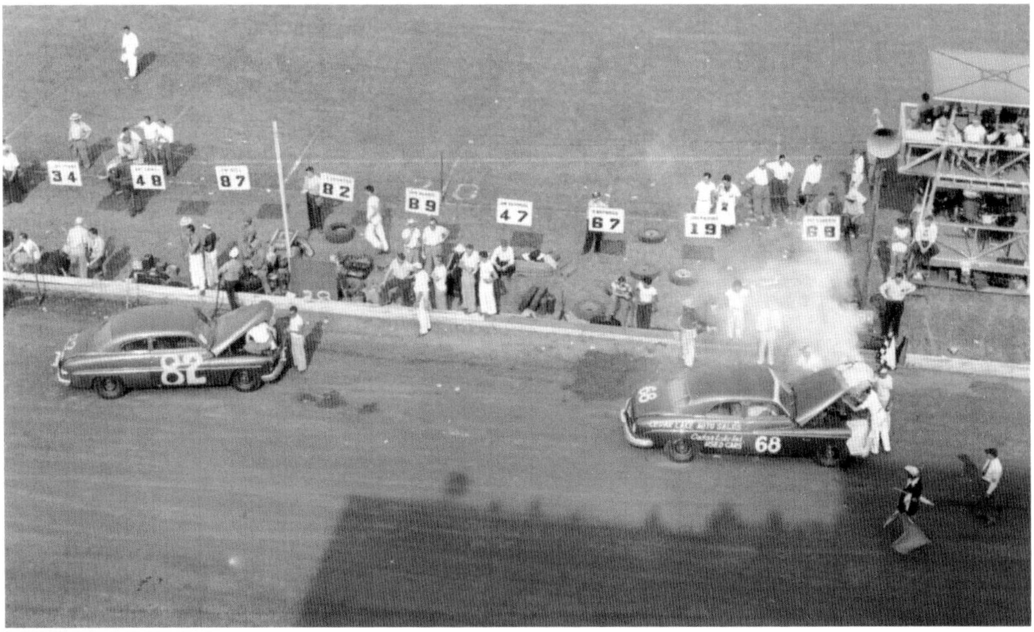

Stock-car races drew large crowds race after race in Milwaukee, and this July 1950 race was no different. There was never a dull moment with stocks; here, No. 68, Pat Flaherty, seems to have sustained more damage than No. 82, Chuck Leighton. Sponsored by the Hurricane Hot Rod Association, Leighton and Flaherty were rising stars in the organization. What seems to be a fender bender might be some staged entertainment added to the event. (GGAK.)

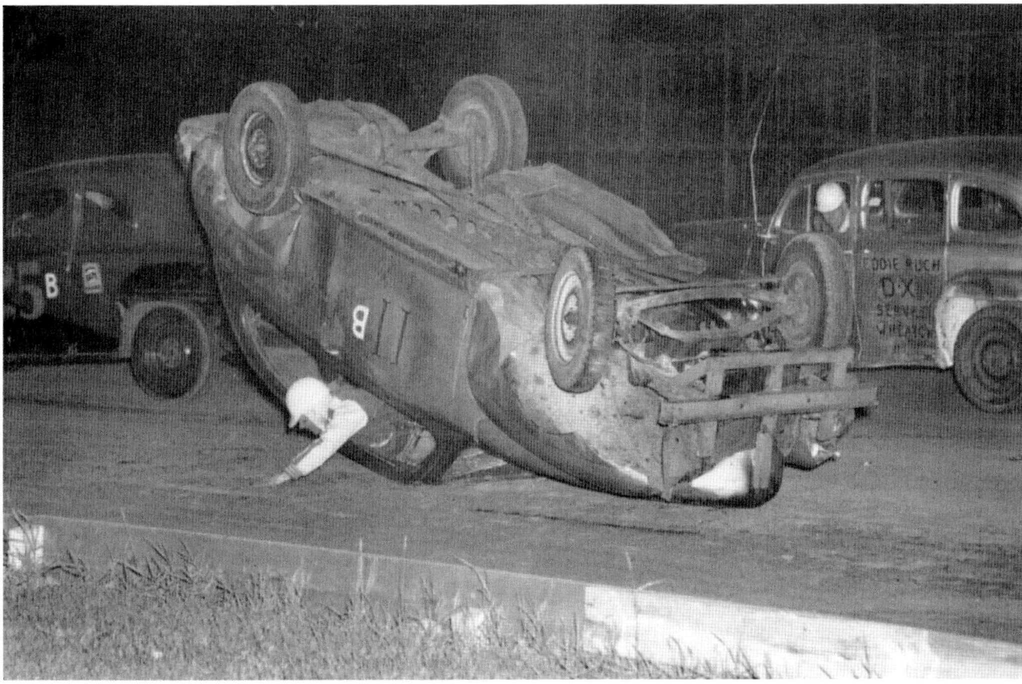

There was nothing better on a summer evening than Thursday night stock-car races. Whether on an outing for date night or family fun, fans could count on an action-packed evening on the quarter mile. This 1950 image shows an unidentified driver scrambling out from under his overturned vehicle. Luckily, the accident was nothing serious, and everyone went home happy. (GGAK.)

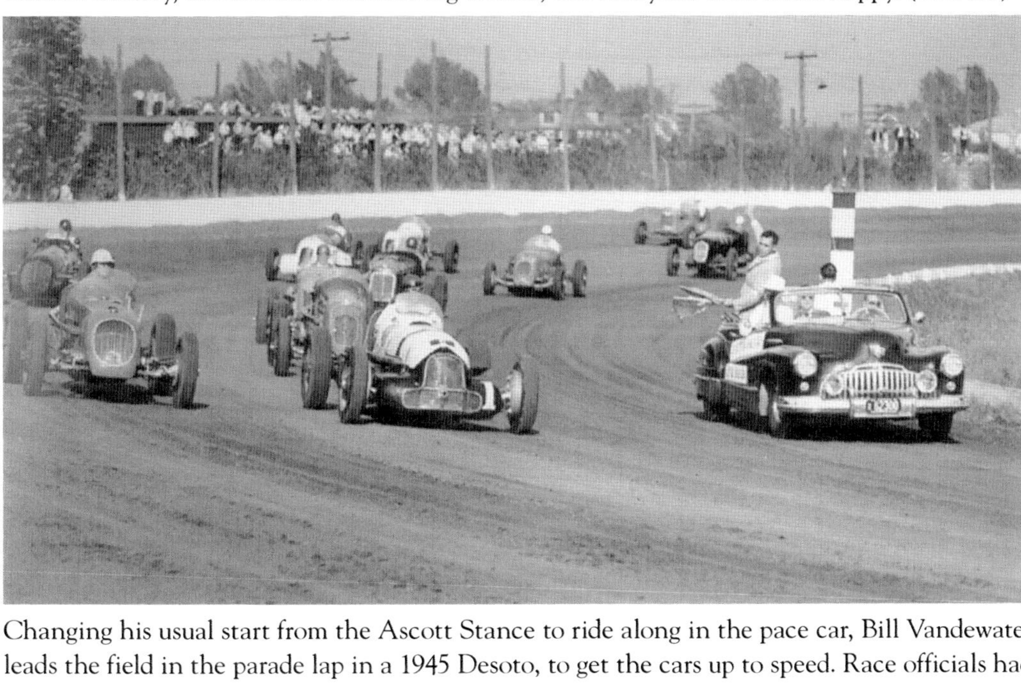

Changing his usual start from the Ascott Stance to ride along in the pace car, Bill Vandewater leads the field in the parade lap in a 1945 Desoto, to get the cars up to speed. Race officials had their own flair, and Vandewater was one of the best. (TMS.)

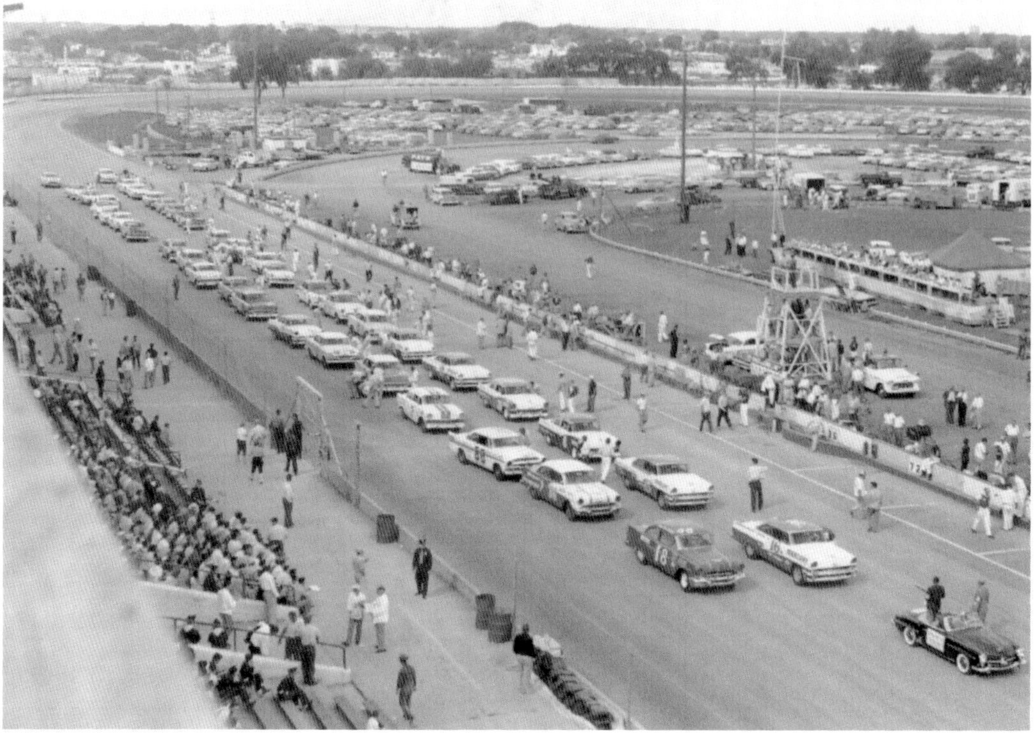

The speedway always was a favorite for drivers; the challenging track and hefty purses made for good turnouts. This 1951 race fielded 40 cars. So popular and profitable was State Fair Park, many drivers would not commit to an event until the State Fair Park's schedule was announced. (GGAK.)

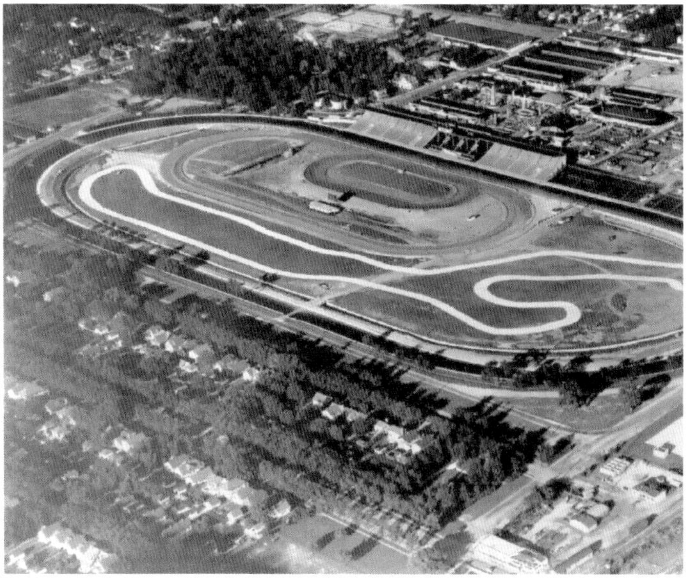

This aerial photograph, taken sometime after 1954, provides a better view than the one at ground level of the Wisconsin State Fair Park tracks. Clearly visible are the quarter-mile dirt oval, half-mile dirt oval, road course, and the paved mile track. The availability of four tracks provided multiple opportunities for varied programming and auto sports. (TMS.)

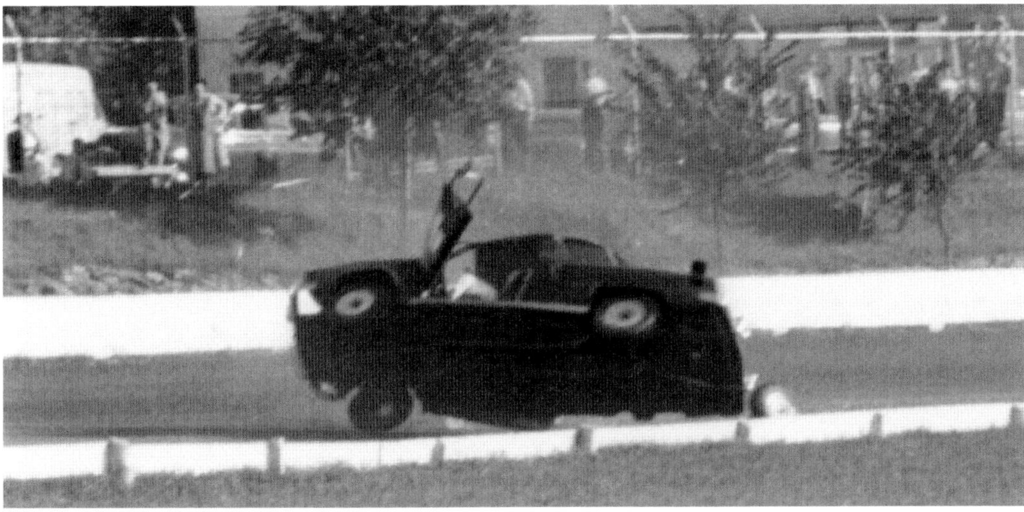

The door flew open as Myron Fohr flipped his stock car between turns one and two on August 23, 1951, severely damaging his vehicle in a race during the state fair. Despite the heavy damage to his car, Fohr, with some assistance, was able to walk away from the wreck. (RL/MC.)

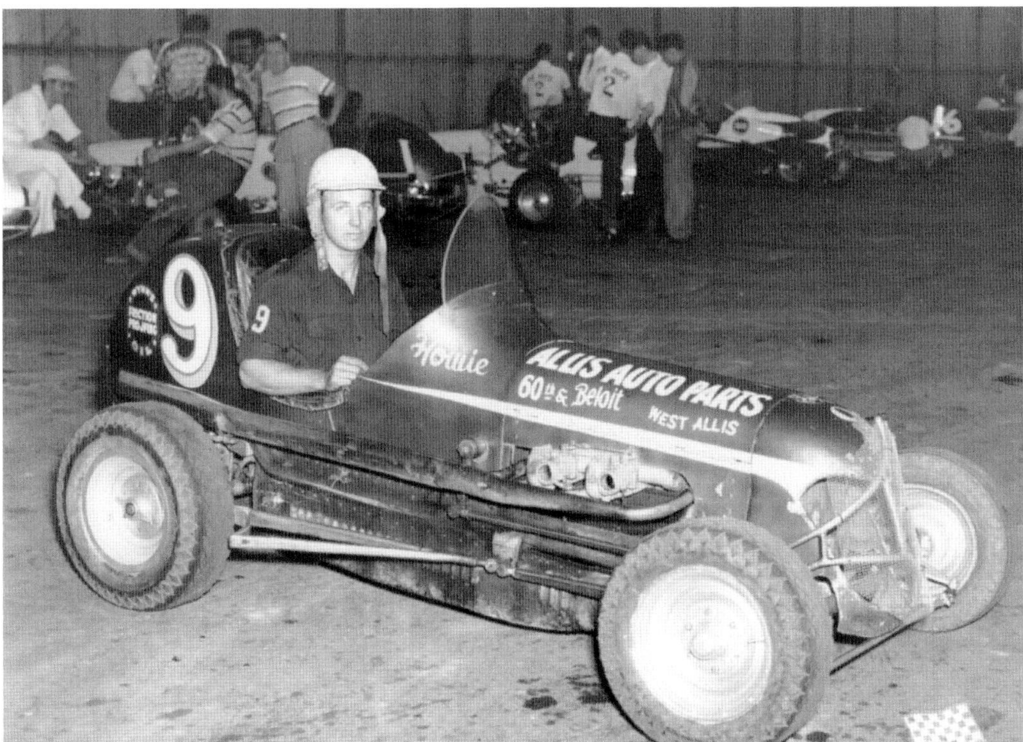

Howie Bradshaw, from West Allis, was a high-scoring midget driver during the 1950s, and like many drivers, he held a full-time job and raced during off hours for the thrills and the extra cash. Most drivers were backyard mechanics, building, maintaining, and driving their own cars; Bradshaw was no different. (BBH.)

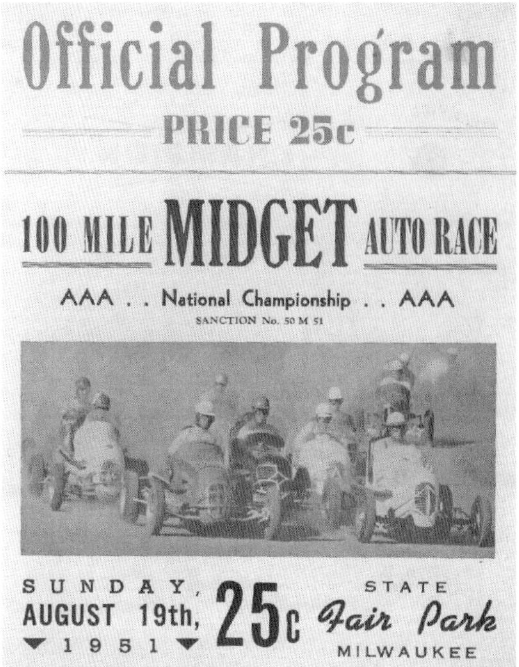

Technology definitely lent a hand in engineering, particularly in the automotive industry. Engine modifications, body style, and components contributed to increased speeds. The race of August 19, 1951, had 30 entries, with an average speed of 90 miles per hour. The winner at the 100-mile midget race that day was Frank Armi, normally an Indy car driver. (JS.)

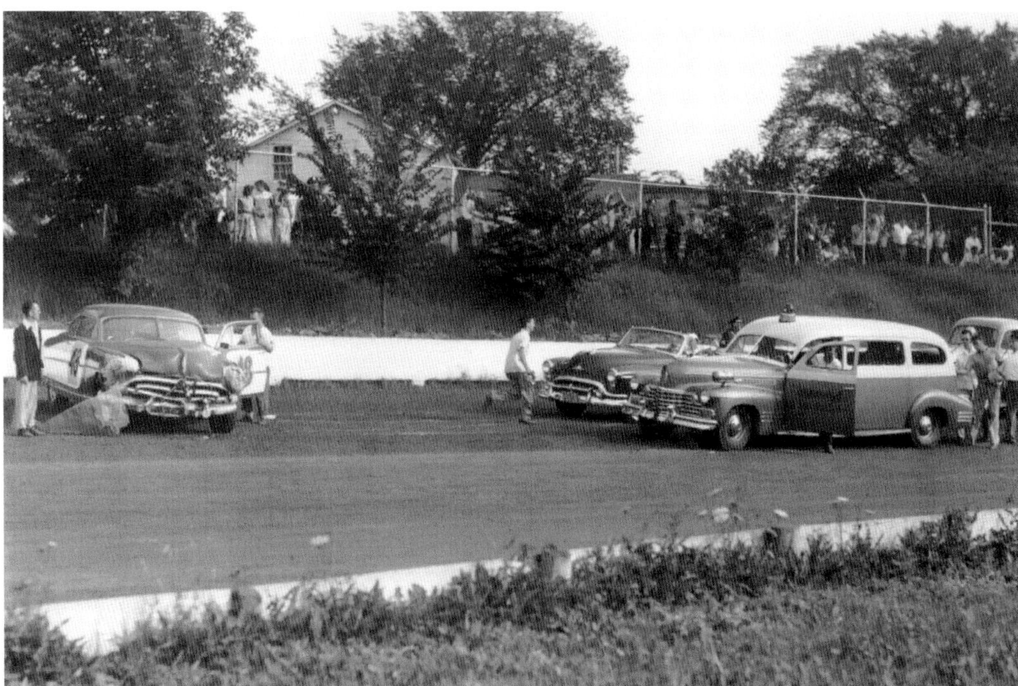

A crowd of gapers gathers outside the speedway's perimeter to observe a crash involving Howard Haberling, No. 48, and an unidentified driver. When seconds count, speedway safety team members arrive on the scene to assess the damage and prep to transport for medical treatment if necessary. Everyone loves a free show. (GGAK.)

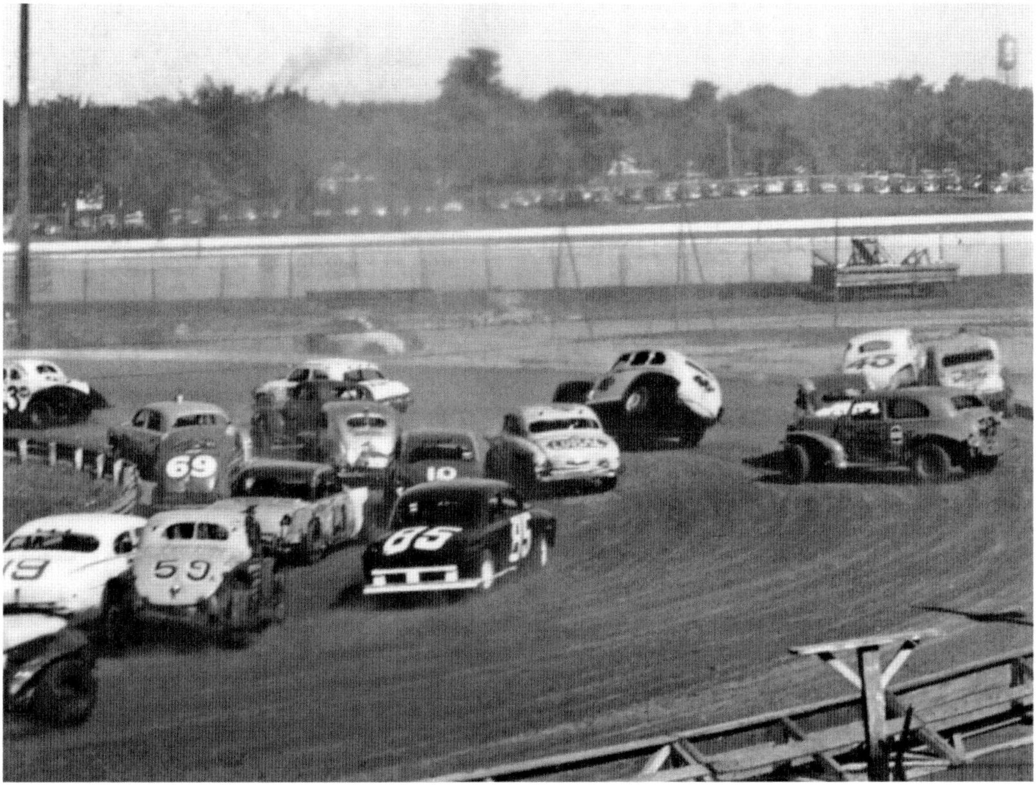

The action was wild and wooly on the quarter-mile track in this 1952 stock-car race, with vehicles all over the track going into the first turn. Little is known about the race, as the records from that era, especially for the quarter mile, are very sketchy. (RL/MC.)

Motorsports were all about pushing the limit on everything, including thrills. This team of daredevils from the Swanson Thrillcade drew thousands of spectators to the speedway. Although the stunts could be dangerous, they were well orchestrated. Sponsoring automobile companies delighted in the antics of stunt teams; if these cars could take the punishment, think of how well they would stand up to the average driver. This picture dates to around 1955. (MCHS.)

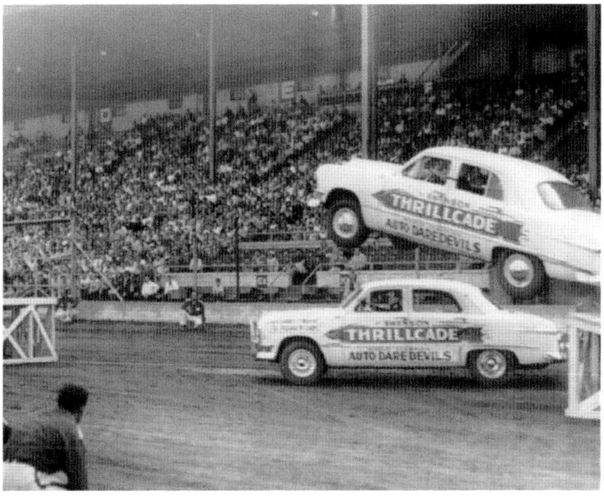

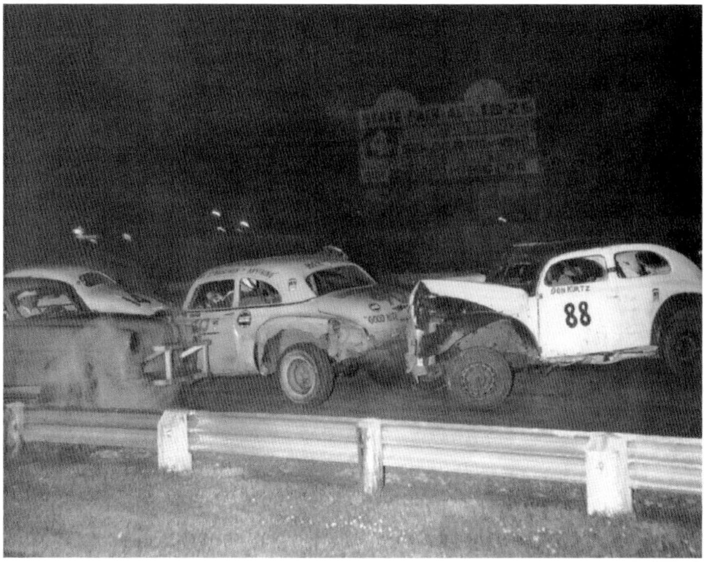

Four drivers duke it out along the quarter-mile track during this 1952 race. No. 88, Don Kurtz, seems to be all right, but his car needs major repairs. In the background, a billboard announces the summer fair schedule. The fair promised something for everyone, and it followed through. There were midget, stock, and big car races—enough variety to please most everyone. (GGAK.)

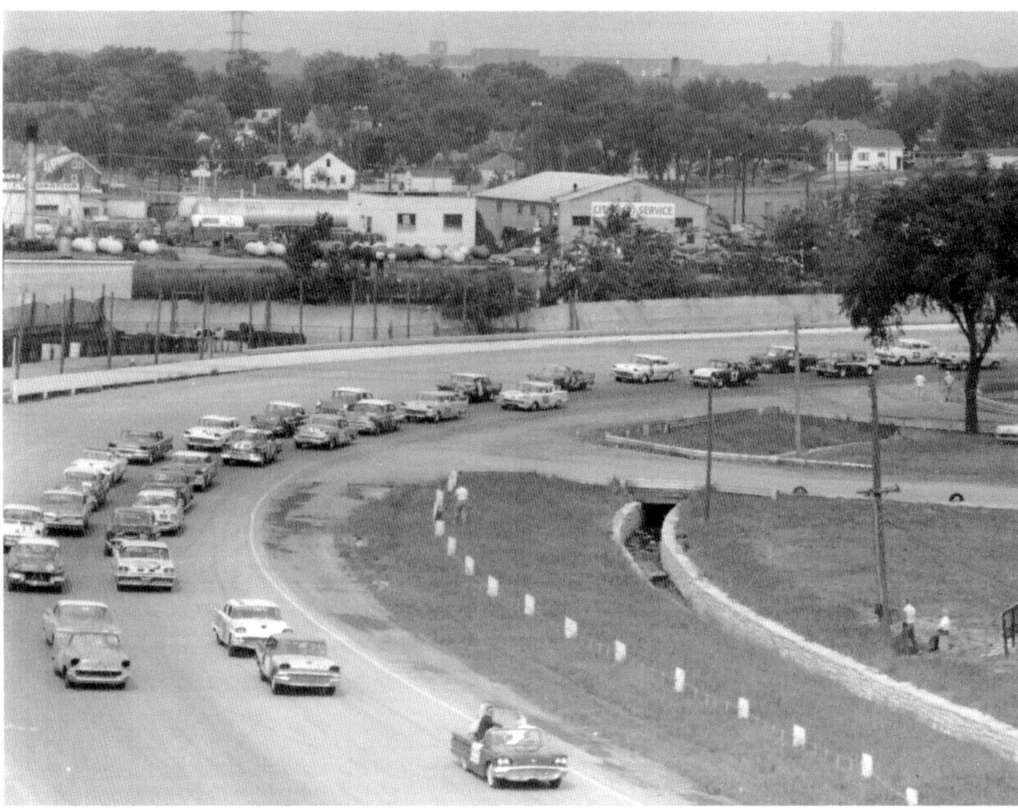

Down the straightaway out of the fourth turn, the field of cars picks up speed. They are led by the pace car in the parade lap of this 1959 USAC 200. Rodger Ward, No. 99, is up front, strategizing how to stay there. He must have had a good plan—he finished first. (GGAK.)

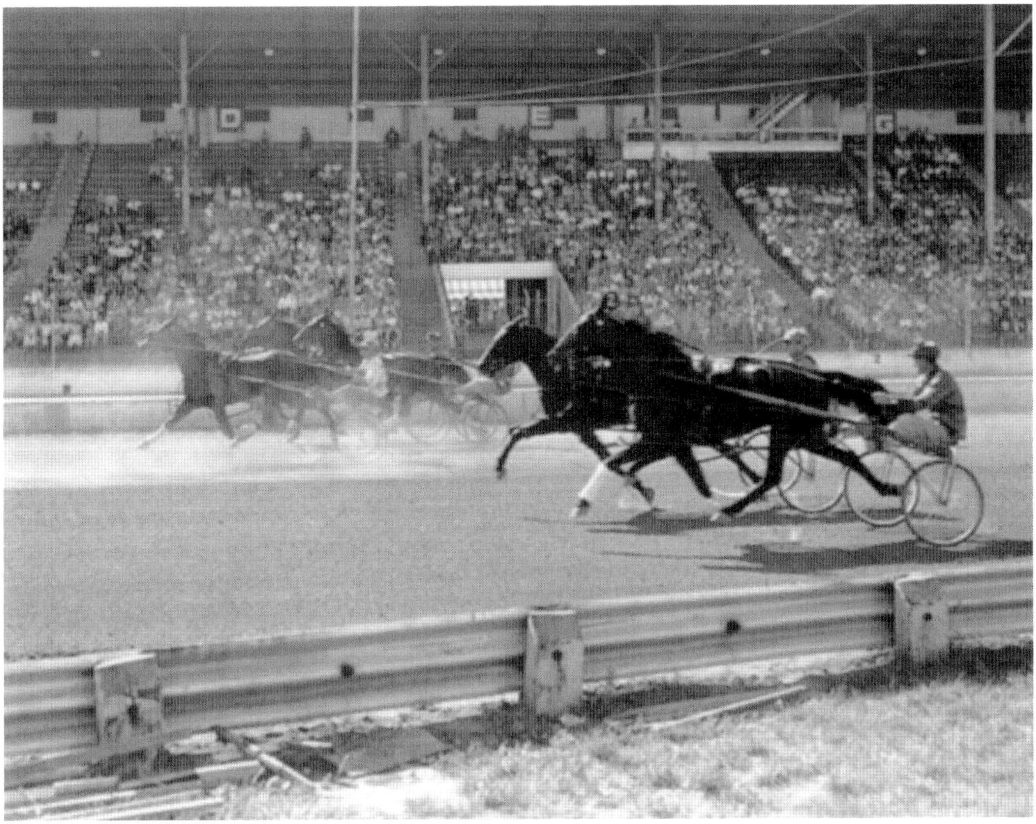

During the 1950s, harness racing remained popular, and the track continued to accommodate both harness and auto racing. It was most certainly a headache for the grounds crew to adjust a packed soil track for autos and soft, loose soil for trotters. Harness racing moved to the interior half-mile track after the oval was paved in 1954. (MCHS.)

A legend in its time, the Hudson Hornet was a driver's dream. Hornets dominated early 1950s stock-car races; this 1953 AAA 100-mile stock-car race was no different. Shot from the upper grandstand, this picture captures Ottis Stine, No. 46, and Don Dumfee, No. 38, piloting Dodges; Jim Rathman, No. 57, in his Olds; and No. 71, Sam Hanks (the winner) driving a Hornet. The top three places went to Hornets, with Marshall Teague taking second and Frank Mundy coming in third. (GGAK.)

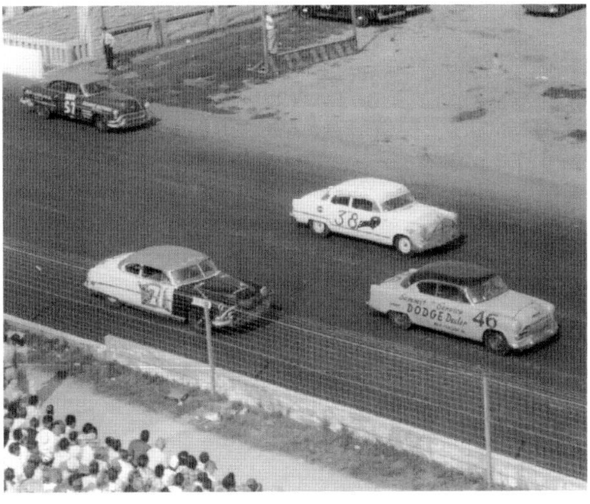

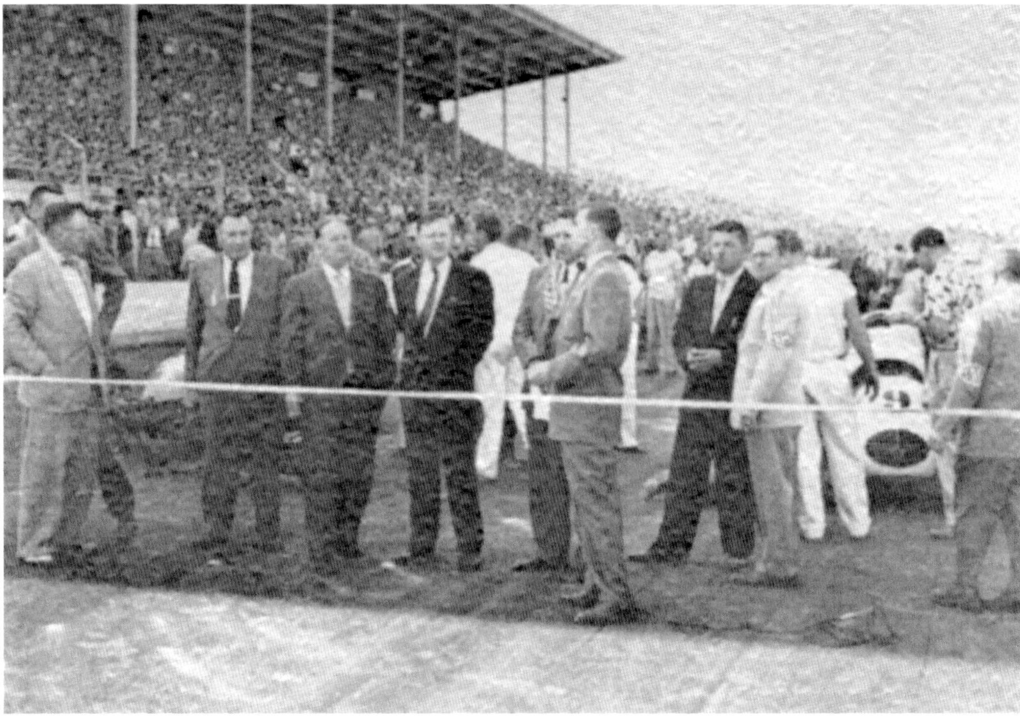

Entering a new era, the Wisconsin State Fair Park Speedway readies for opening day on June 6, 1954, with the Rex May Classic. Dignitaries, politicians, and fans gather for the ribbon cutting to officially open the season. Auto racing of all types was extremely popular during the 1950s, as can be seen by the sellout crowd in the grandstand. (JS.)

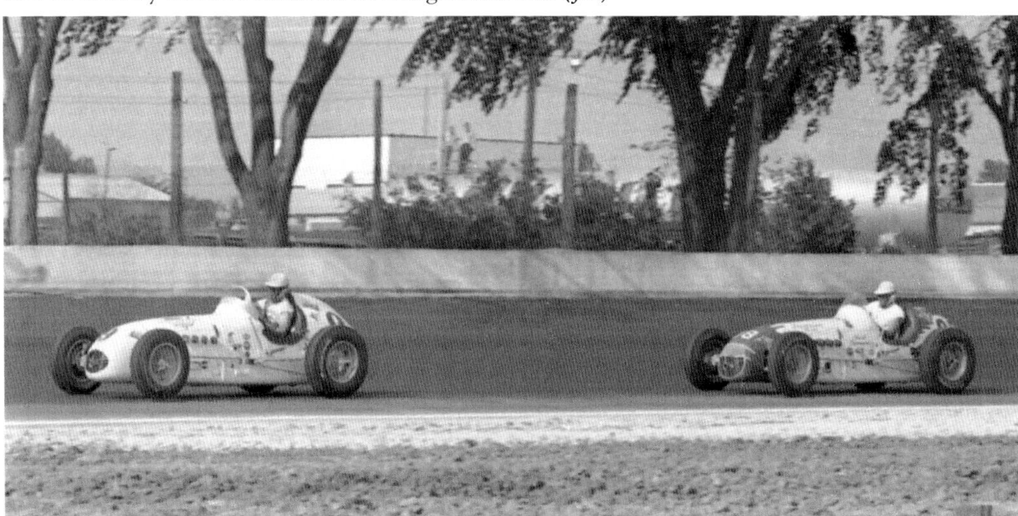

The first race held on the track after it was paved was a 100-mile AAA-sanctioned big car race on June 6, 1954. The Milwaukee big car race was traditionally held the week after the Indianapolis 500. Indianapolis 500 winner Bill Vukovich (No. 9) is shown leading eventual Milwaukee race winner Chuck Stevenson (No. 98), through turns three and four. (RL/MC.)

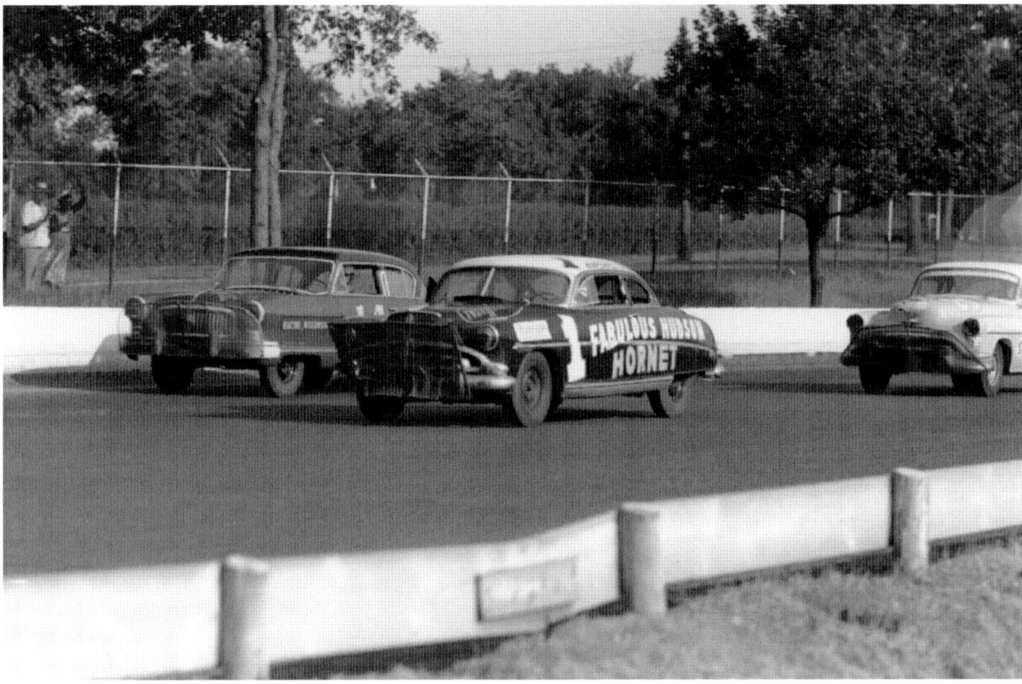

Those Fabulous Hornets, as Marshal Teague declared, were the most popular and dominant stock cars from 1951 to 1954. In an effort to gain factory sponsorship, Teague convinced the Hudson Motor Car Company they needed him. Teague got what he wanted: corporate sponsorship included cars, expenses, and all entry fees. The popular Hornet's unibody chassis, light weight, and powerful six-cylinder motor consistently won over the larger, more-modern engine cars. (GGAK.)

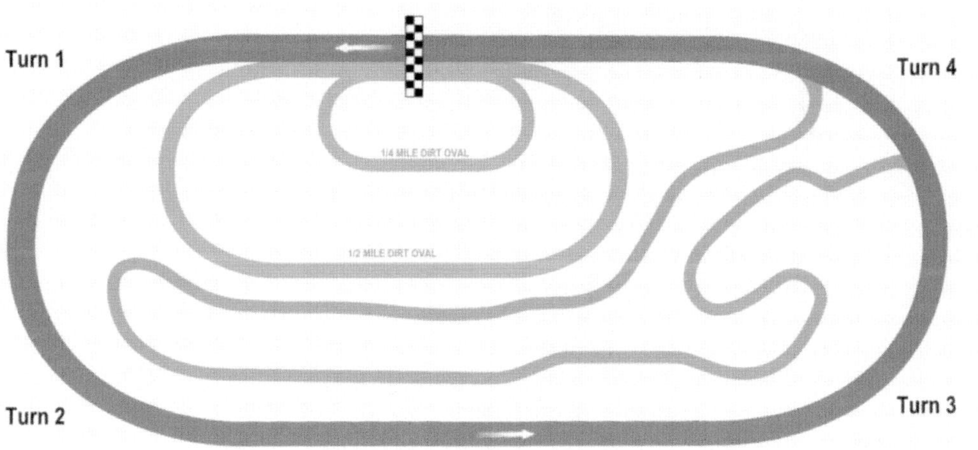

This diagram depicts the State Fair Park Speedway as it was in 1954. Looking from the inside out is the quarter-mile dirt track for sprint cars, followed by the half mile dirt track for harness racing, the infield road course layout, and the mile oval at the outermost edge. Paving the track in 1954 meant spectators were no longer subject to clouds of choking dust. It also allowed the track to compete with other national tracks for sanctioned races. (NTRC.)

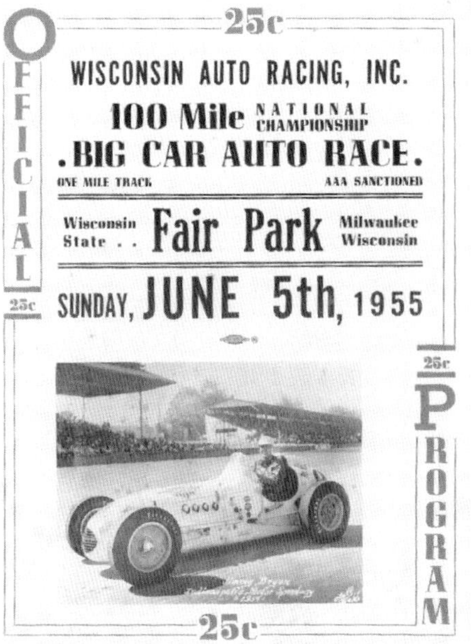

The cover of the program for the fifth annual Rex Mays Classic for 1955 features Jimmy Bryan. By the 1950s, technology was influencing both speed and safety in auto racing. Top speed that day was 98.84 miles per hour, clocked by Johnny Thomson in the win. Helping to fatten the purse to $22,480 were more than 25,000 fans.

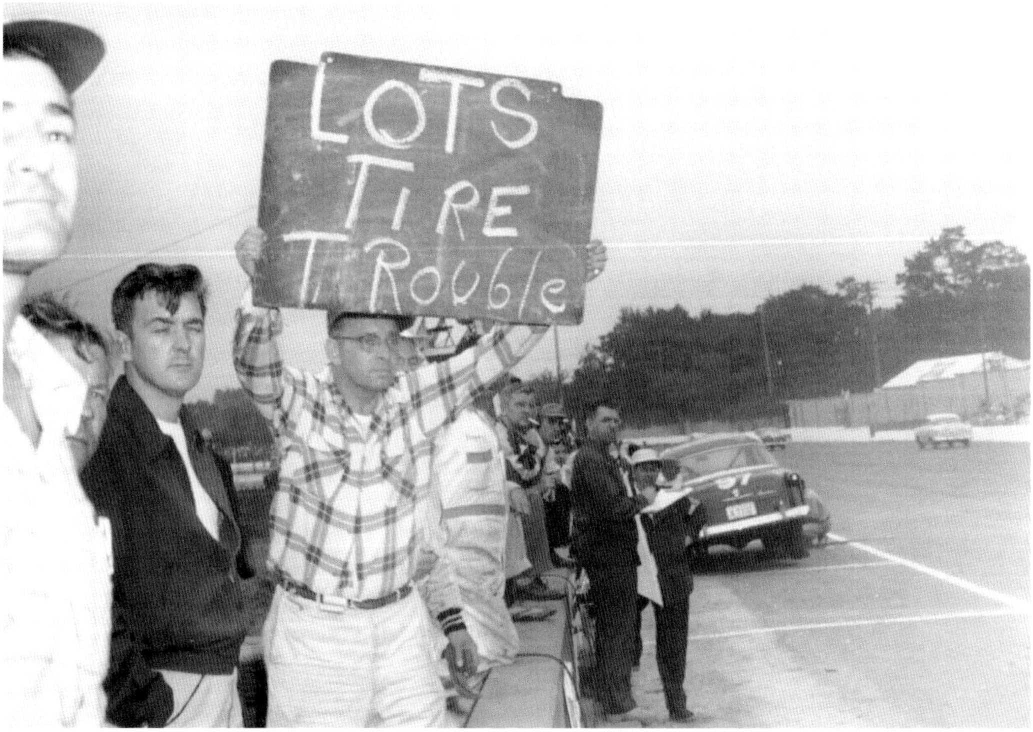

Visual signals, like the pit board seen here around 1955, at one time were the standard form of communication between driver and pit crew. Thankfully, technology has advanced communication between team members, integrating radio into the car's body and the driver's helmet. Always seeking to enhance a fan's race-day experience, NASCAR allows fans to listen in on driver-crew talk. Thankfully, the pit board has disappeared. (WHS.)

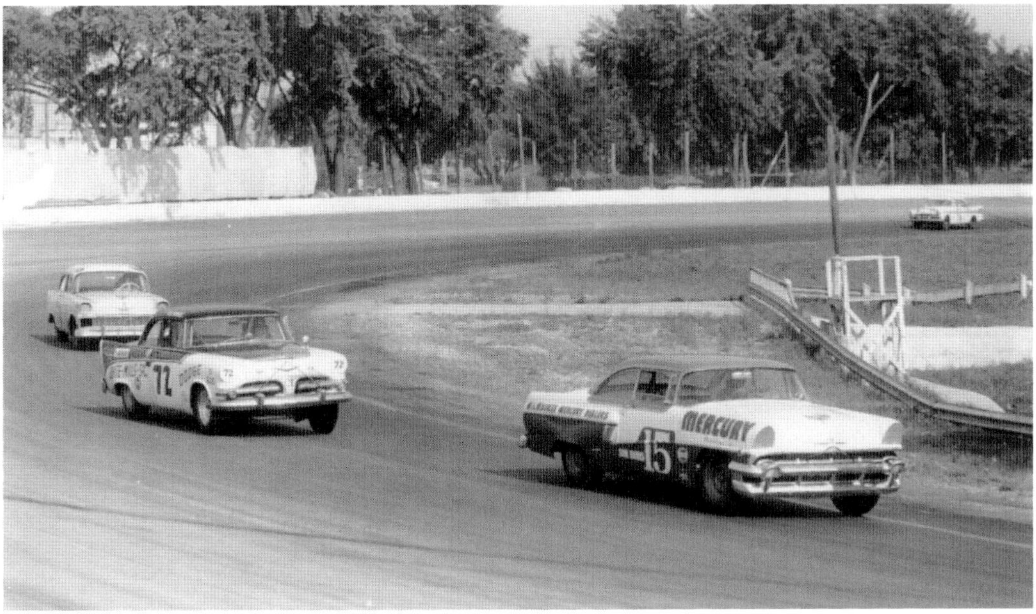

The US Auto Club (USAC) had just begun sanctioning races at the time of this 1956 USAC 250. Sam Hanks, No. 15, driving his 1956 Mercury just out of the fourth turn, holds onto first. He is followed by Bill Granger, No. 72, in his Dodge, with Marshall Teague, No. 6, driving his Chevy in last place. (GGAK.)

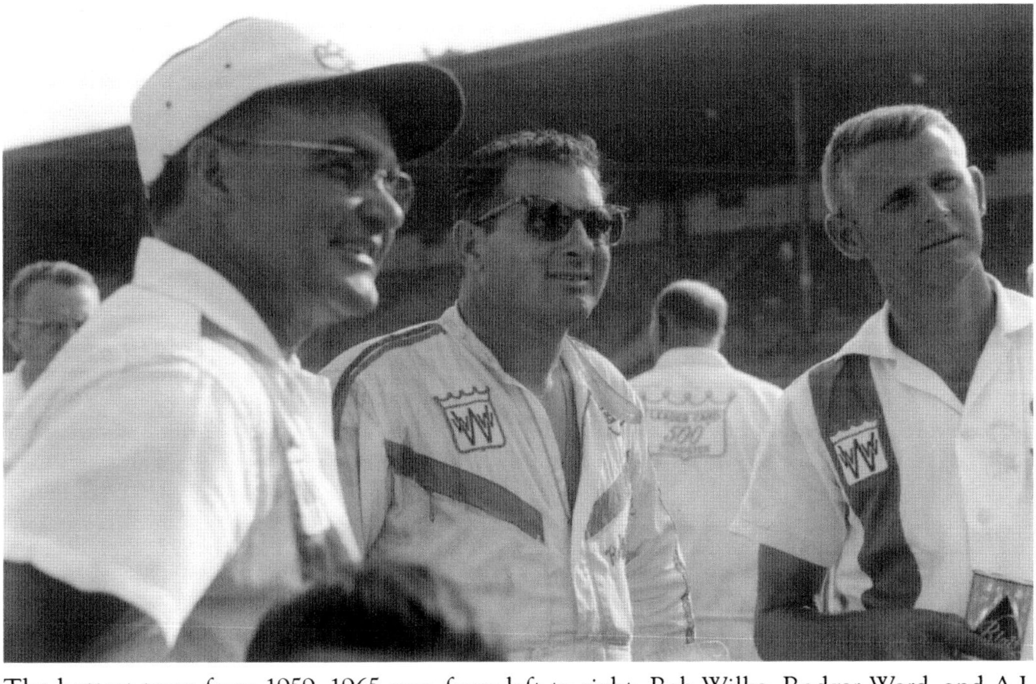

The hottest team from 1959–1965 was, from left to right, Bob Wilke, Rodger Ward, and A.J. Watson. Known as "the three Ws," They could be found on most tracks, coast to coast. Anyone lucky enough to beat them knew they had beaten the best. (MWLPP.)

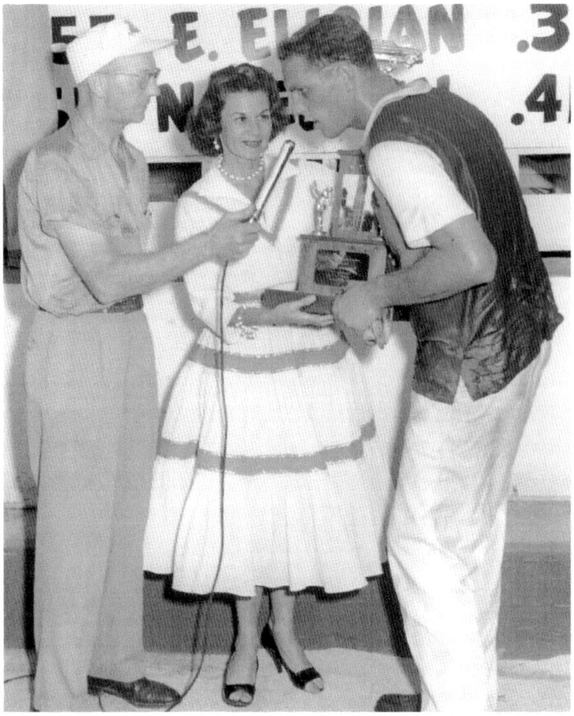

The July 15, 1956, USAC 150 stock-car race was certainly one for the record books, with 56 cars entered for 40 positions, but Troy Ruttman pulled off the win. Awarding the trophy is Betty Skelton, "First Lady of Firsts," the fastest woman on earth. She was a land-speed record holder, stock-car driver, and aerobatics pilot who set 17 aviation records and several automobile records. To her right is Ed "20 Grand" Steinbach. (GGAK.)

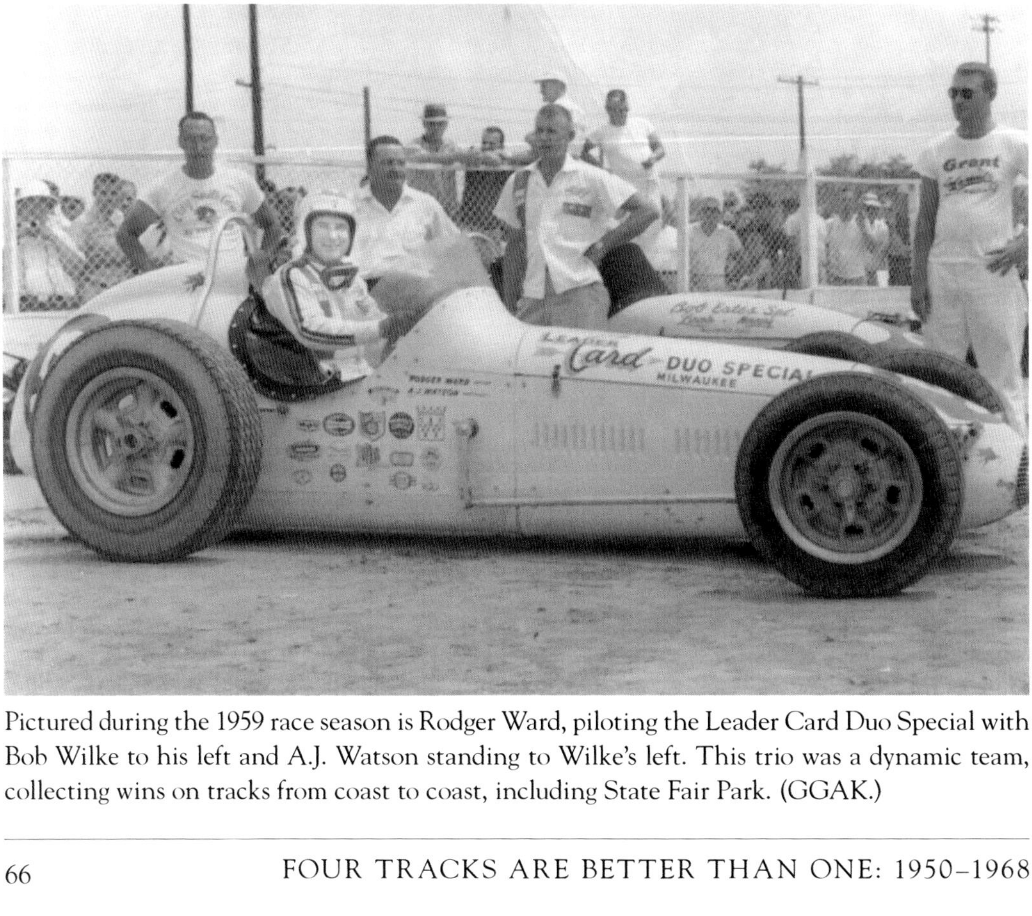

Pictured during the 1959 race season is Rodger Ward, piloting the Leader Card Duo Special with Bob Wilke to his left and A.J. Watson standing to Wilke's left. This trio was a dynamic team, collecting wins on tracks from coast to coast, including State Fair Park. (GGAK.)

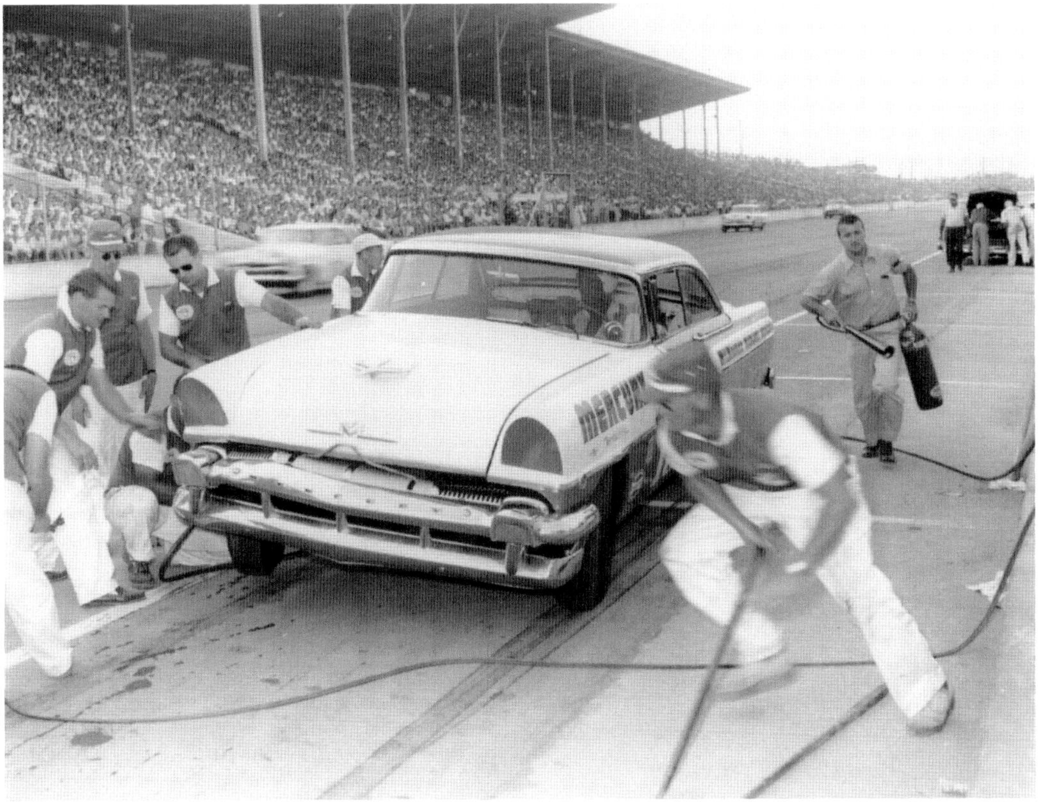

Troy Ruttman pulls into the pits as his crew scurries to perform needed services. It is the crew's responsibility to perform the tasks faultlessly and make any adjustments at this time so that the driver does not lose position. The driver's job is to execute mistake-free entries and exits. (GGAK.)

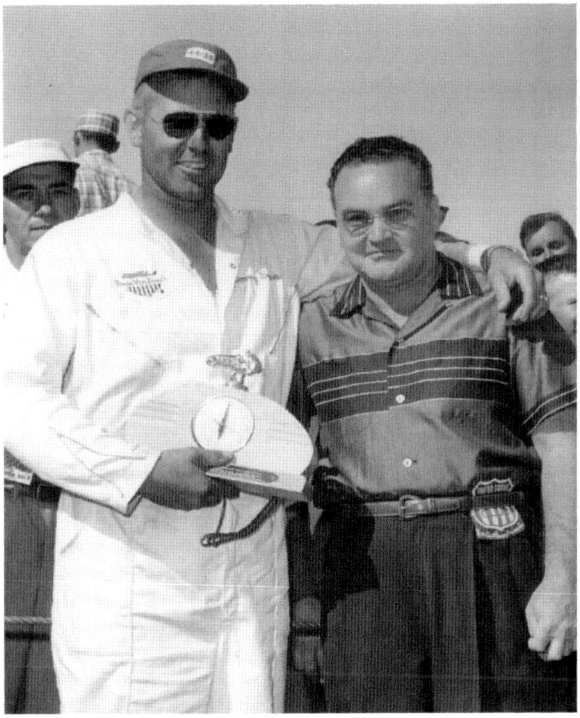

Jimmy Bryan, left, driving for Dean Van Lines, receives the Leader Card trophy from Bob Wilke for fast time in the June 9, 1957, Rex Mays Classic. Driving his 1957 Mercury, Bryan placed fourth that day, not bad for starting out at 16th. (MWLC.)

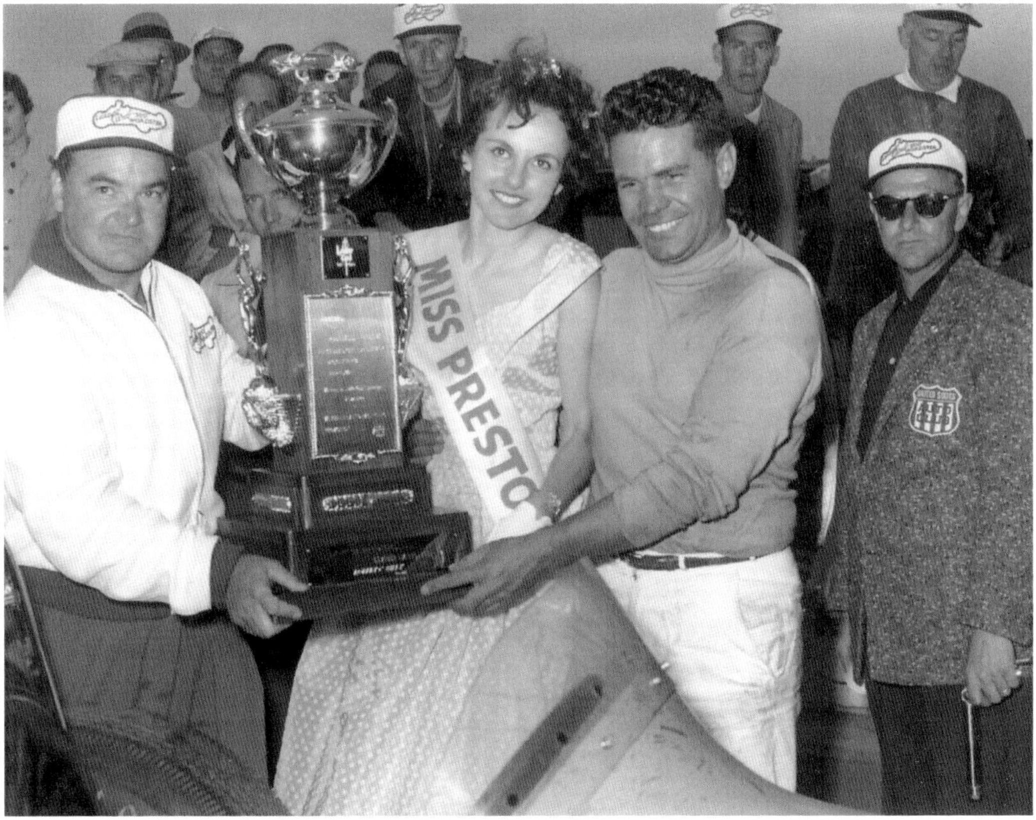

With a grin from ear to ear, Art Bisch, left of Miss Prestone Darlene Paulak, accepts the Leader Card trophy from Bob Wilke, far left, after winning the June 8, 1958, 100-Mile Rex Mays Classic. Dominating the race, Bisch held off threats from Tony Bettenhausen to claim his prize. Tragically, Art Bisch lost his life a month after this race at Lakewood Speedway in Atlanta. (MWLPP.)

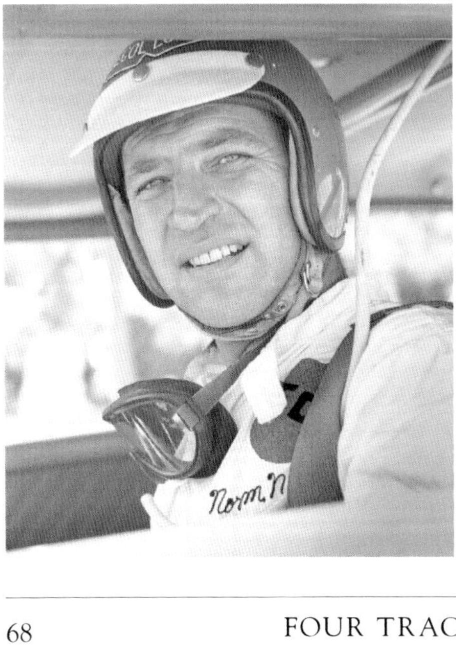

Nicknamed the "Great Dane," Norm Nelson from Racine, Wisconsin, had a career that spanned almost three decades, pulling double duty as driver and owner. Behind the wheel, Nelson won three USAC championship races—1960, 1965, and 1966—and five owner championships with great drivers like Roger McCluskey, Jim Hurtubise, and A.J. Foyt. Out of his 35 USAC victories, 11 races were won before his friends, family, and fans at the State Fair Park. (GGAK.)

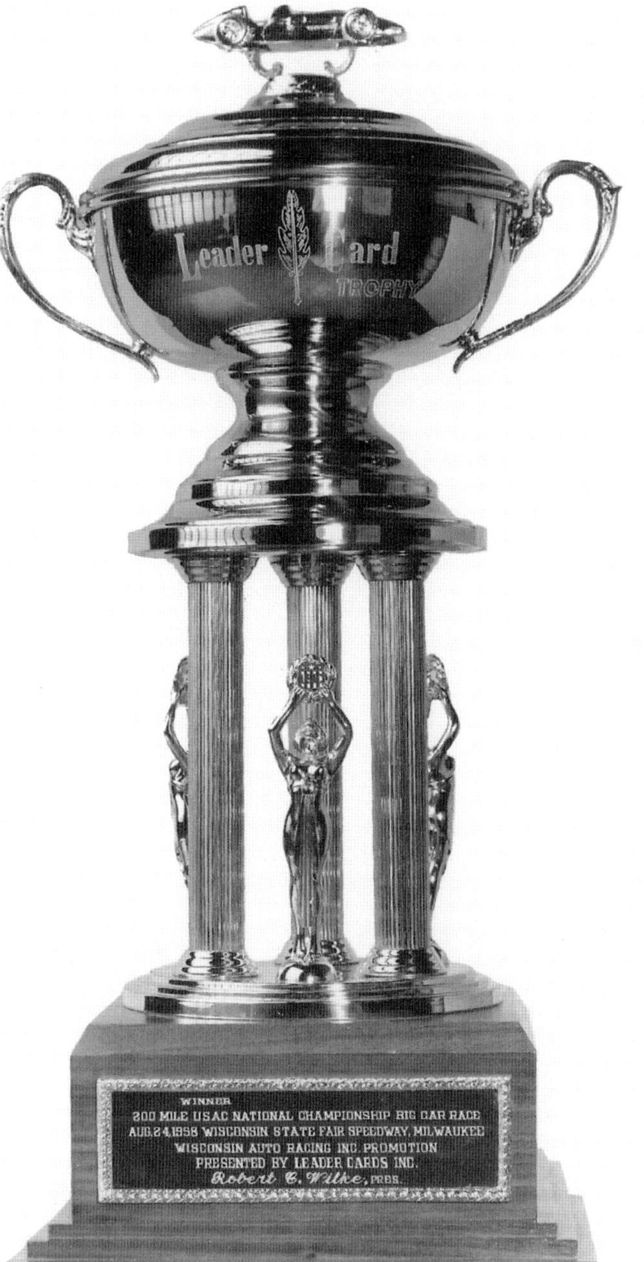

In racing, whether on an oval, quarter mile, or back roads, drivers compete for glory and bragging rights. As racing became more organized, winners vied for the purse and, along with it, a trophy—the reward and recognition of distinction. This 1958 Leader Card trophy was presented to Rodger Ward. For years, Bob Wilke and Leader Cards Inc. sponsored trophies at the Milwaukee Mile races for big cars, stock cars, and midgets. (MWLPP.)

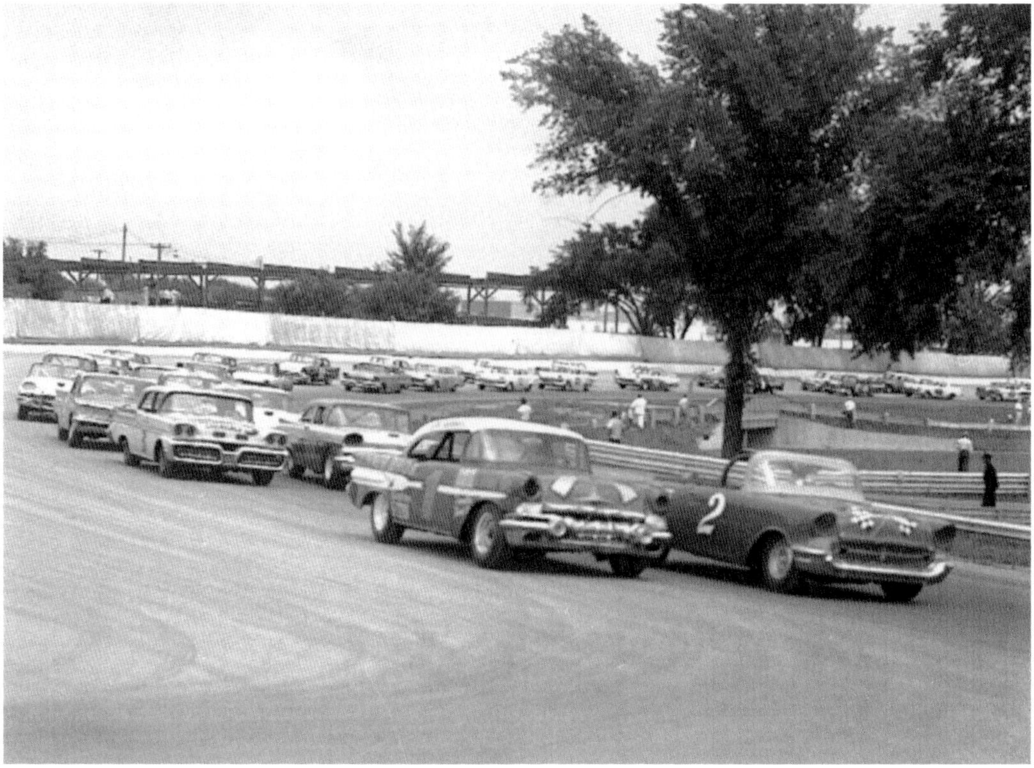

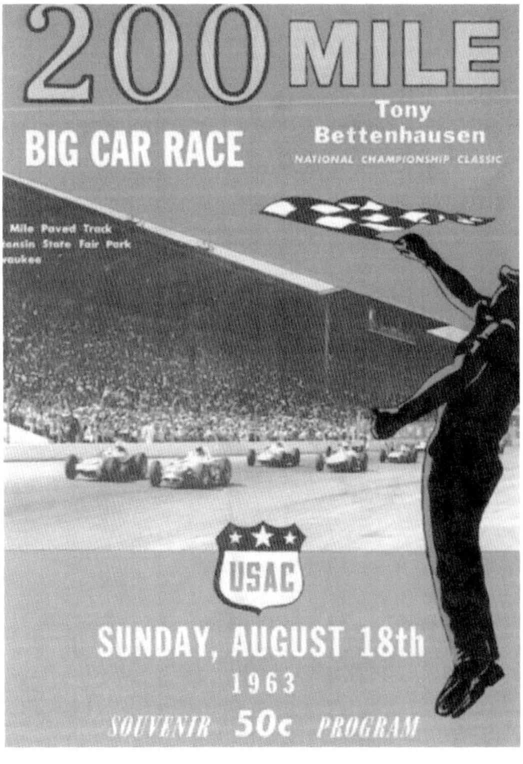

The field rounds turn four and heads for the start of the July 19, 1959, USAC/ARCA co-sanctioned 150-mile stock-car race. Nelson Stacy (No. 2), in his convertible stock car, and Don Oldenberg (No. 1) were at the front of the 42-car field. In the background, just to the right of the tree, the concrete area where the creek passed under the track is visible. (RL/MC.)

Designated the Tony Bettenhausen 200 in 1961, this August event honored one of the most respected and popular drivers of the era. Bettenhausen earned champ status driving both midget and Indy cars in AAA and USAC champion series. Nicknamed "the Tinley Park Express," Bettenhausen, a fearless driver who lived life with gusto, was killed during a practice crash at Indianapolis in 1961. The August event was eliminated in 1982. (JS.)

Tony Bettenhauser, left, chats with Rodger Ward during some downtime before the race. Both drivers were geared up and ready to get it done. Bettenhausen raced for Firestone, while Ward raced for Bob Wilke on the Leader Card team. (MWLPP.)

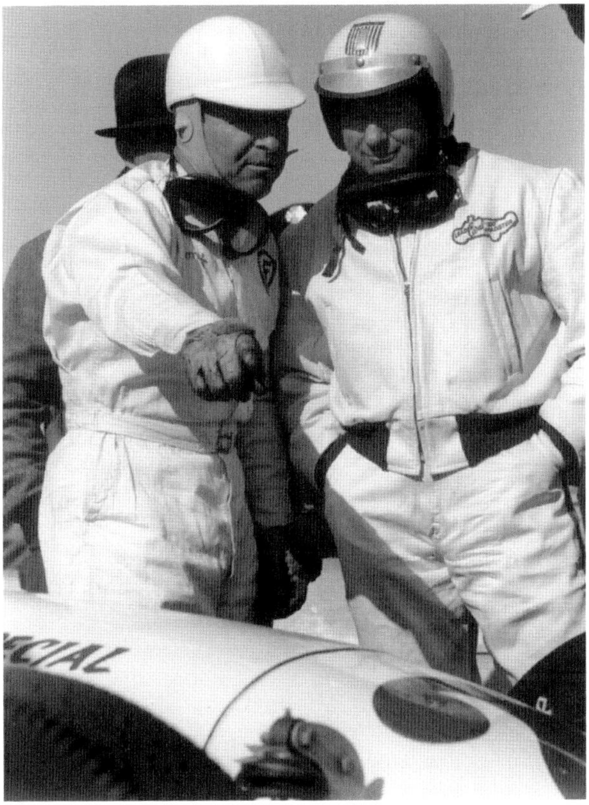

Modifieds, those quirky cutaway vehicles, hit their peak from the mid-1950s to the early 1970s, and for the mechanically inclined, they were the car of choice. Down the straightaway on the quarter-mile dirt track at State Fair Park, modifiedes give this Saturday afternoon crown in 1965 quite a show. These "Doodle Bugs" had a following and fans were crazy about them. (JS.)

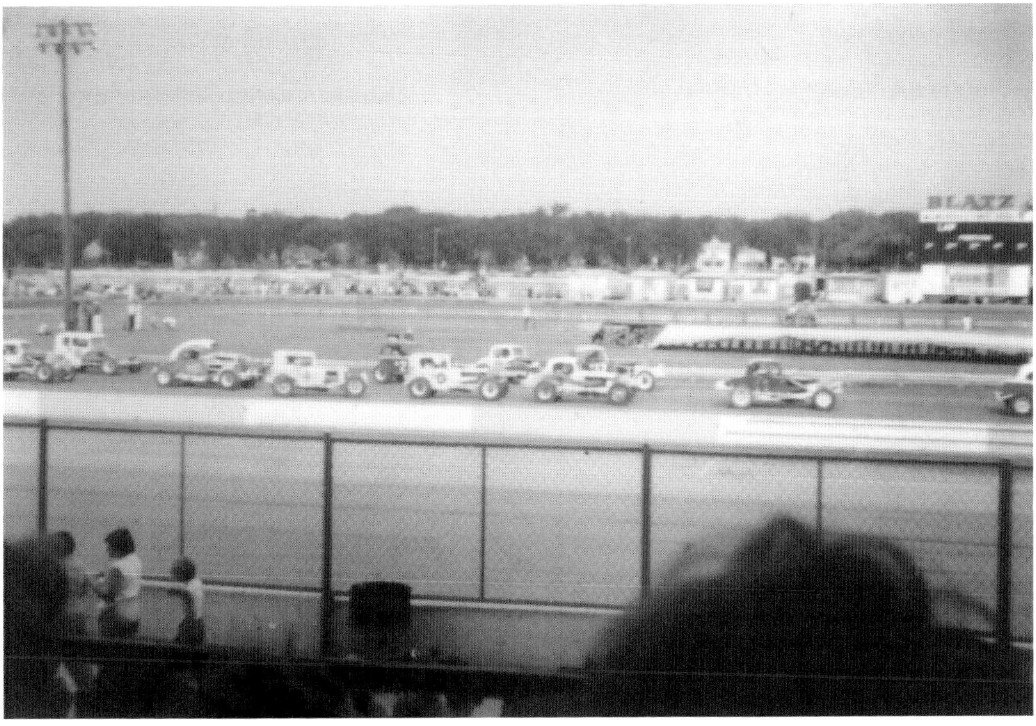

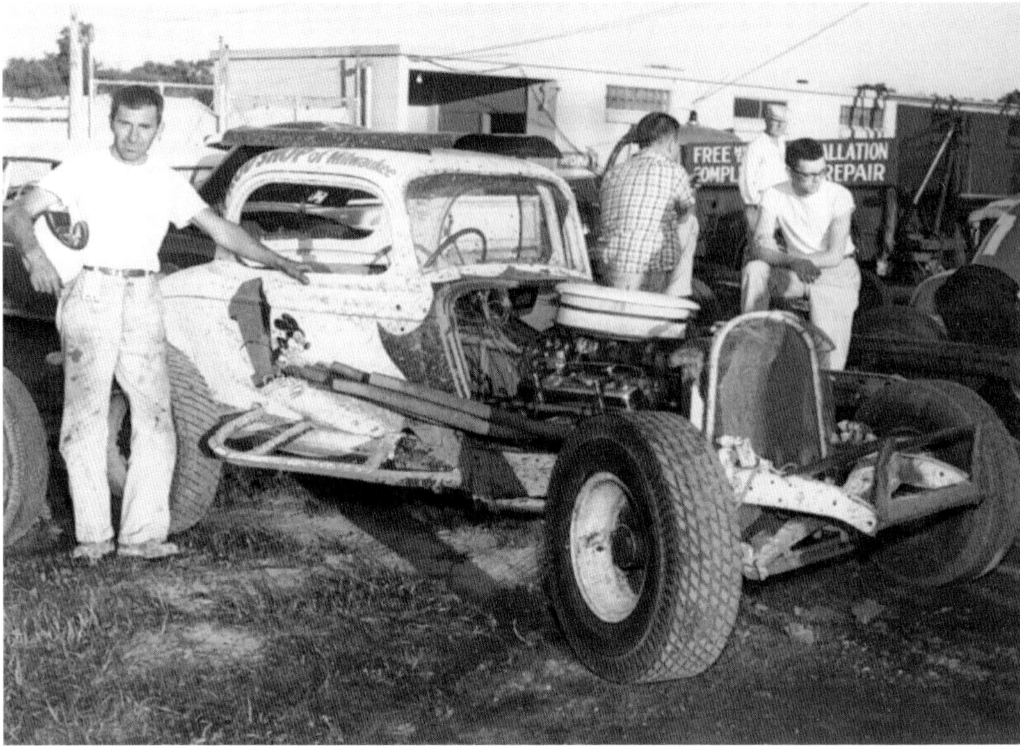

Miles "Mouse" Melius posed with his modified stock car in the infield of the track in August 1959. The modifieds raced on the quarter-mile dirt track every Thursday night. The dirt track was removed when the speedway was renovated, and a new pit lane was built before the 1967 season. (RL/MC.)

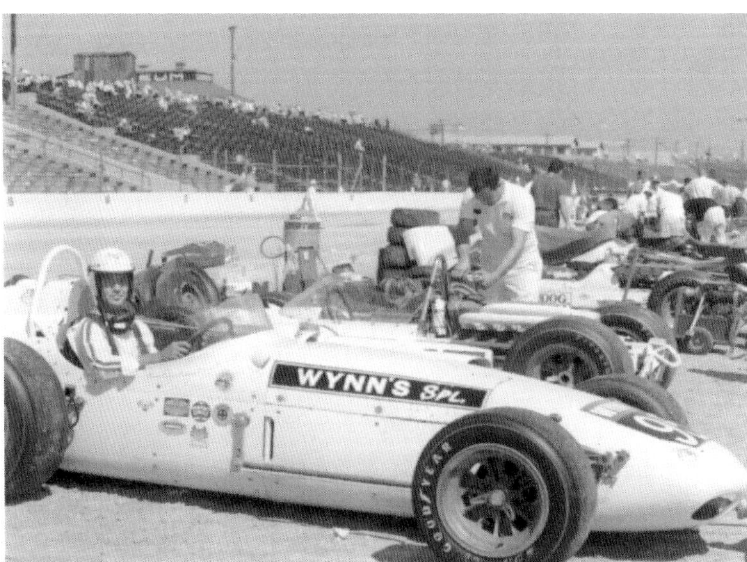

Driven by Bobby Grim in the August 14, 1965, USAC Indy car 150, this roadster was fabricated by A.J. Watson for Bob Wilke of Leader Card Racers. Designed and built by Larry Shinoda, Leroy Payne, and fabricators Willie Davis and Roger Beck, the roadster was Watson's first semi-monocoque design. (MWLPP.)

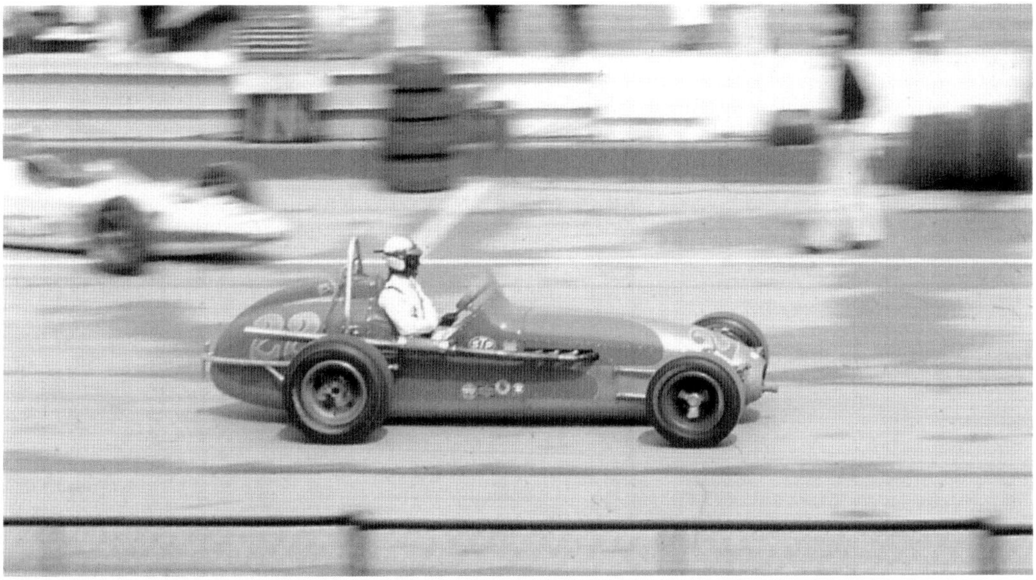

Racing is inherently dangerous, given the speed, a tank of gas, and the human desire to win. This photograph, taken in the mid-1960s, shows Ronnie Duman at speed down the straightaway at the State Fair Park. Note the unidentified driver and car behind him in the pit. The excitement of the race, when good judgment should be at its highest, can sometimes get the better of drivers. (JS.)

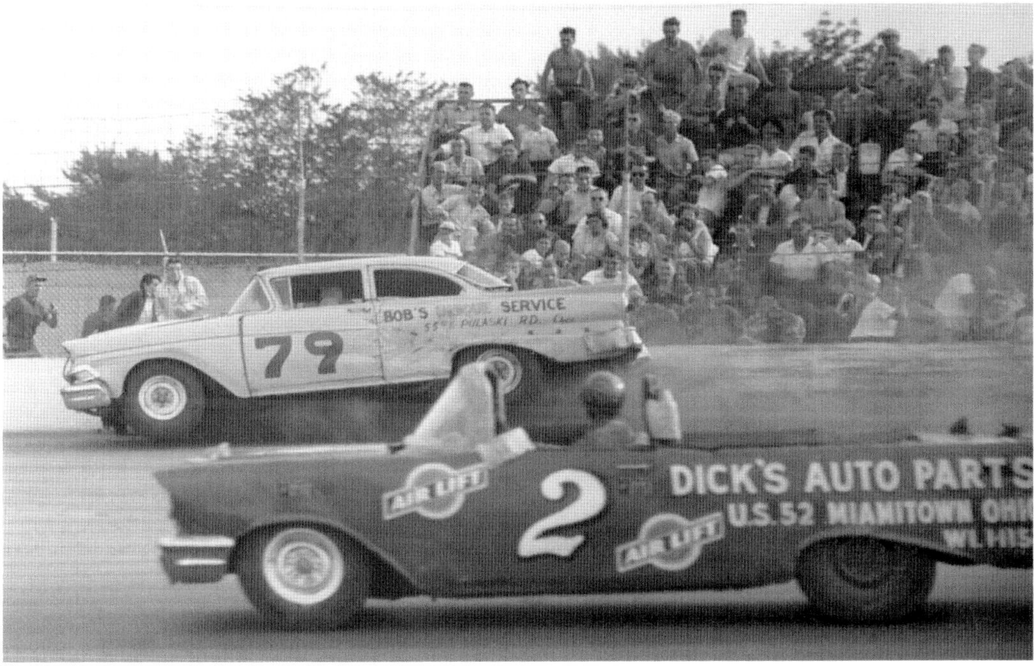

Jack Shanklin (No. 79) puts his 1958 Ford stock car up on the turn one wall during a USAC/ARCA co-sanctioned 250-lap stock-car race on September 20, 1959. Nelson Stacy (No. 2), passing on the inside in his 1957 Chevy convertible, is turning his head to get a better view of Shanklin's accident. Convertibles ran with the hard-top stock cars in the 1950s and into the early 1960s. (RL/MC.)

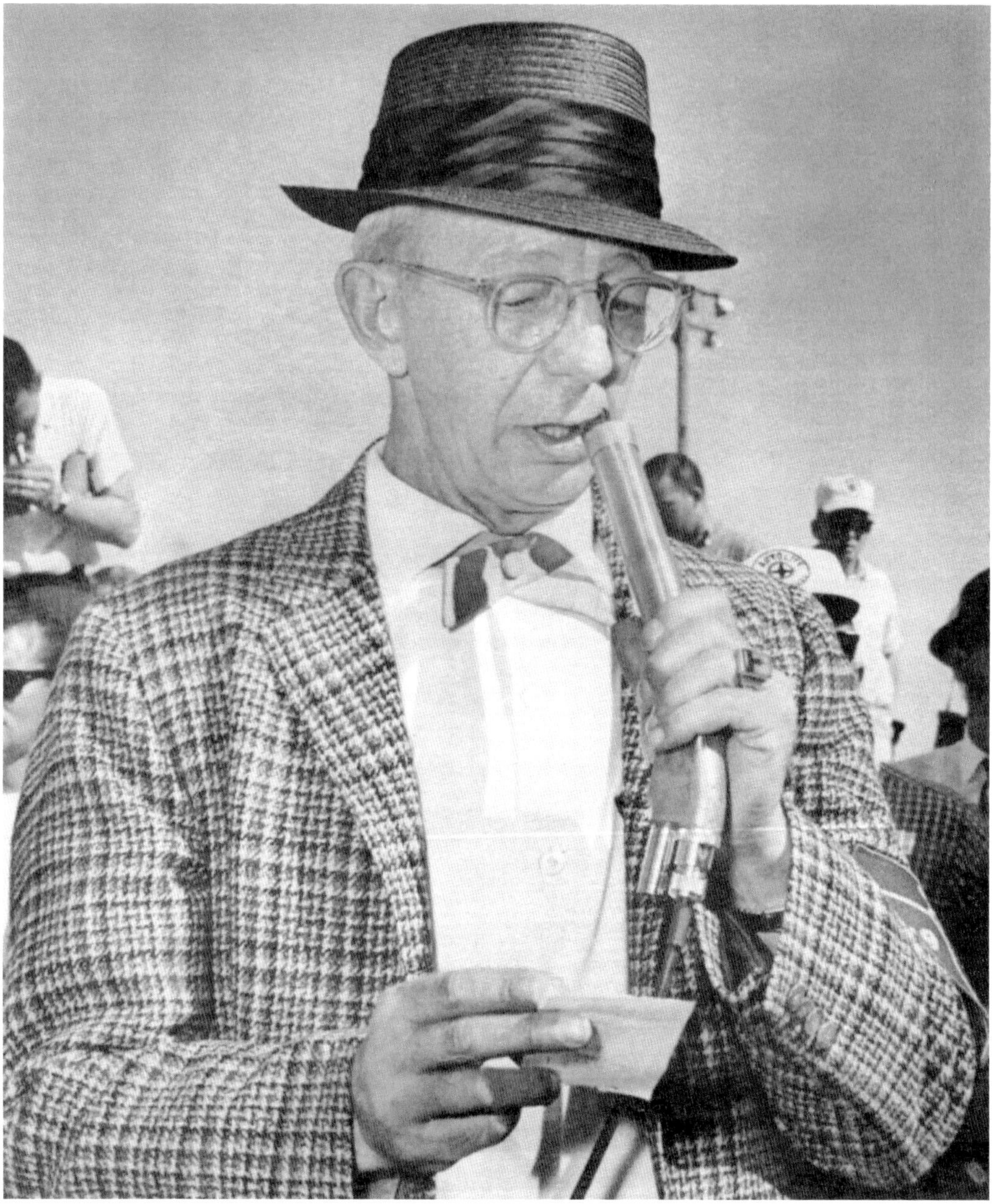

Race fans around the world are drawn by the sheer speed and environment of the track, including the announcer's commentary, which add another dimension to the race. One such great was Ed "Twenty Grand" Steinbach, pictured around 1959. Knowledgeable and entertaining, Steinbach had the uncanny ability to relate the excitement and emotions of racing to his audience; from his first call in 1938 until his death in 1964, Steinbach thrilled race fans. (JS.)

Driver Lloyd Ruby (left) and car owner John Zink accept the Leader Card trophy for the win at the 1961 Tony Bettenhausen 200-mile Indy car race. Presenting the trophy was the newly crowned 1961 Alice in Dairyland, Carol Jean Anderson. (MWLPP.)

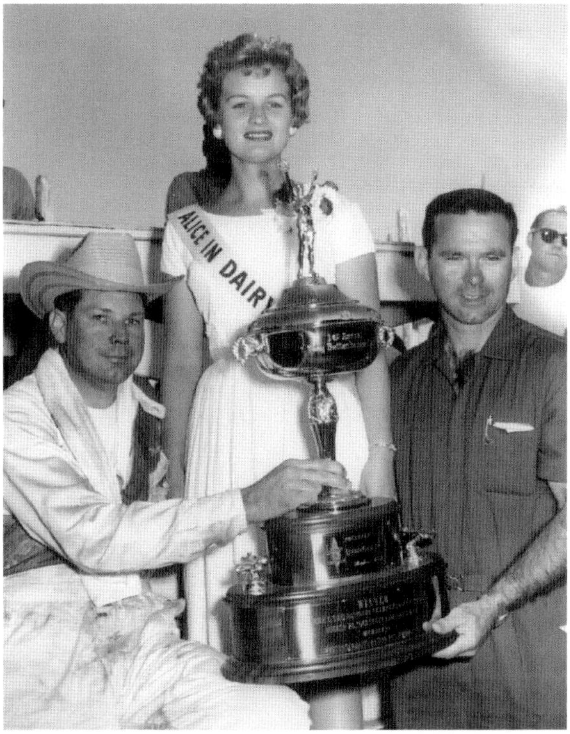

On June 26, 1960, the USAC sprint cars, which are slightly smaller than the traditional dirt car and very powerful, ran twin 50-lap features on the one-mile track. Parnelli Jones (No. 51), who is pictured leading a group of cars into turn three, won the first feature, while Don Branson won the second race and was the overall winner based on cumulative finishes in both races. Unfortunately, the other drivers are unidentified. (RL/MC.)

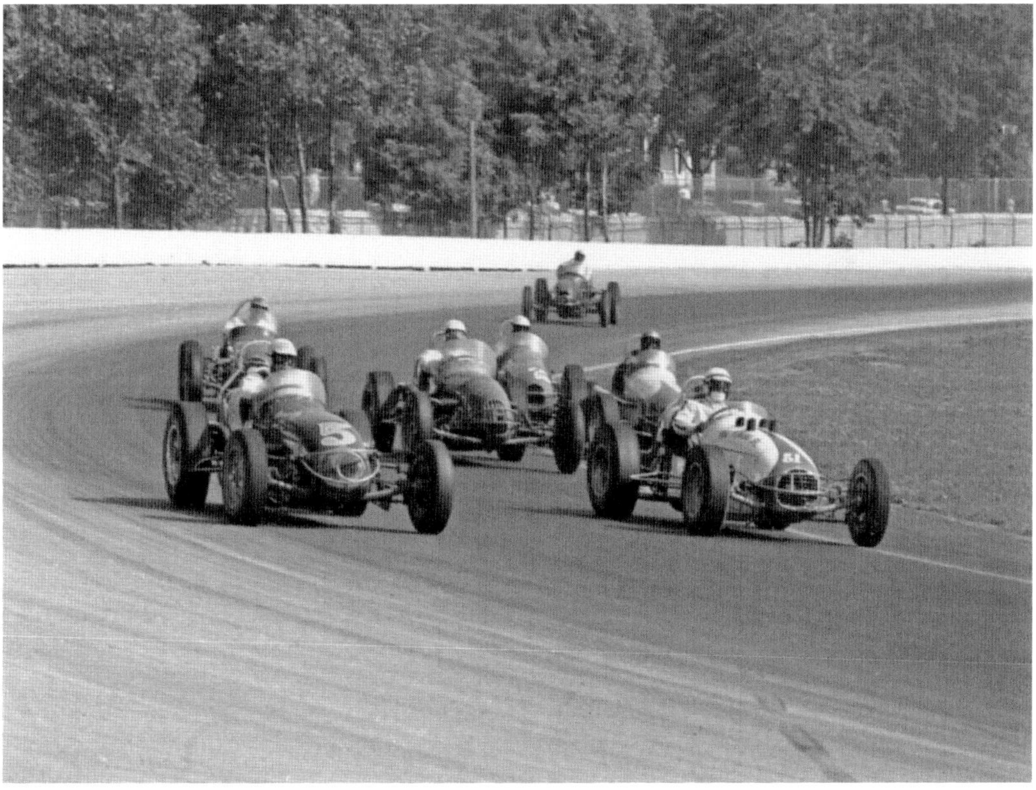

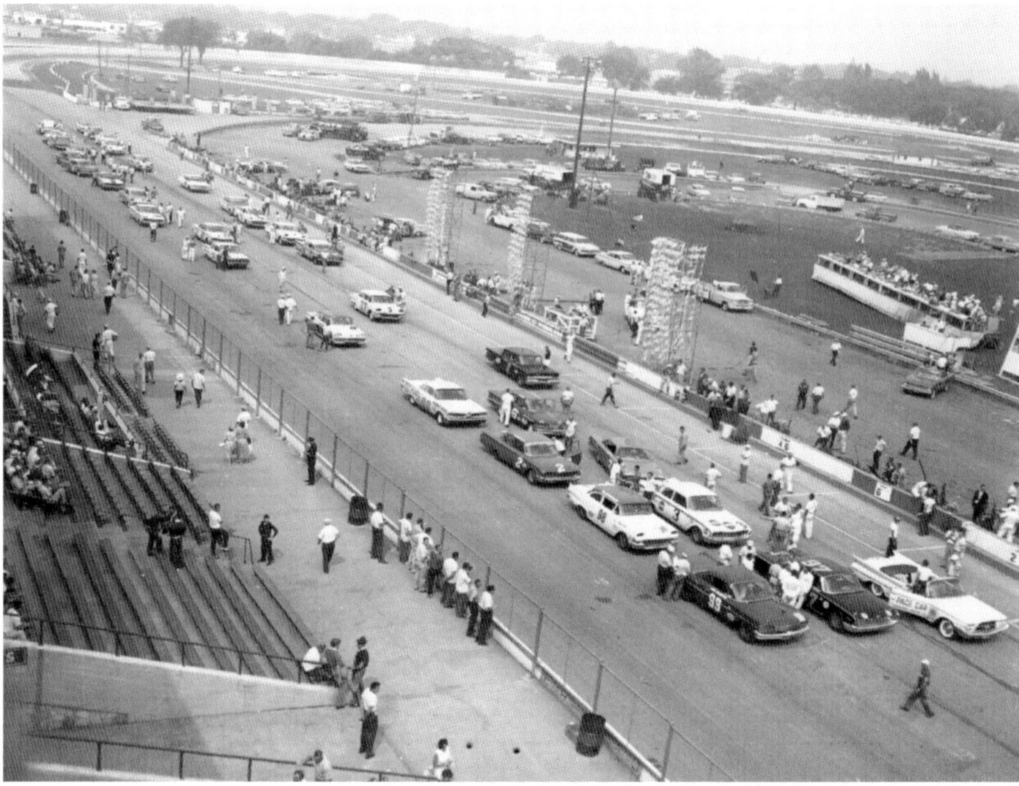

The field is lined up on the front straightaway getting ready for the start of a 200-mile stock-car race on August 25, 1960. It is evident that this race was held during the state fair, as the light towers for the evening stage shows were just off the track surface. Tony Bettenhausen (No. 98), who started fourth, won the race, while Norm Nelson (No. 3) started third and finished second, and Paul Goldsmith (No. 99), who started second, finished third. (RL/MC.)

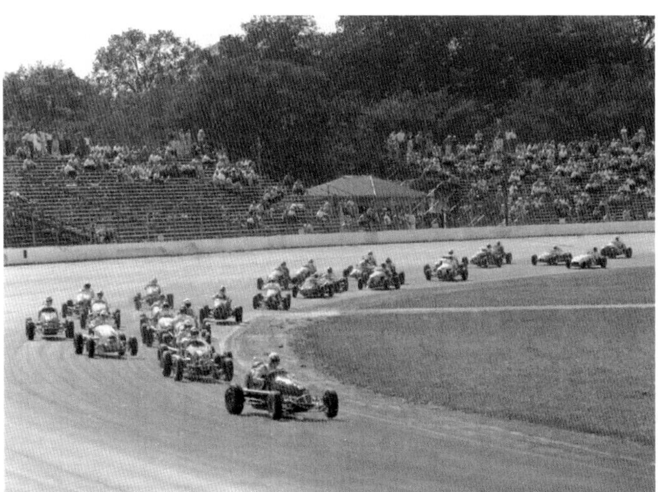

Tony Bettenhausen leads the field onto the back stretch on the opening lap of a USAC 100-mile midget race on August 27, 1960. Bettenhausen went on to win the event, but other results for the race could not be located. Bettenhausen lost his life the following May during practice for the Indianapolis 500. Because of his popularity in Milwaukee, the August big car race was named in his honor. (RL/MC.)

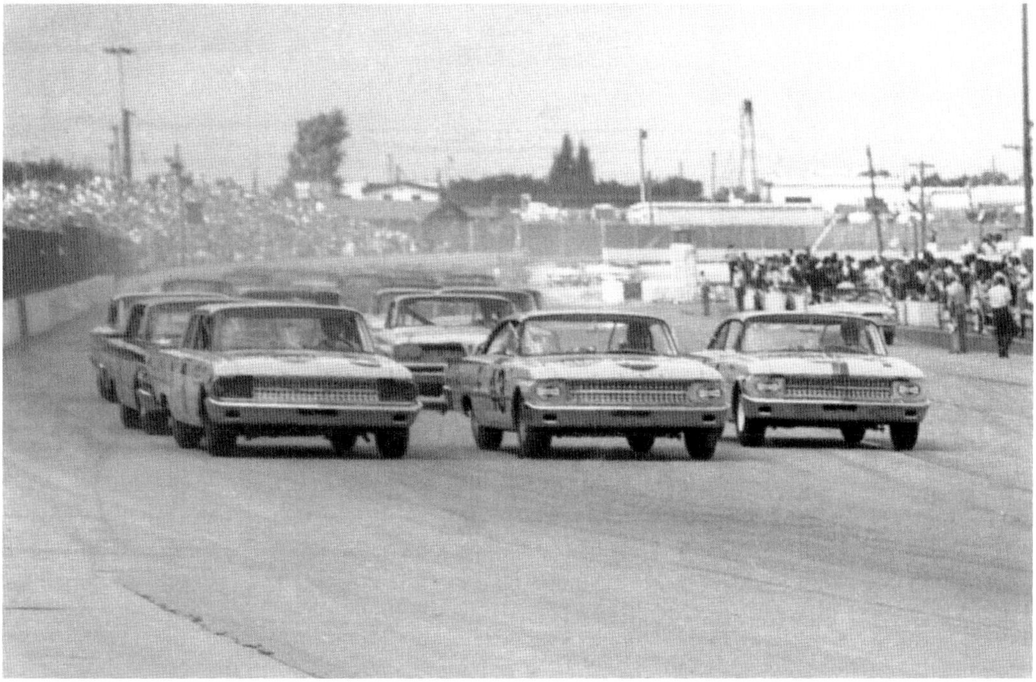

This ground-level shot of the start of the July 16, 1961, USAC 200-mile stock-car race shows pole-sitter Dick Rathmann in the middle of a stock-car sandwich, as Eddie Sachs (No. 3) is outside of Rathmann, while Don White (No. 4) is on the inside, both challenging Rathmann for the race lead. (RL/MC.)

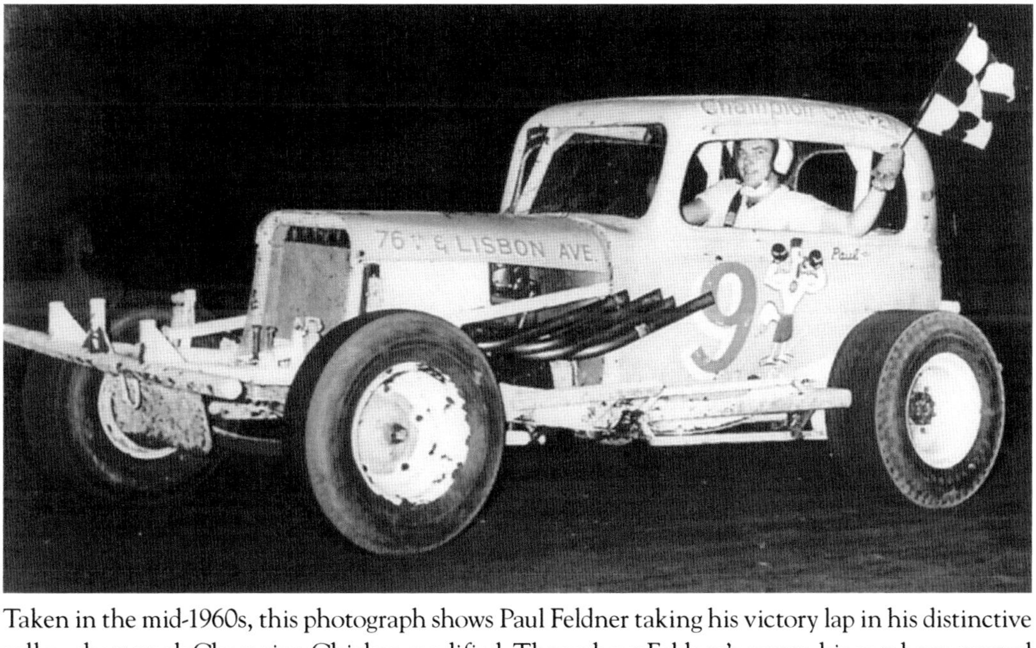

Taken in the mid-1960s, this photograph shows Paul Feldner taking his victory lap in his distinctive yellow short-track Champion Chicken modified. Throughout Feldner's career, his cars have sported several numbers, determined by his previous year's point standings. (GGAK.)

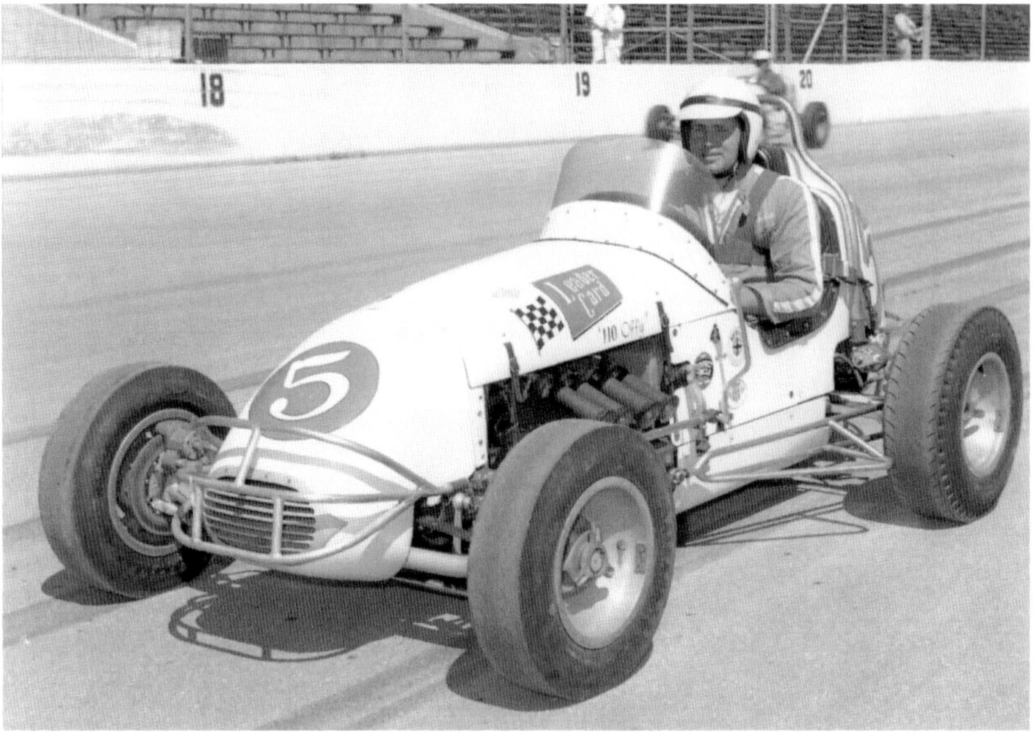

On a great day for a race, Jim Hurtubise readies for the August 12, 1961, 100-mile USAC midget race at State Fair Park Speedway. Driving No. 5, Hurtubise was able to finish in a respectable second place, while teammate Len Sutton, in No. 4, was close behind at third. Both drivers raced for Bob Wilke of the Leader Card Co. (MWLPP.)

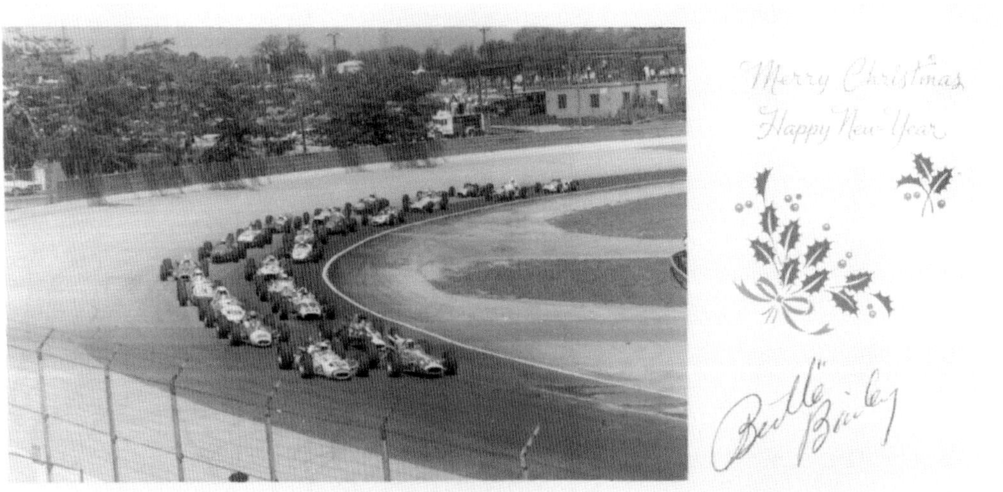

This Christmas card with a photograph of the August 14, 1965, race at the State Fair Park Speedway captures drivers coming out of the fourth turn in what seems to be a pace lap, allowing engines to warm up and drivers to prepare for a fast start. The sender of this card must have been a big race fan—enough to share their experience with everyone. (MWLPP.)

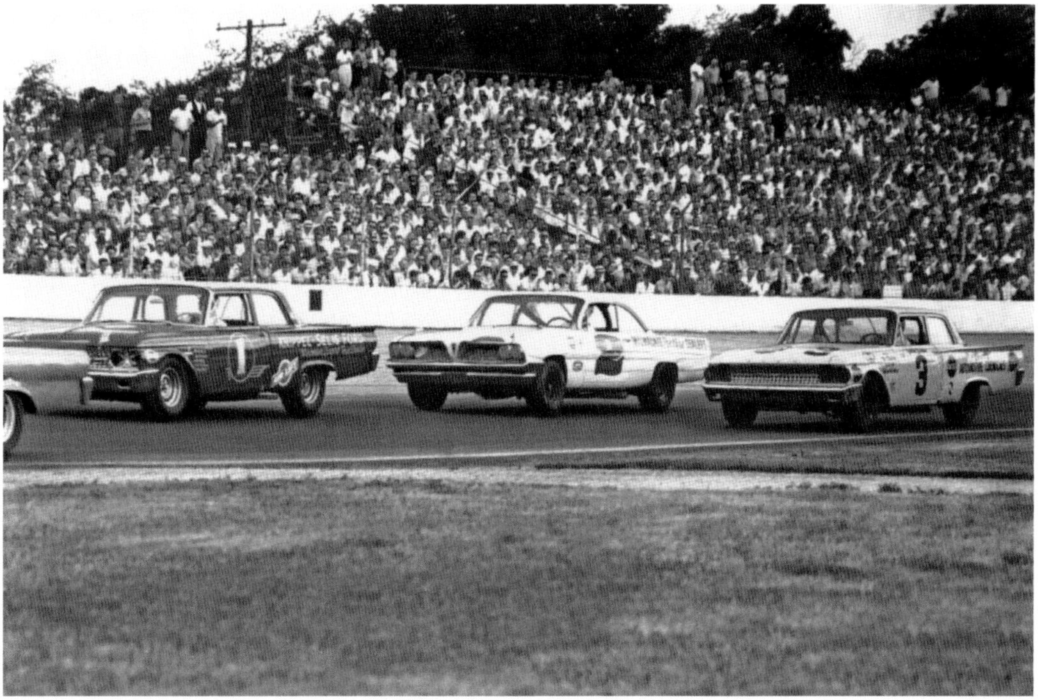

During the July 16, 1961, USAC 200-mile stock-car race, Norm Nelson (No. 1), Paul Goldsmith (No. 2) and Eddie Sachs (No. 3) ran in numerical order as they battled for position during the race, seen here in front of full bleachers in turn two. Sachs won the race, and Nelson finished third. Goldsmith had trouble with his mount and ended up finishing 25th. (RL/MC.)

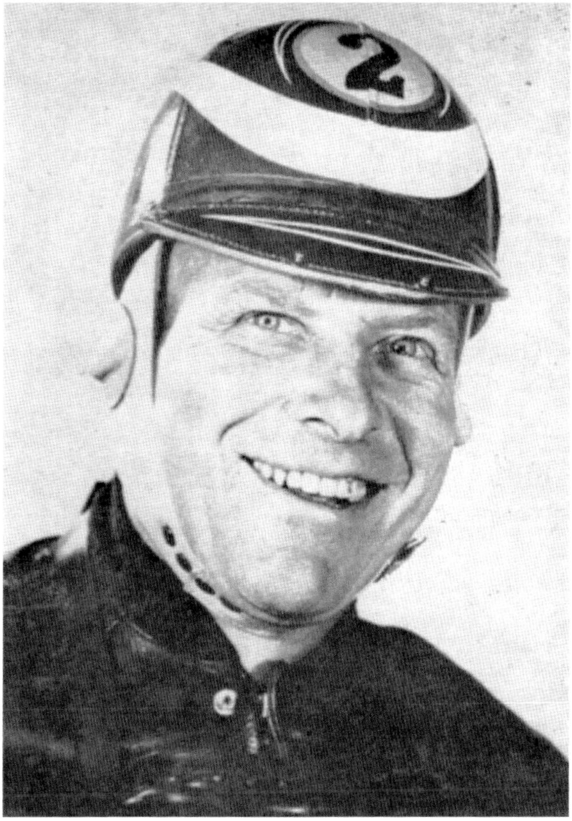

Fatally injured while testing at the Indianapolis Motor Speedway on May 12, 1961, Tony Bettenhausen was a champion among champions. A talented and versatile driver, Bettenhausen piloted stock, midget, and Indy cars, winning in every category. He was recognized for his influence on auto sports, and the Tony Bettenhausen 200 was named in his honor. (JS.)

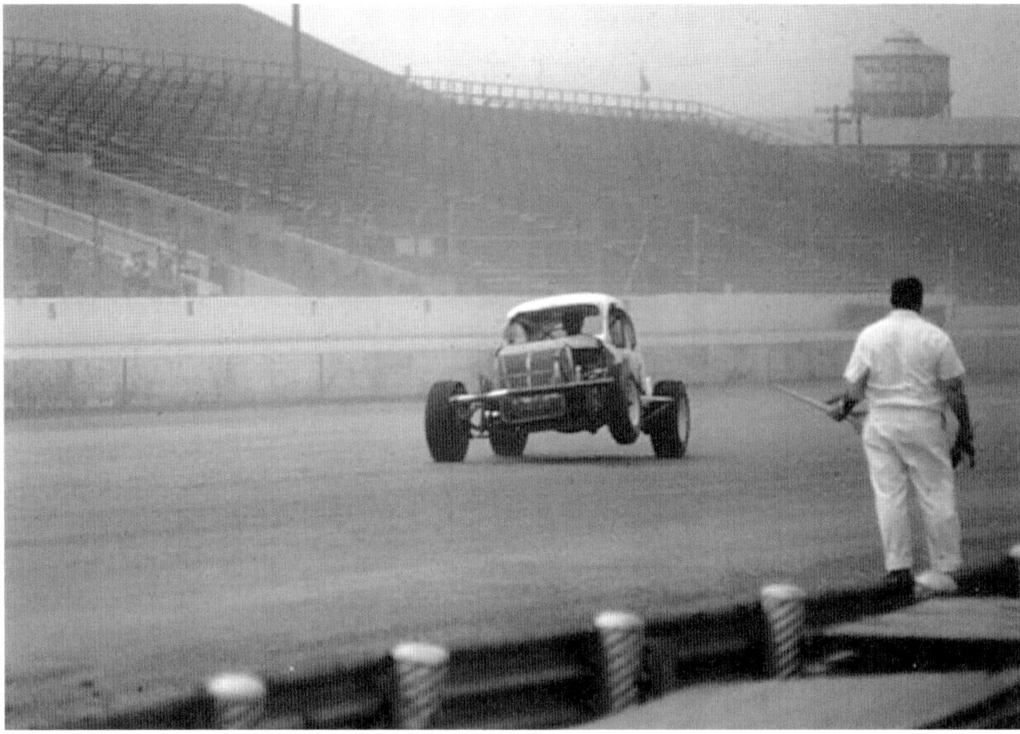

Coming down the straightaway, Miles "the Mouse" Melius is seen in this 1962 photograph on three wheels. Screeching tires and near rolls are an exciting part of modified racing. Starter Duane Sweeney stands at the ready, with his set of flags (which his wife had sewn) in hand. Sweeney, a familiar figure at Milwaukee for decades, later became a starter at the Indy 500. (JS.)

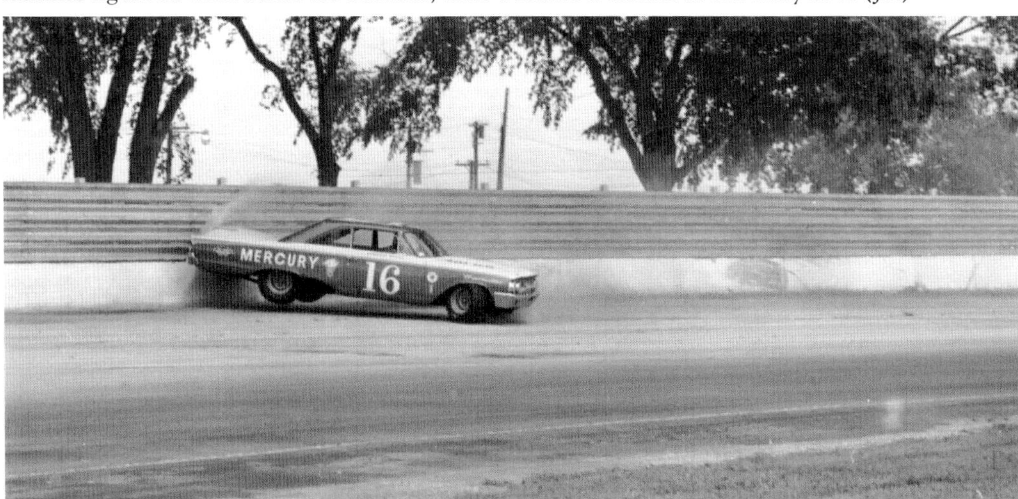

Driving his 1963 Mercury, No. 16, during the USAC 150 in August 1963, Rodger Ward hits the third turn wall. Years of experience—and the ability to get out of a sticky situation—helped Ward regain control and finish the race. Placing fourth helped split the purse, worth over $16,000, for owner Bill Stroppe. (GGAK.)

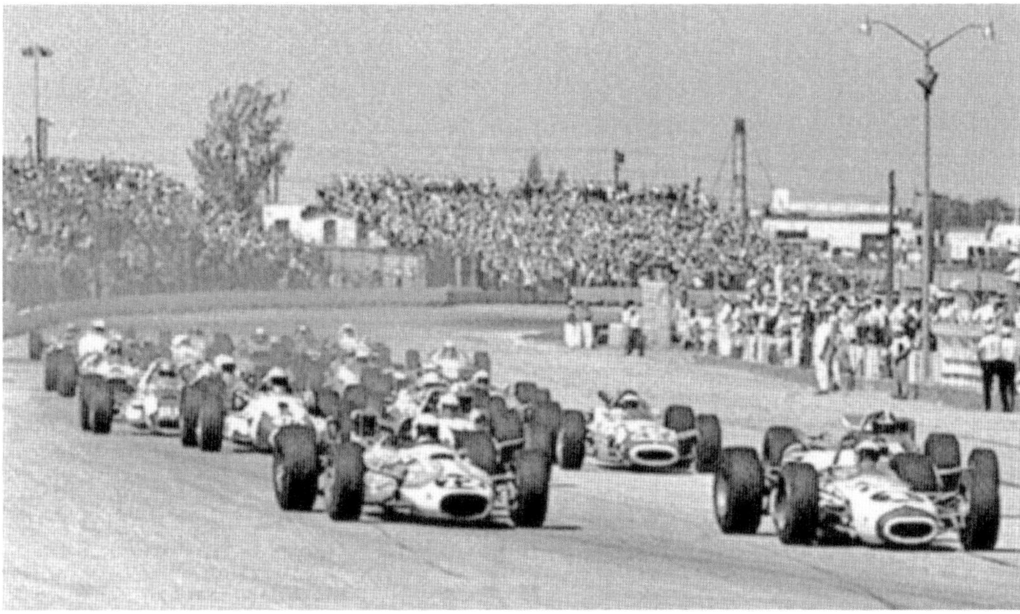

Mario Andretti (No. 1) and Gordon Johncock (No. 72) lead the field to the start of the Tony Bettenhausen 200-mile big car race in front of a packed grandstand on August 27, 1966. Andretti and Johncock dueled for the lead throughout the race, with Andretti finally taking the win and Johncock finishing second. Andretti won both big car races at the track in 1966. (RL/MC.)

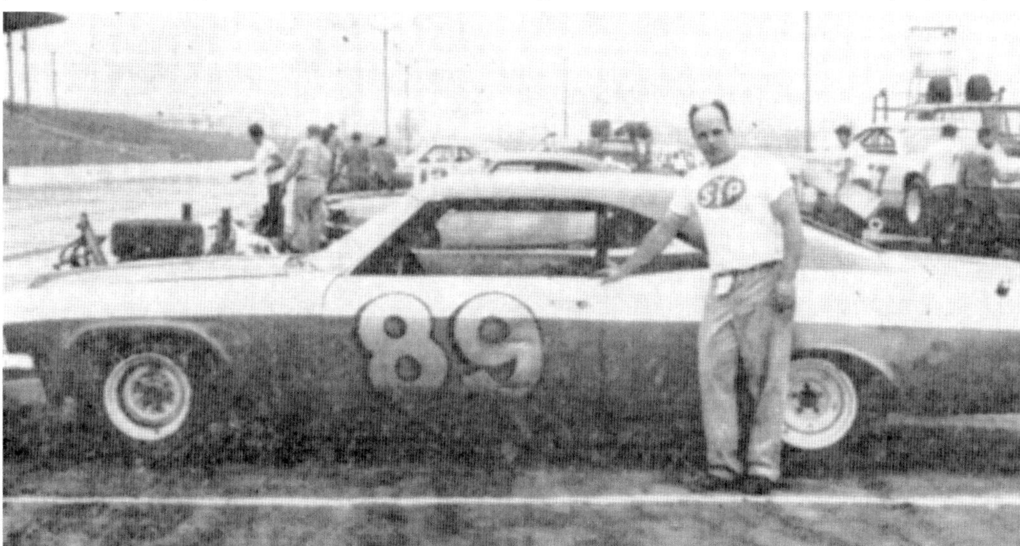

Tom Klippel of Wauwatosa, Wisconsin, seen here with his 1967 Chevy, was an accomplished late-model stock-car and sportsman driver. One of a group of drivers who would race five to six nights a week throughout Wisconsin, he had a fan base that was spread wide. Known as "the Voice," Klippel offered color commentary that entertained fans for 22 seasons at the Hales Corners Speedway. Klippel was a 2012 inductee into the Southeastern Wisconsin Short Track Hall of Fame. (GGAK.)

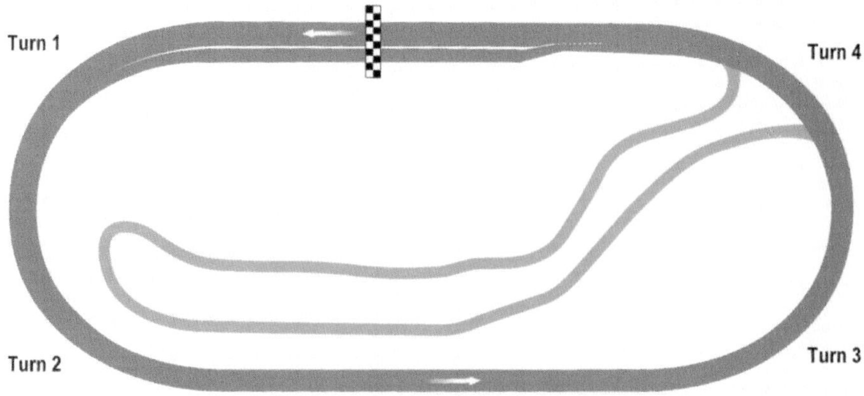

This is a rendering of the State Fair Park track as it would have been driven from 1967 to 1995. Two tracks remain: the interior road course and the mile oval. An enlarged paddock removed the quarter- and half-mile tracks, now only accommodating race cars. At the finish line, the pit lane was separated from the main track by a wall for safety reasons. (RC.)

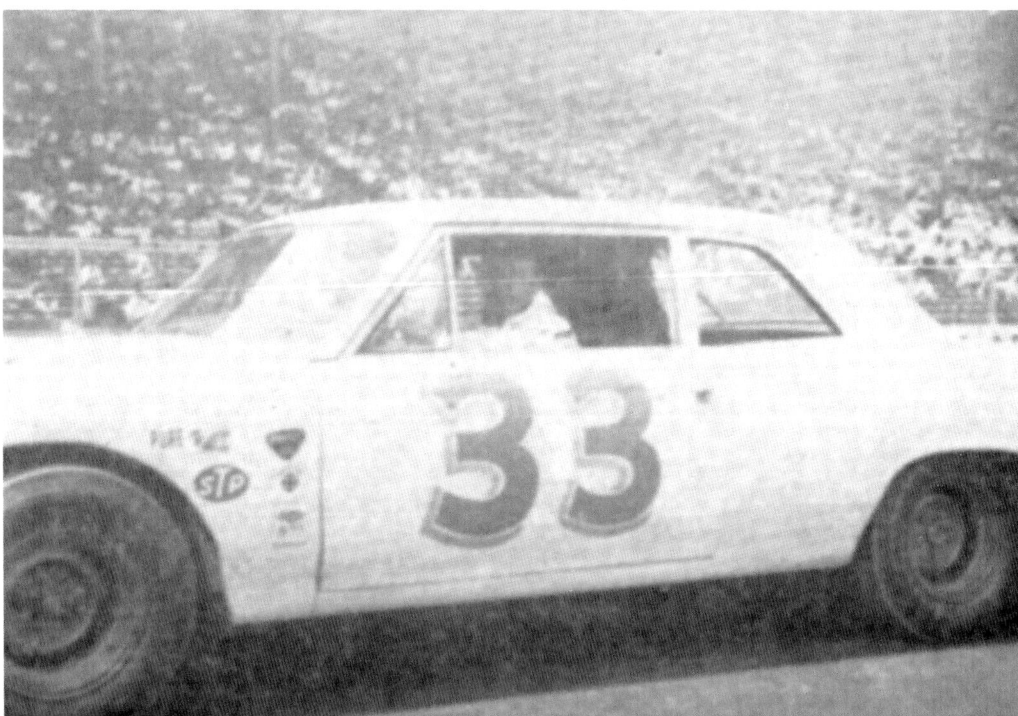

Dave Koehler, from Kiel, Wisconsin, started his career in Milwaukee racing modifieds and eventually switched to stock cars. He is shown here driving his 1967 Chevrolet Chevelle at the Governor's Cup 250. After a tragic accident in 1970 left him partially paralyzed, Koehler overcame tragic odds to do what he loved: race. He returned to racing for the 1975 Miller High Life 200, placing 23rd out of a field of 40. (JS.)

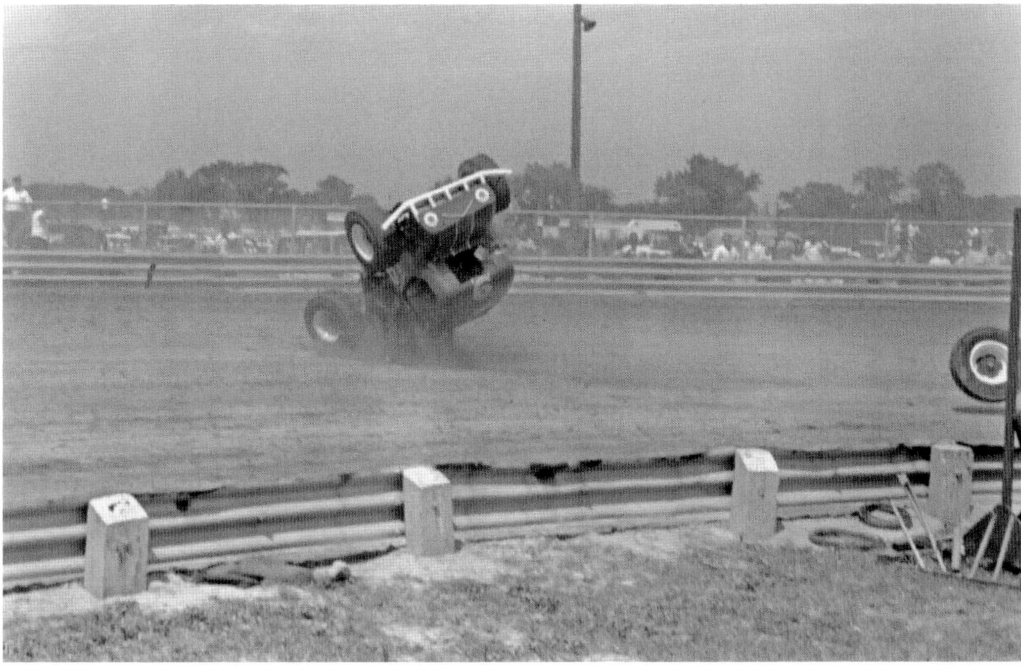

Veteran driver Bay Darnell flips his modified stock car in the north turn of the quarter-mile dirt track on August 8, 1963, during a special 100-lap race on a Saturday afternoon during the state fair. The modifieds normally ran on the quarter mile on Thursday nights. (RL/MC.)

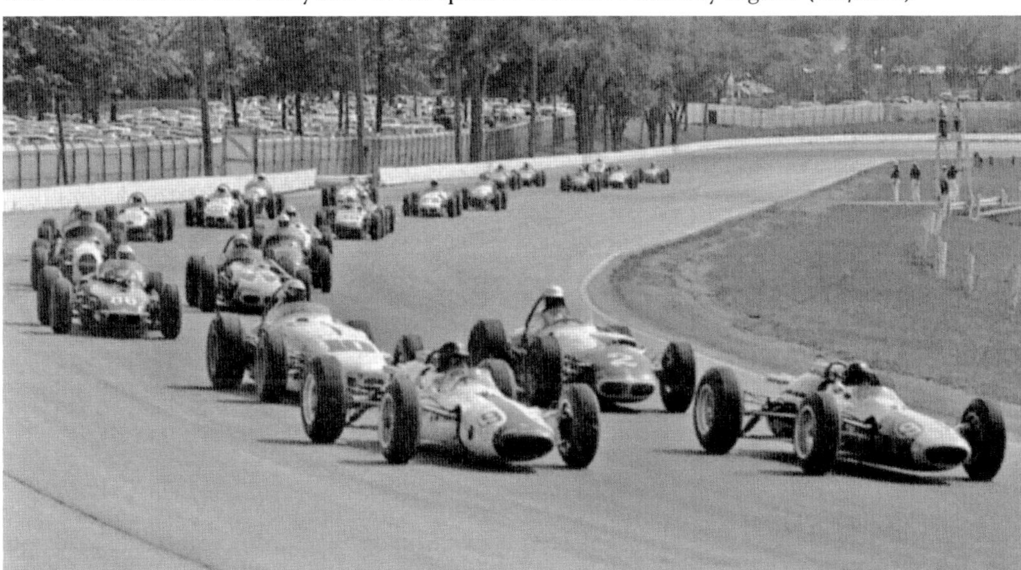

Jimmy Clark (No. 92), in a rare champ car appearance (other than the Indy 500), and Dan Gurney (No. 93), pace the field in a rear-engine Lotus before a crowd of more than 35,000 people at the Tony Bettenhausen 200 on August 18, 1963, during the state fair. In the second row are A.J. Foyt (No. 2) and Chuck Hulse (No. 10), both driving front-engine cars. Foyt finished second in the race, while Gurney was third, behind race winner Clark. (RL/MC.)

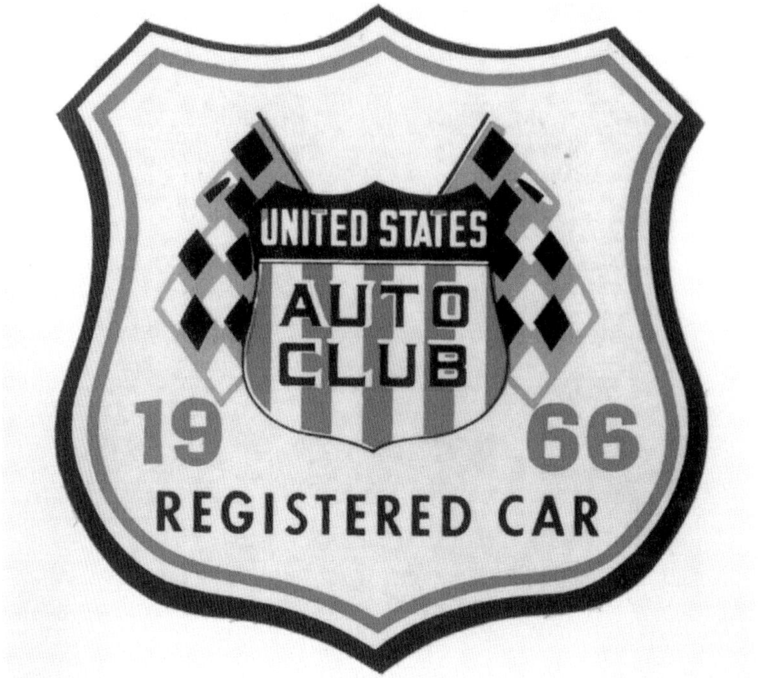

As a result of the 1955 Le Mans disaster, AAA, which sanctioned auto races from 1904 to 1955 and established American Championship Car racing, dissolved. The following year, 1956, it was replaced by USAC as the governing body. This 1966 badge was displayed or carried by team members for entrance onto the speedway. (MWLPP.)

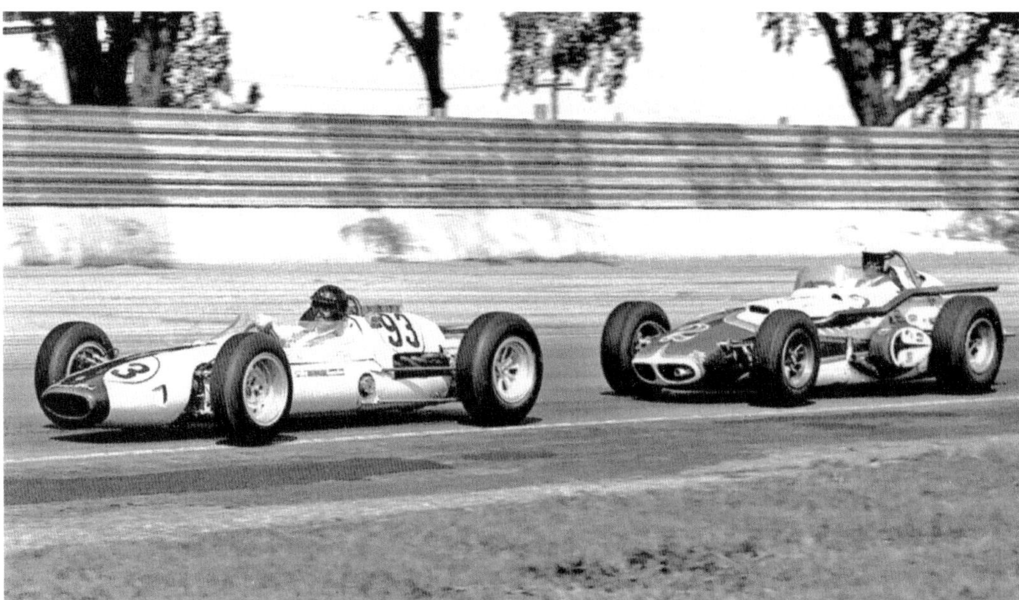

Dan Gurney (No. 93) and A.J. Foyt (No. 2) fight for position as they drive between turns three and four during the 200-mile big car race on August 18, 1963. Gurney started second, and Foyt third, but the pair reversed positions at the finish, as Foyt was second and Gurney was third behind pole-sitter and race winner Jimmy Clark. (RL/MC.)

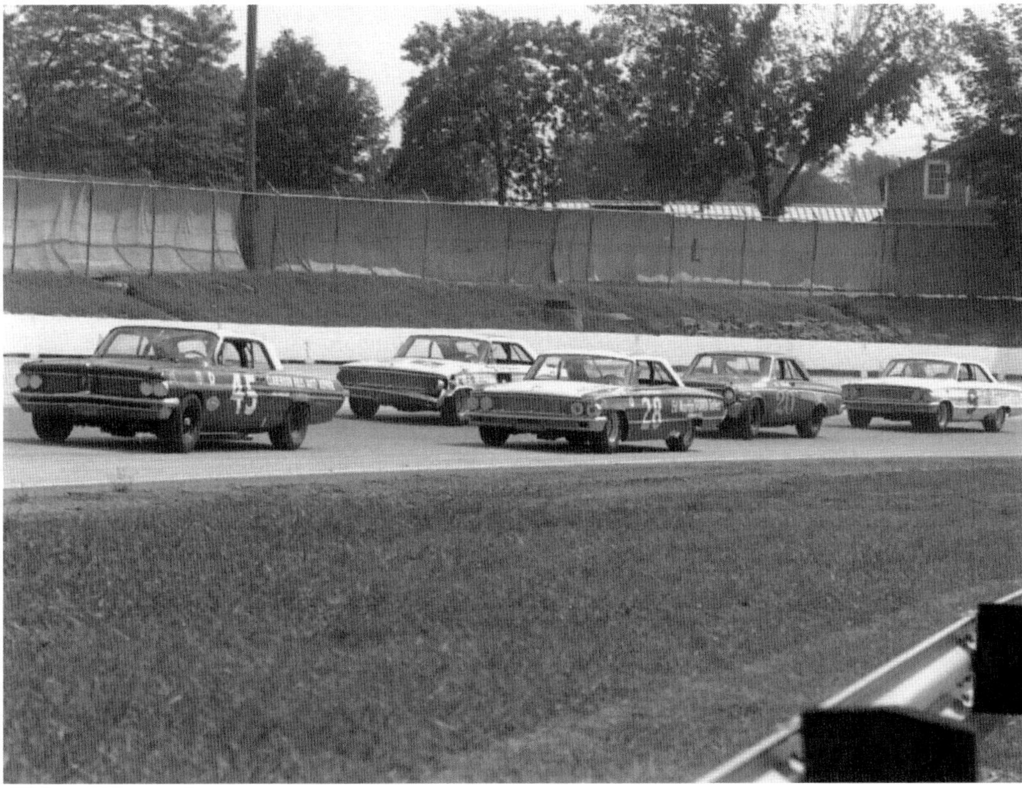

The mid-pack action is hot and heavy as this group of cars enter the back stretch during the August 16, 1964, USAC Fair Stock 150-mile race. Leading the group is Ralph Trumbull (No. 54), who is trailed by Whitey Gerken (No. 28), Bobby Marshman (No. 2, alongside Gerken), Joe Leonard (No. 20), and John Rostek (No. 9). Gerken was the highest finisher of the group, posting a sixth-place finish. (RL/MC.)

From his first experience at 13 years old, racing in a youth league—Formula Junior in Ancona, Italy—Mario Andretti was hooked on racing. His first US oval race was in 1959 and, as they say, the rest is history. In Milwaukee, Andretti swept the Rex Mays 100 and 200 Classics in 1966, and the 200 again in 1967. Andretti is seen here with crew chief and owner Steve Stapp. (GGAK.)

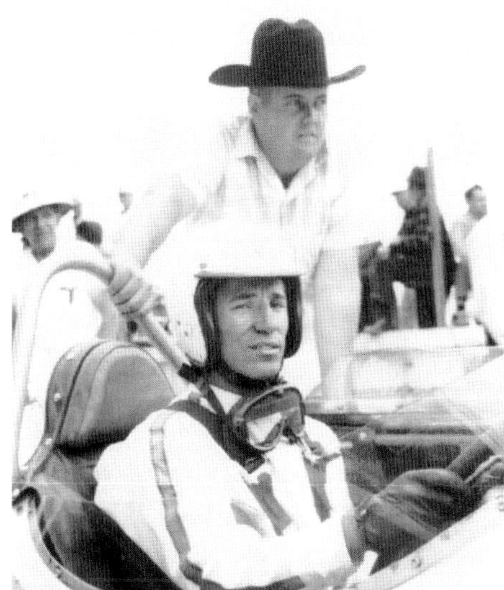

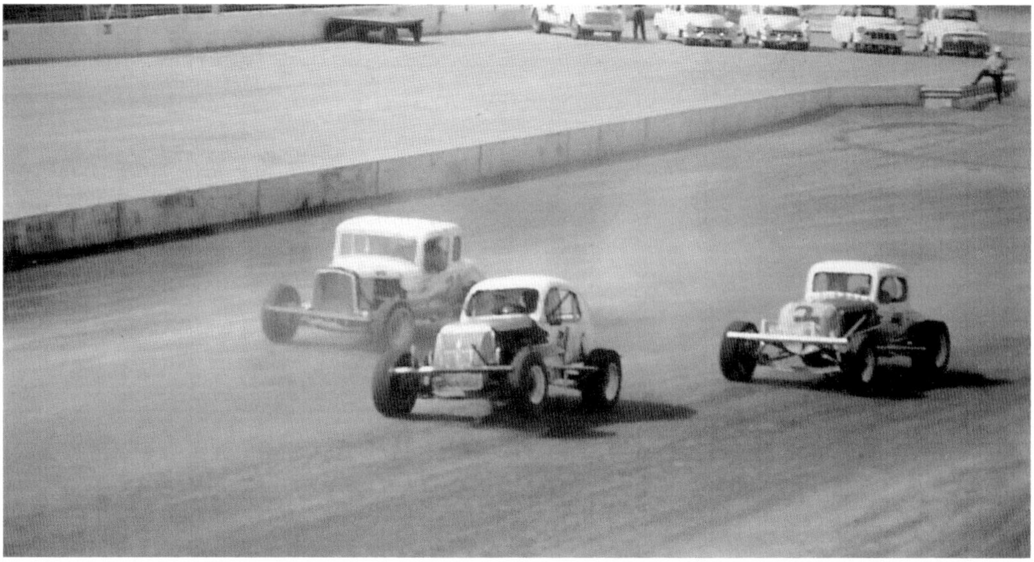

Hard-driving, dirt-kicking modifieds running on the quarter mile at the State Fair Park in 1962 made for a great day at the races. Modifieds lured their own fan base. The excitement fans felt as their driver rounded a turn on three wheels, or spun out, was enough to give everyone something to talk about. (GGAK.)

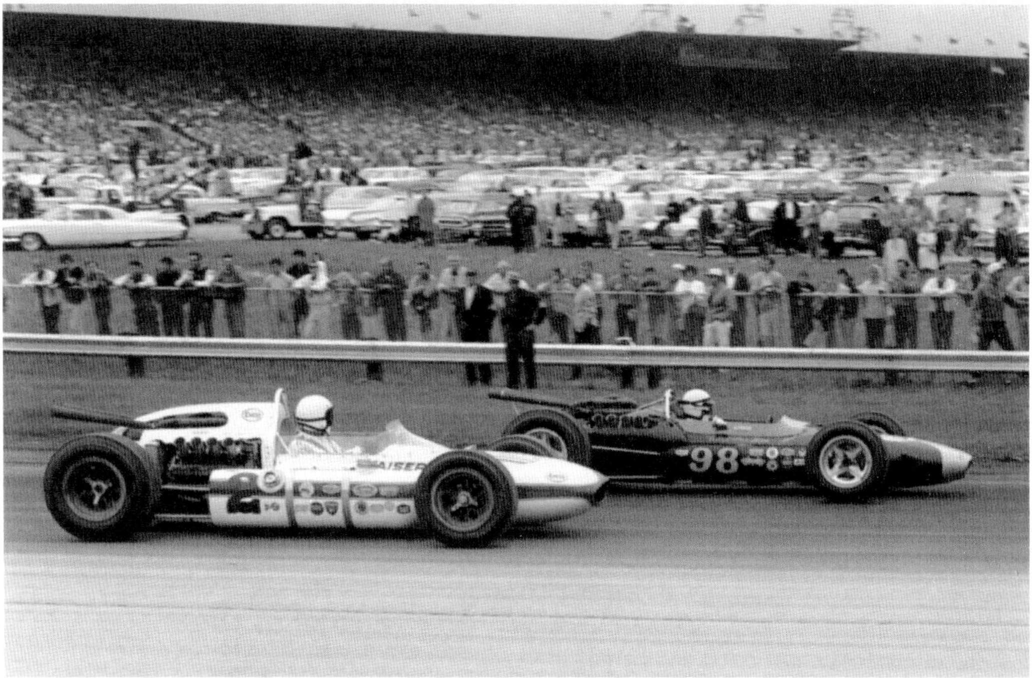

Driver Rodger Ward (No. 2) glanced over at his rival, Parnelli Jones (No. 98), on the pace lap prior to the start of the state fair champ car race on August 23, 1964. By late 1964, the transition of champ cars from the higher front-engine cars to the low-slung rear-engine machines was almost complete. (RL/MC.)

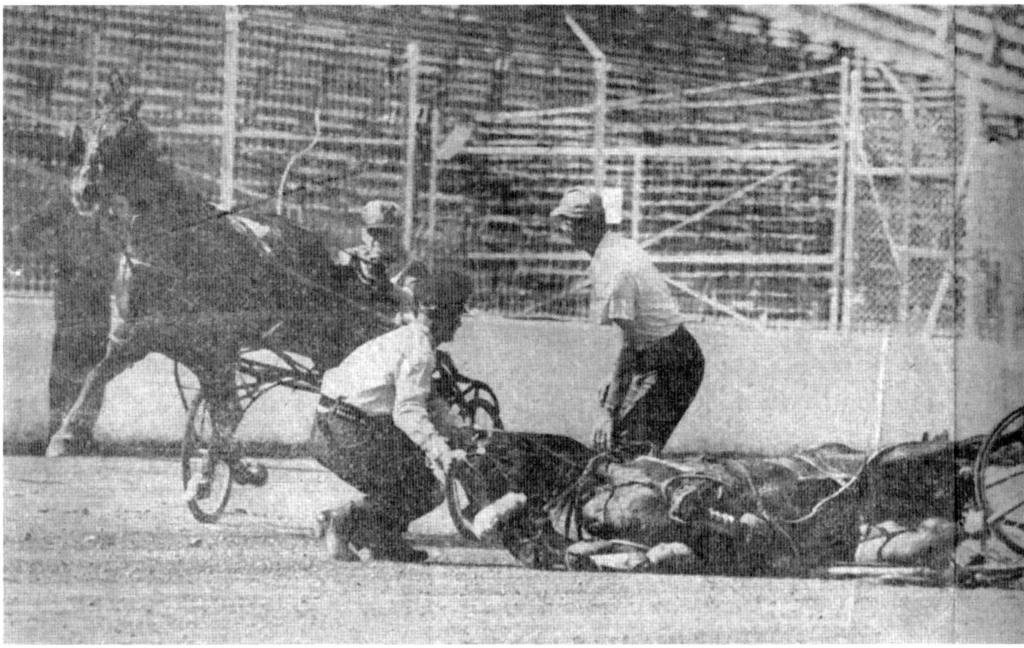

Harness racing can also have its accidents, as seen with this pileup during a summer race at the State Fair Park sometime in July 1957. June Eighth, a fallen mare, broke behind the motor barrier and threw her driver, G.W. Minshall. Minshall lay unconscious while the reinsmen attended to the horse and protected both as the remaining field finished the race. (WAHS.)

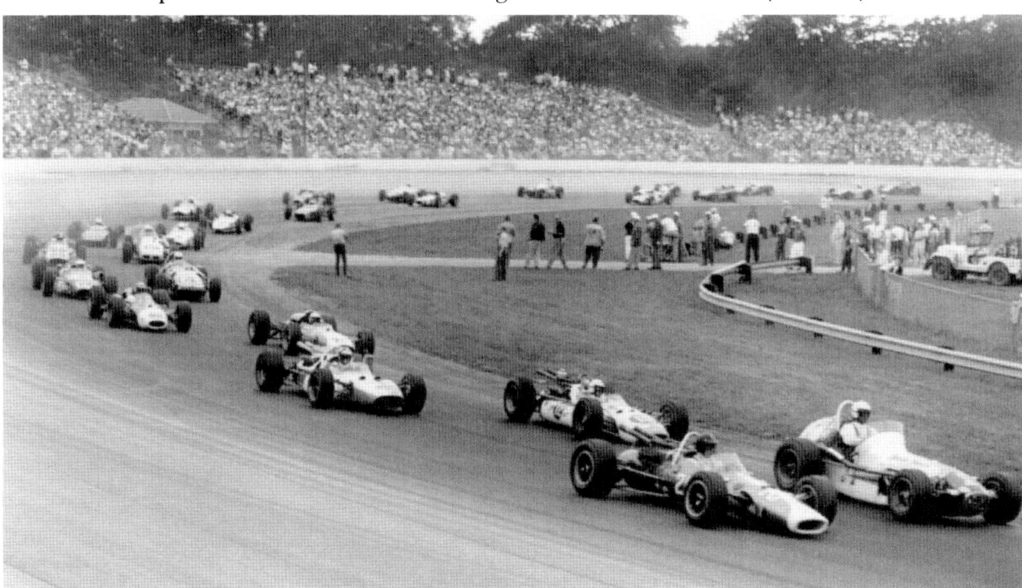

A.J. Foyt (No. 1) sat on the pole for the state fair champ car race on August 22, 1965, in his front-engine dirt-track machine after his speedway car failed to show up at the track. Foyt's was the only car in the field designed to run on dirt, not pavement. He drove to a second-place finish in the car, with which he had won a dirt-track race at the Illinois State Fair the previous day. (RL/MC.)

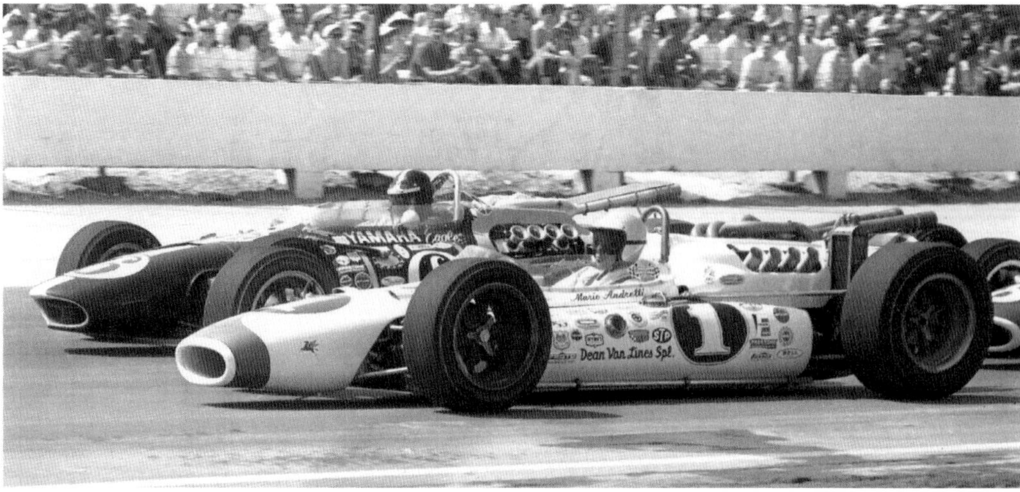

Mario Andretti (No. 1), on the pole, and Joe Leonard (No. 6), on the outside of the front row, pace the field prior to the start of the sold-out Rex Mays 100 bi-car race on June 5, 1966. Andretti went on to win the race, while Leonard finished third. (RL/MC.)

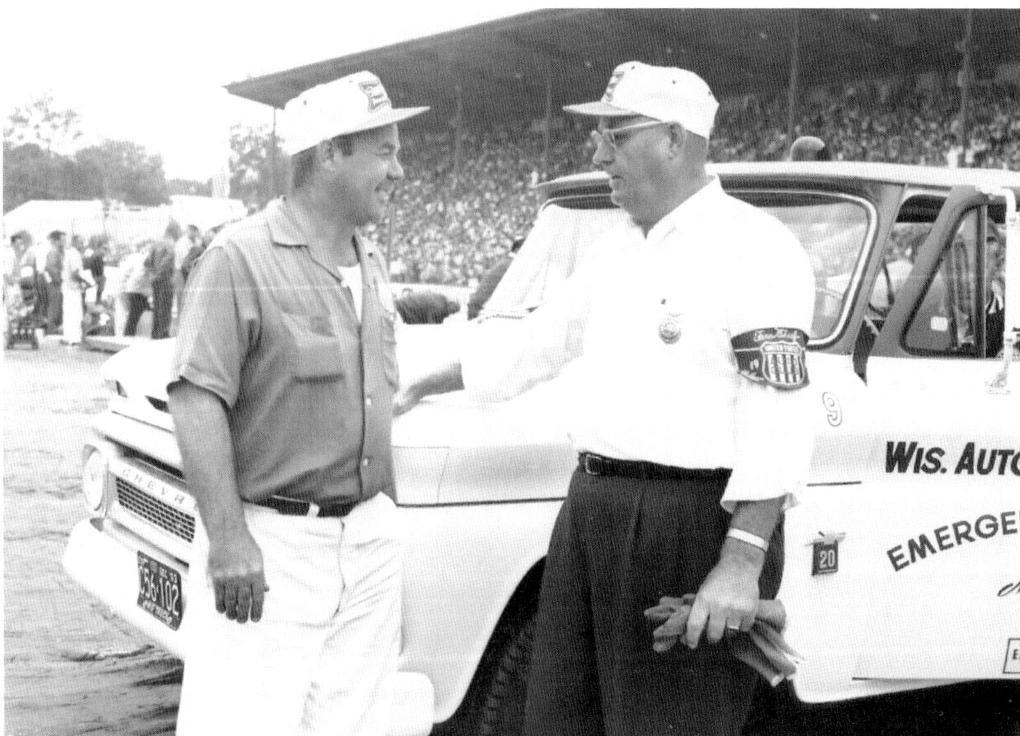

Pre-race strategy prevents disasters, and that is exactly what chief George Carolan, right, of Miller Brewing Company's fire department, is discussing with one of his team members, Steve Klamik, before the Tony Bettenhausen 200-mile classic in 1964. Miller Brewery donated the use of $2,000 worth of extinguishers for each race at the State Fair Park. When seconds count, count on the safety staff at the park. (MWLPP.)

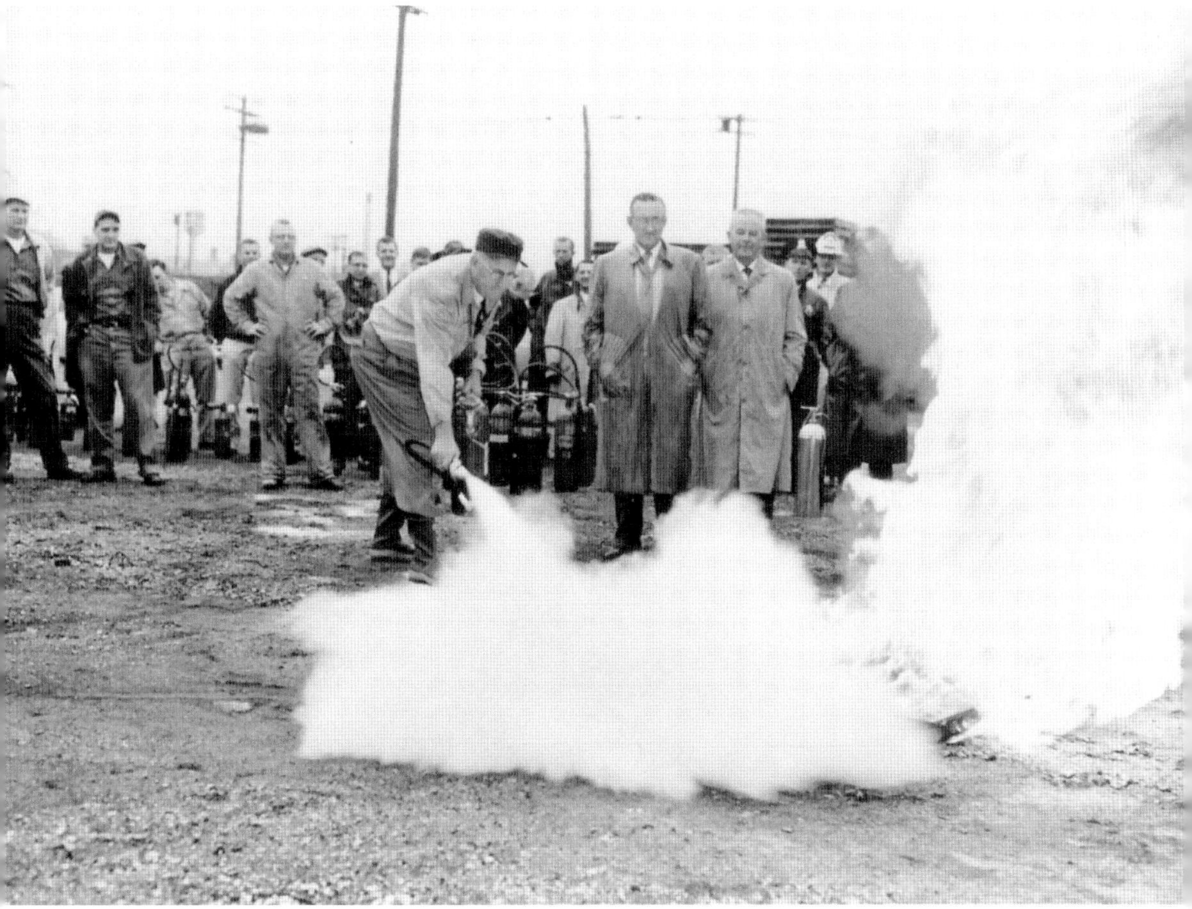

One of the deadliest threats in motor sports is fire. Speed and mishaps make for a dangerous mix. Taking precautionary measures seriously here in 1962 is George Carolan, chief of the Miller Brewery's fire department. In 1952, Miller Brewery, at Chief Carolan's suggestion, donated the use of fire extinguishers at every race. Carolan's team of 90 well-trained volunteers stood at the ready to extinguish the threat. Here, George Carolan demonstrates the proper technique to douse fires. (MWLPP.)

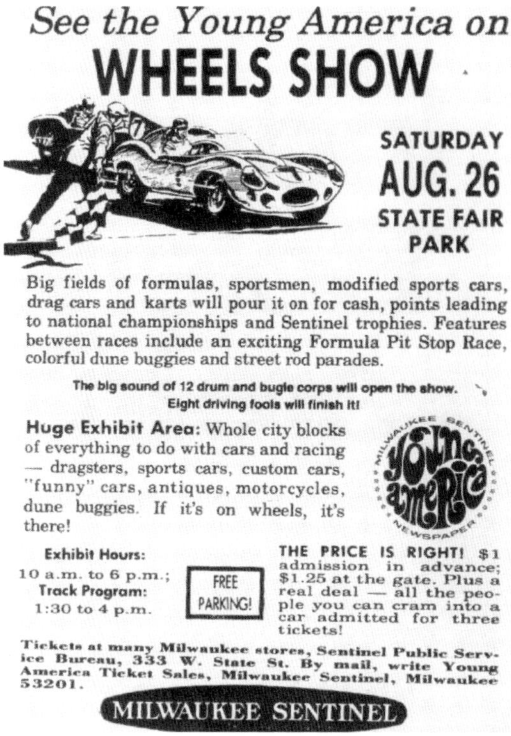

Sponsored by the *Milwaukee Sentinel*, Young America Week ran during the 1960s and 1970s, targeting the young citizens of Wisconsin. The event featured arts, fashion, music, and other "swinging, happening" summer events. The auto portion, Young America on Wheels, featured show races, daredevil escapades, auto displays, and meet-and-greets with race drivers. (MCHS.)

Three different styles of big cars were running in the 200-mile race on August 27, 1966. Greg Weld (No. 95) was driving a roadster, Wally Dallenbach (No. 24) was wheeling a dirt car, and Lloyd Ruby (No. 29) was driving a rear-engine car. The days were numbered for the front-engine cars, which were already considered dinosaurs by 1966. Ruby finished eighth in the race, while Weld and Dallenbach finished 14th and 15, respectively. (RL/MC.)

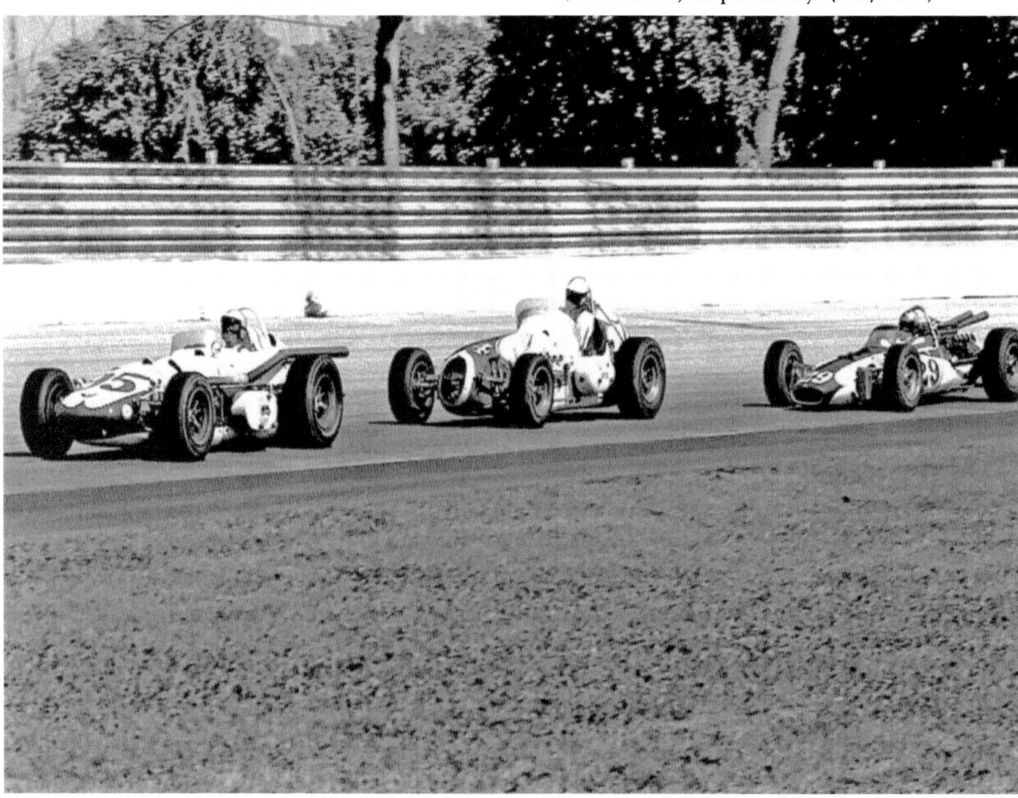

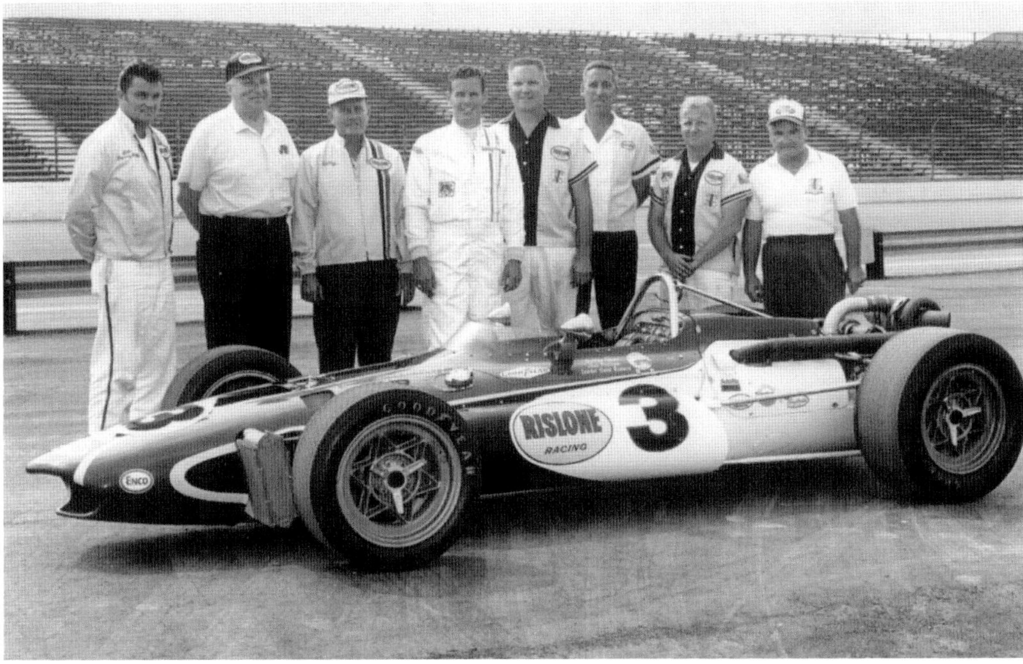

In town for the June 1968 Rex Mays 150, Bobby Unser is seen here with car owner Bob Wilke (far right) and other Rislone racing staff members. Little did anyone know at the time of this picture that the day's race would take a tragic turn when Ronnie Duman was killed in an accident at the start of the third lap. (MWLPP.)

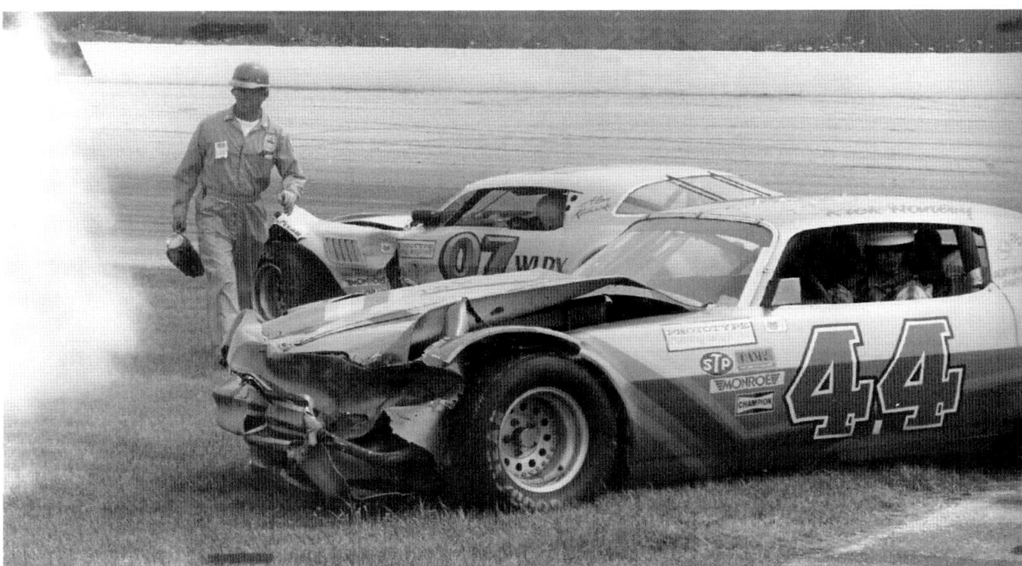

Dueling for the win during a USAC 1981 season race, these two drivers wound up in quite a fender-bender. Alan Kulwicki, driving his 1980 Chevy Camaro No. 97, doesn't seem too happy, but neither does Rick Hanley in No. 44. It's a lucky day when drivers can walk away from a wreck. (GGAK.)

SEPT. 17—250 MILE LATE MODEL STOCK CAR RACE

For information regarding auto races — call EVergreen 4-2240
Races under auspices of Wisconsin Auto Racing, Inc.

Trophy Awards to Fastest Qualifier and to Winner of Race —
Courtesy of Pure Oil Co. — A Division of Union Oil Co. of California

Pace Car — The "All New" 1968 Chrysler 300 Convertible —
Courtesy of Mayfair Chrysler/Plymouth
Highway 100 just South of North Avenue, Milwaukee

Emergency Equipment Jeeps — Courtesy of Bob Eisen Motors, Milwaukee, Wis.

CAR NO.	DRIVER, FROM	ENTRANT, FROM	CAR NAMES	YEAR MADE	TIME
1	NORM NELSON Racine, Wis.	Nelson Racing Enterprises Racine, Wis.	Plymouth	1967	
2	DON WHITE Keokuk, Iowa	Ray Nichels Highland, Ind.	Dodge Charger	1967	
3	AL UNSER Albuquerque, N. M.	Rudy Hoerr Peoria, Ill.	Dodge Charger	1967	
4	SAL TOVELLA Addison, Ill.	Sal's Auto Sales Chicago, Ill.	Dodge Charger	1967	
4	SHAD WHEELER Fredrickstown, Ohio	Carroll Barnhart Marysville, Ohio	Ford	1966	
7	KEITH PLOUGHE Indianapolis, Ind.	Keith Ploughe Indianapolis, Ind.	Dodge Charger	1965	
8	ROGER REGETH West Allis, Wis.	Jim & Jerry's Service South Milwaukee, Wis.	Ford Galaxie	1966	
9	PAUL FELDNER Colgate, Wis.	Paul Feldner Colgate, Wis.	Ford	1967	
11	MARIO ANDRETTI Nazareth, Pa.	Holman-Moody Inc. Charlotte, N. C.	Ford	1967	
12	DAVE WHITCOMB Valparaiso, Ind.	Dave Whitcomb Valparaiso, Ind.	Plymouth	1965	
15	PARNELLI JONES Palos Verdes, Calif.	Holman-Moody Inc. Charlotte, N. C.	Ford	1967	
21	JACK BOWSHER Springfield, Ohio	Jack Bowsher Springfield, Ohio	Ford	1967	
25	JOHNNY ROBERTS Breckenridge, Mich.	Johnny Roberts Breckenridge, Mich.	Ford Fairlane	1967	
27	A. J. FOYT Houston, Tex.	Holman-Moody Charlotte, N. C.	Ford	1967	
33	DALE KOEHLER Glendale, Wis.	Dale Koehler Glendale, Wis.	Chevelle	1967	
40	BOBBY COE	Bobby Coe	Ford	1966	
41	BILL CHEESBURG Tucson, Ariz.	Stephenson/Layton/Greene Salem, Ohio	Ford	1966	
42	JIM MARTIN Fort Wayne, Ind.	Bill Budd Fort Wayne, Ind.	Chevelle	1965	
43	TOM JONES North Brook, Ill.	Erwin Nowosel Glenview, Ill.	Chevrolet Impala	1966	
45	JERRY SMITH Appleton, Wis.	Al Piette Appleton, Wis.	Plymouth	1965	
47	J. C. KLOTZ Fort Wayne, Ind.	Ernie Harris Fort Wayne, Ind.	Plymouth	1965	
	DICK MITCHELL Trenton, Mich.	Alan Stockton Detroit, Mich.	Ford	1967	

250 MILE STOCK CAR RACE — *Page Seven*

Legends of racing appear in this 1967 stock-car roll call, which is literally a page out of history. It lists everyone who is anyone: Mario Andretti, Al Unser, A.J. Foyt, and others. Each driver—hometown or not—paid their dues, moved the fans, and created more memories than one could count. These drivers, as well as those not so famous, brought fans back week after week. (JS.)

5

Flexing Muscle

1969–1980

As the 1960s wound down, major renovations affected track programming. Safety issues were prioritized, and in 1967, a new pit lane was installed, resulting in the loss of the quarter-mile dirt track and eliminating short track racing at the State Fair Park forever. In 1968, the entire track was repaved. Leadership also changed when Tom Marchese sold a percentage of his Wisconsin Auto Racing Association Inc. to John Kaishian, a Milwaukee dirt track owner and promoter who partnered with Marchese as the track's co-promoter.

The golden years of stock-car racing would arguably be considered the mid-1960s through the early 1970s, when every automobile manufacturer flexed their muscle. Thanks to these new hot wheels, drivers raced to the roar of sold-out crowds, making stock-car racing the fastest-growing sport with the biggest following. Detroit-backed racing entered all areas of auto sports, none more thrilling than stock-car racing. From Hudson Hornets to Dodge Daytonas, Chevy Camaros, Plymouth Superbirds, and Ford Torinos, they all had their day, but there was no better day for Detroit than the day after race day, when sales soared. "Win on Sunday, sell on Monday" was a well-known saying. Consumers wanted the cars drivers were winning in.

The 1970s brought some interesting spins to the track when Al Unser Sr. dominated the 1970 Bettenhausen 200 and Rick Mears made his first Mile appearance in a USAC stock car in 1977. Women drivers were not new to racing, but Janet Guthrie made her mark as the first woman Indy car driver to race at the Milwaukee Mile in 1979.

The year 1978 saw the first American Speed Association (ASA) Late Model Series event held at the park, won by Michigan's Bob Senneker. Championship Auto Racing Teams (CART), founded in 1979 by team owners dissatisfied with the USAC, began sanctioning Indy car events at the track in August 1980. USAC's once popular stock-car series began to decline through mismanagement, and its final Milwaukee event was sanctioned in 1983; one year later, the division ended.

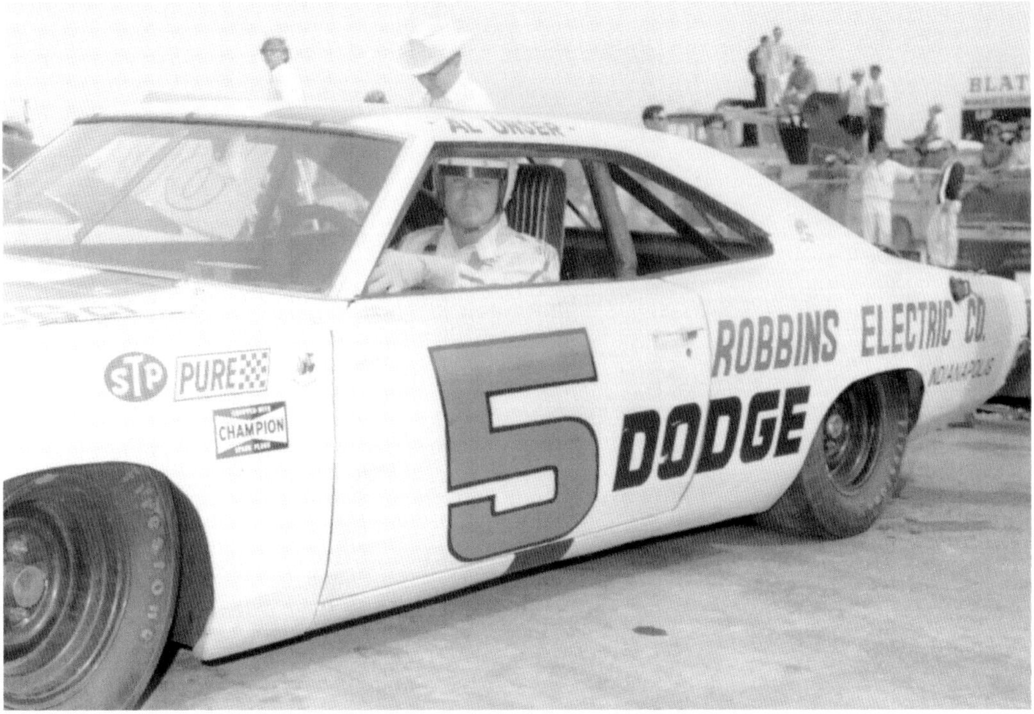

The Milwaukee Mile has witnessed many legends in its time, and Al Unser is one of them. Unser, a member of one of racing's few dynasty families, not only found a great fan base in Milwaukee, but much success as well. His first USAC Indy car race win at the Mile was during the Tony Bettenhausen 200 on August 17, 1969. (GGAK.)

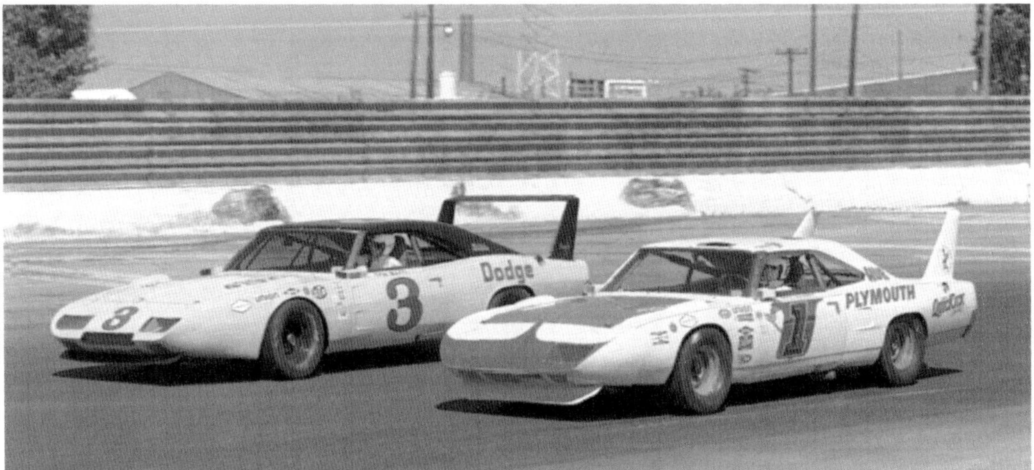

Two of the legendary winged stock cars competed at the State Fair Park speedway during the traditional Thursday Fair Stock 200 on August 20, 1970. The No. 3 Dodge Daytona, driven by Don White, and the No. 1 Plymouth Superbird, piloted by Roger McCluskey, ran side by side during the race. McCluskey finished third, while White dropped out with mechanical problems. (RL/MC.)

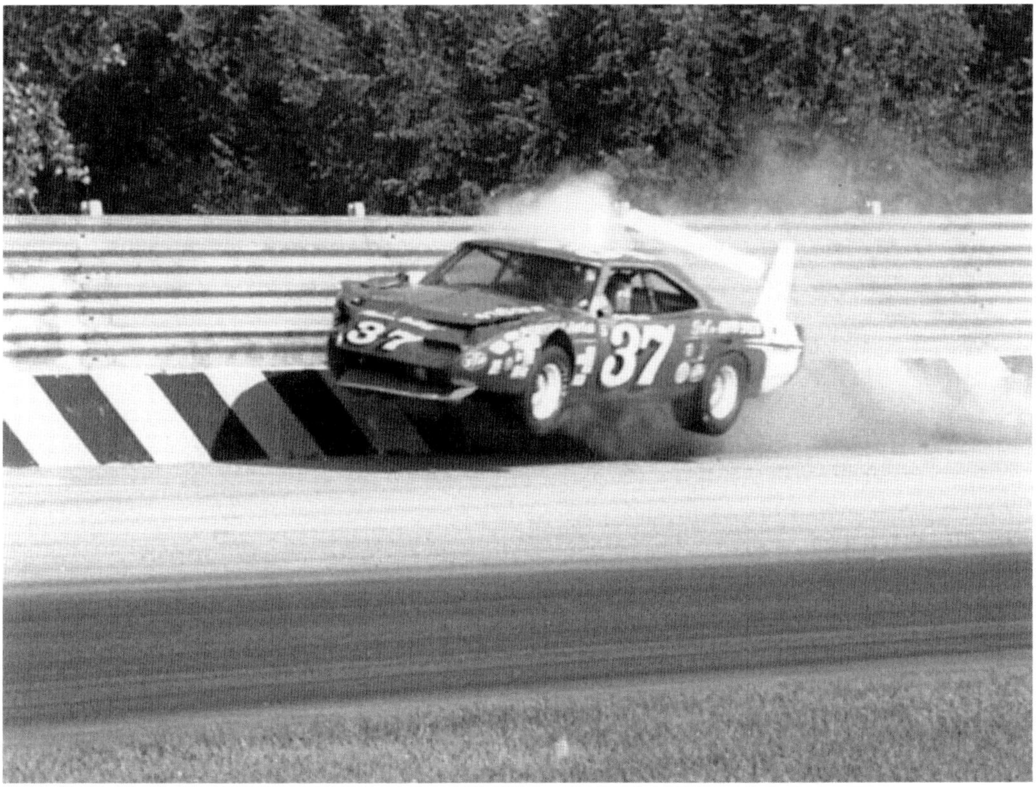

Sal Tovella blew a tire on his 1970 Plymouth Superbird as he headed into turn three during the September 20, 1970, 250-mile USAC stock-car event. The force of the crash lifted all four wheels off the track as he hit the wall. He was not hurt, but his car was severely damaged. (RL/MC.)

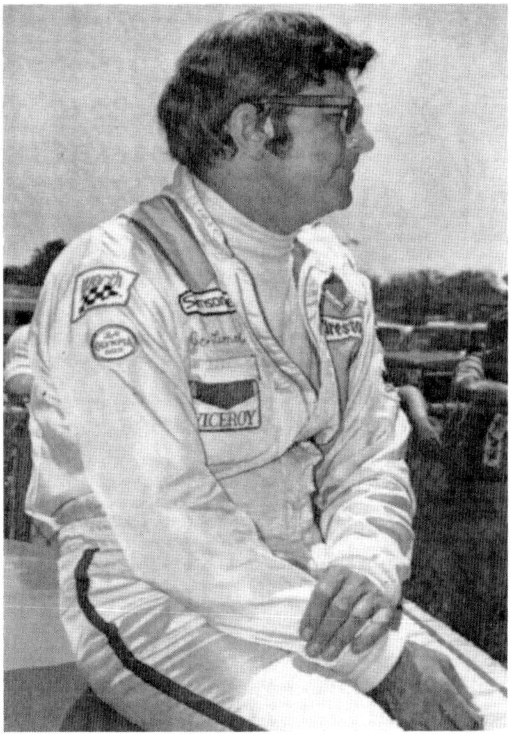

Joe Leonard experiences something unusual: a quiet moment at the track. Leonard was a racer's racer; he did it all, and he did it his way. Motorcycles were his first love, and in 1954, he became the first to win the AMA Grand National Championship Series. After seven years on two wheels, he teamed with Dan Gurney and gave Indy cars a go. His first win at Milwaukee was during the USAC Indy car race on August 14, 1965. (JS.)

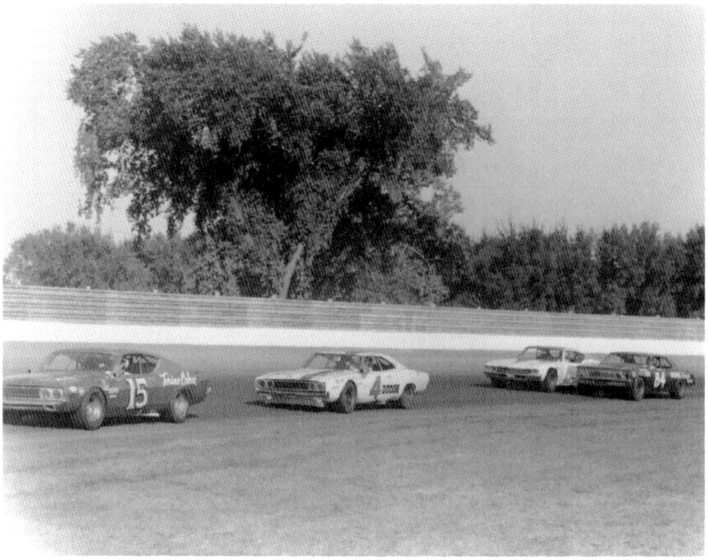

The Governor's Cup 250, the September 1969 USAC stock-car race, saw Al Unser, No. 4, caught in his 1969 Dodge Charger between brother Bobby, driving his No. 15 Ford Torino Cobra, and Gene Marmor, No. 50, tailing his rear bumper in his Chevrolet Chevelle. By the end of the race, Bobby was still up front as they crossed the finish line second and third, respectively. (GGAK.)

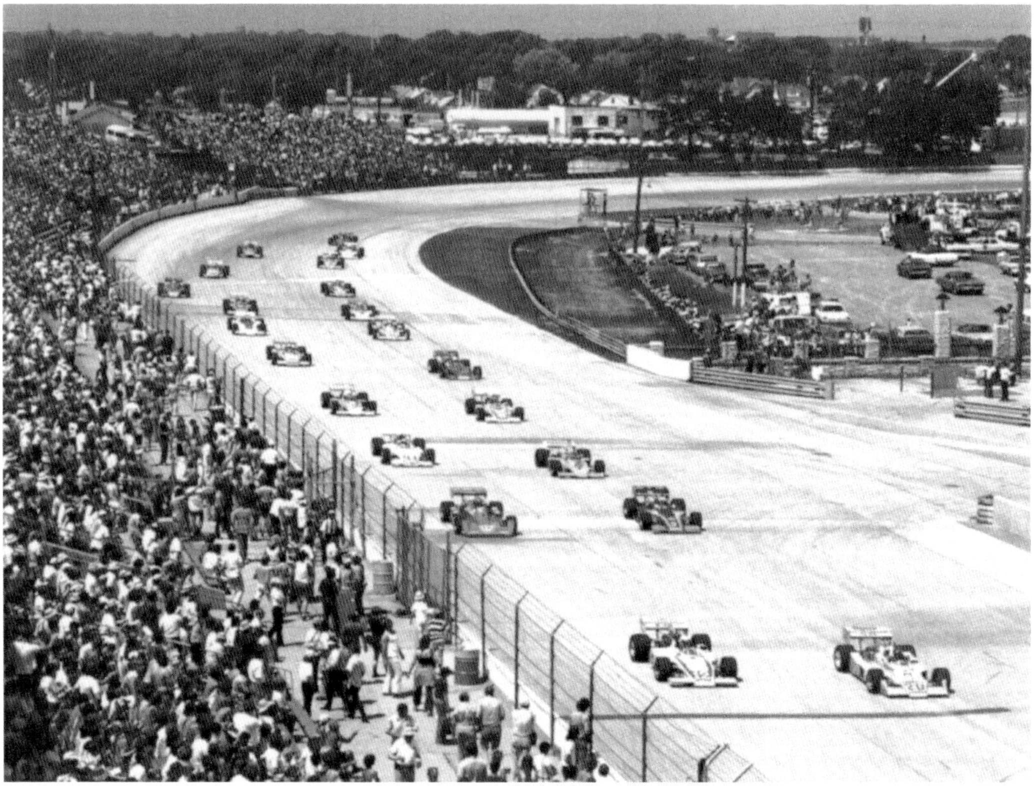

Gordon Johncock (No. 20) and Mike Mosley (No. 12) lead the field to the start of the Rex Mays 150 USAC Champ Car race in front of a full house on June 13, 1975. Although he started second, Mosley led the entire 150 laps, while Johncock finished second. They were the only two to finish on the lead lap. (RL/MC.)

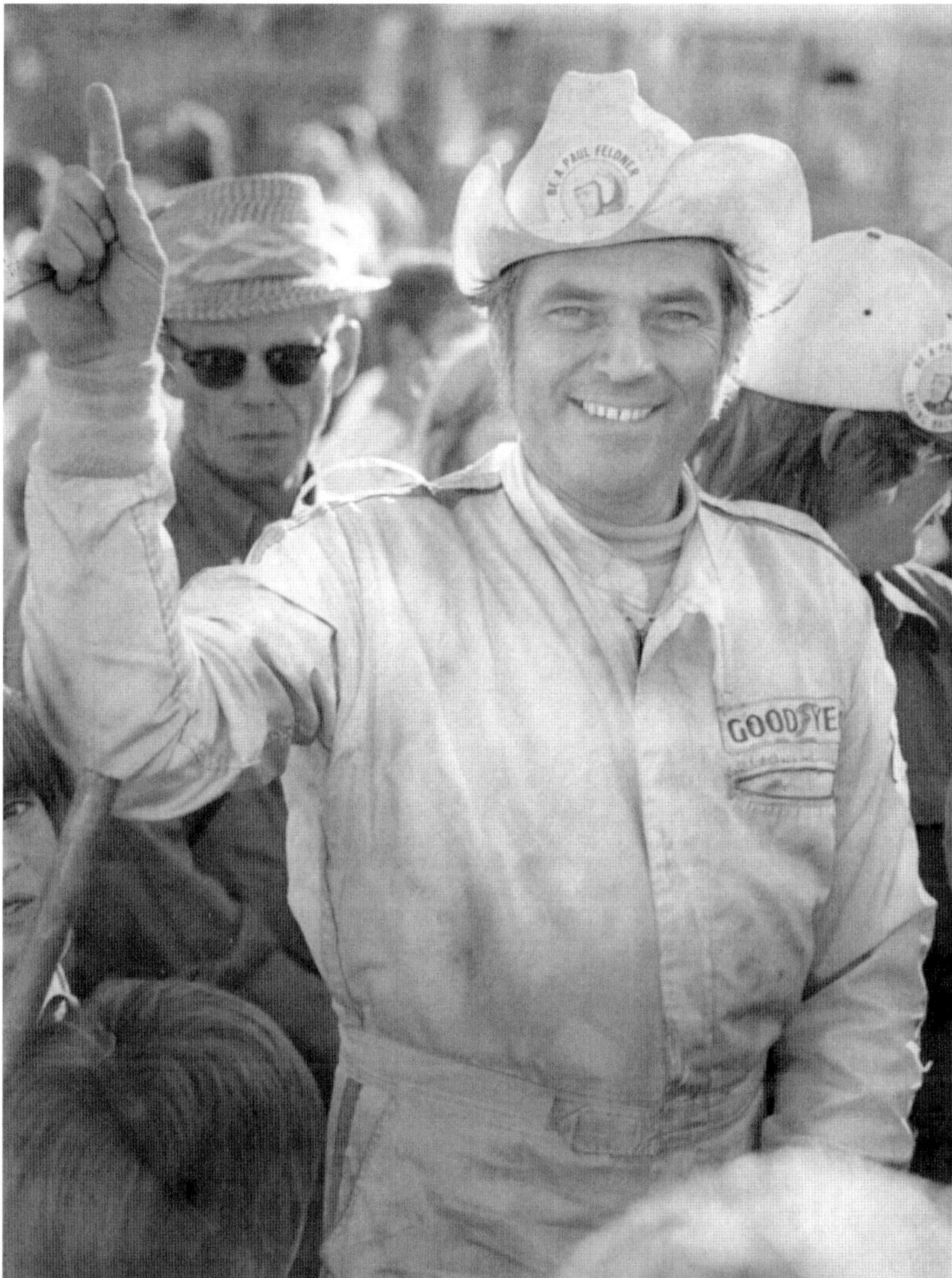

Drivers race for many reasons, but Paul Feldner raced for fun. Racing was a family affair: his wife, Joan, owned the cars, and Paul raced the circuit. From modifieds to stock cars, he was a consistent performer. From 1970 to 1975, Feldner finished in the top 10 spot, and in 1977 was the USAC stock car champ. He loved his fans and they loved him. (WAHS.)

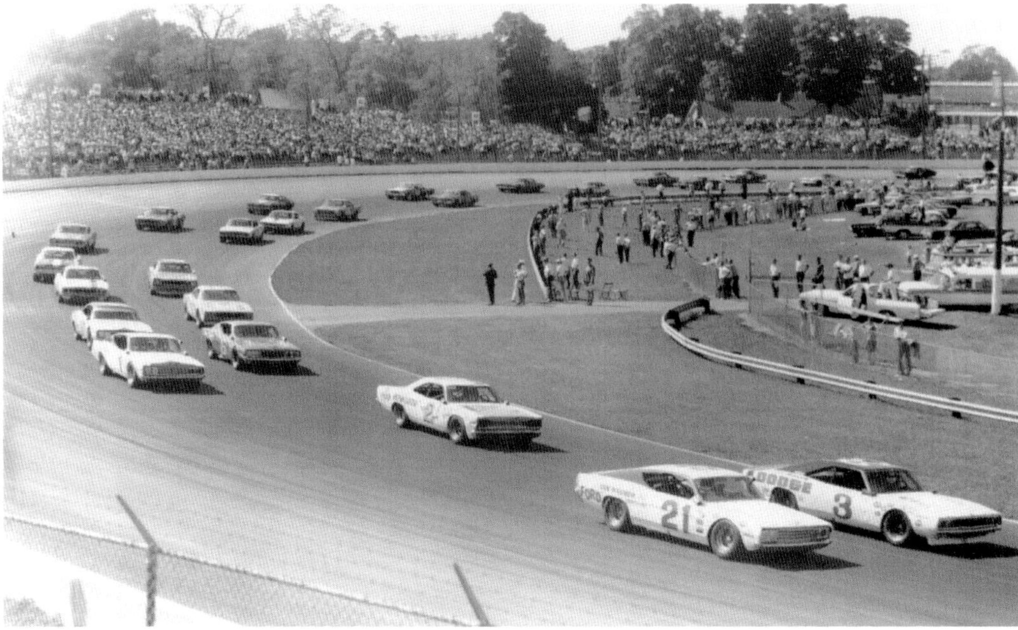

The year 1969 saw an even bigger rivalry between the top three muscle car manufacturers, but it was Dodge and Plymouth that occupied most of the field at the July 1969 Miller 200. Don White, No. 3, driving his 1969 Dodge Charger, inches out Jack Bowsher in his 1969 Ford Torino, while Dave Whitcomb, No. 2, chases both in his 1969 Plymouth Road Runner. (GGAK.)

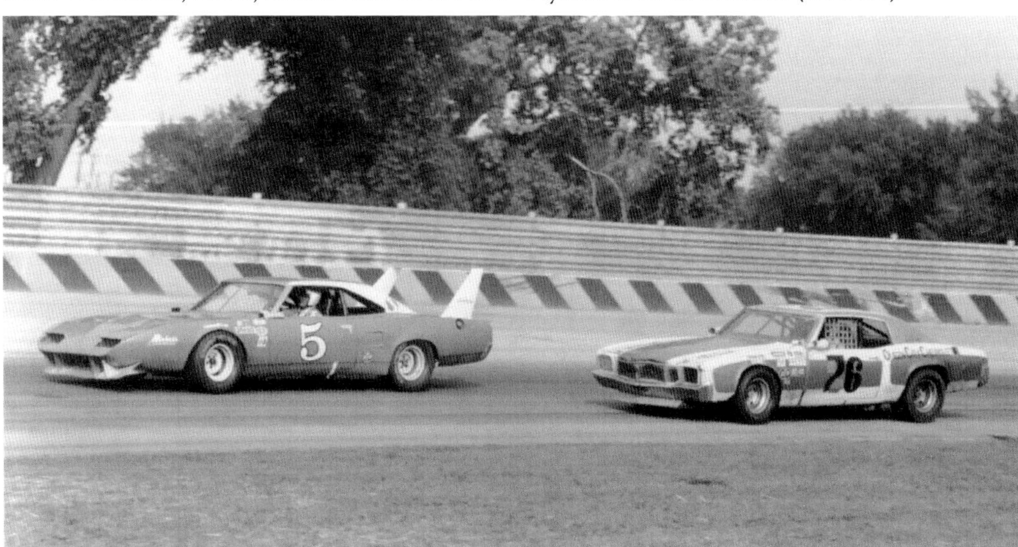

Bobby Unser, driving the new 1970 Plymouth Superbird (No. 5) in the 1972 USAC 150, flies by Ralph Latham in his 1971 Chevy Monte Carlo. The Superbird, the 1970 answer to the Dodge Daytona, was short-lived as well, in production for only one year (despite its cool appearance). Although Unser started out first, he finished second to Gordon Johncock's 1972 Chevrolet Chevelle. (GGAK.)

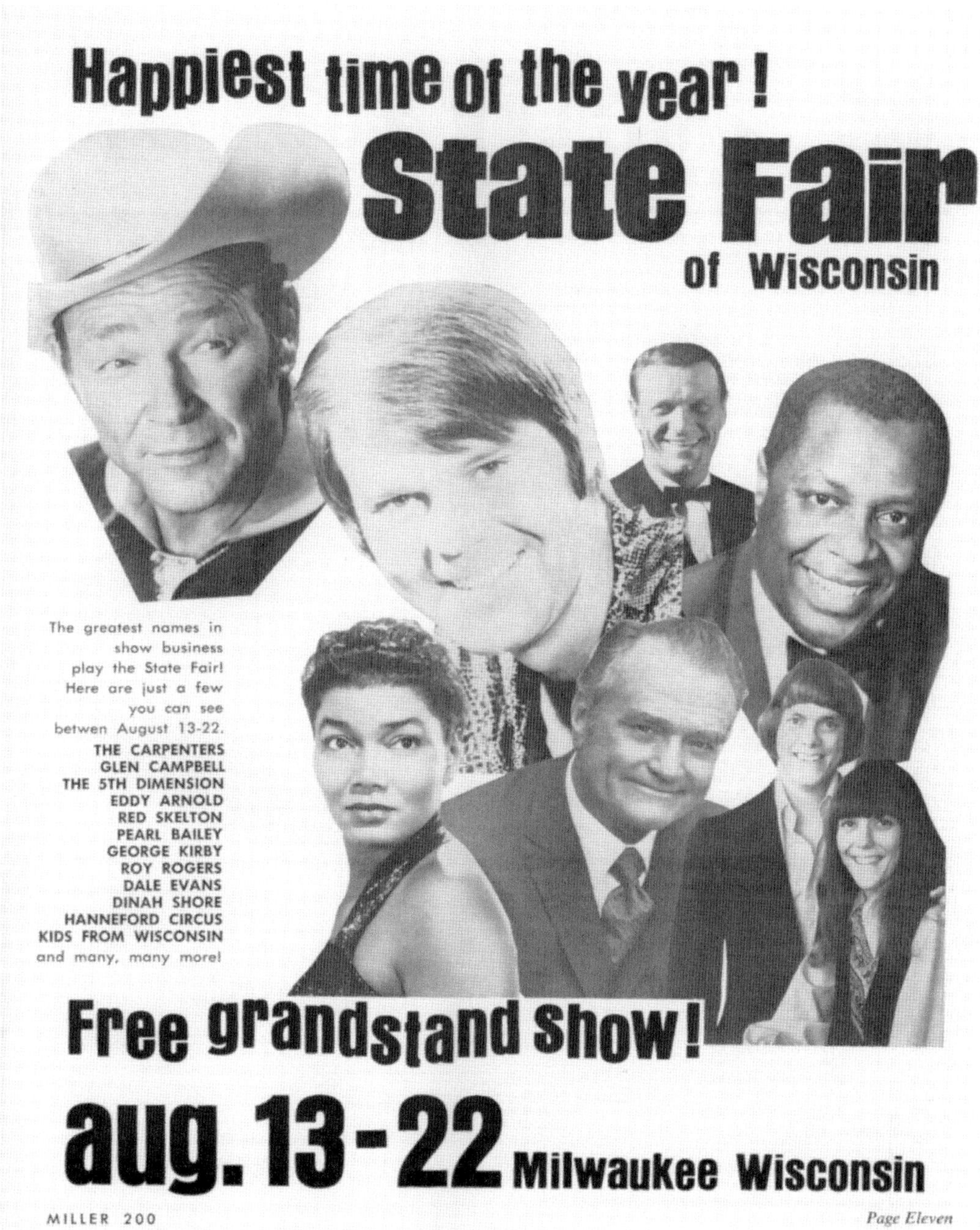

The state fair drew thousands of spectators who came for cream puffs, races, and a walk through the cow barn. There was definitely something for everyone. This grandstand billboard promotes the upcoming talent for the August 1971 shows. The featured entertainment crosses several generations of television, music, and comedy entertainment familiar to everyone. Acts ranging from the Carpenters to Pearl Bailey, Red Skelton, and every young boy's hero, Roy Rogers, entertained sold-out crowds for a week during the state fair. (JS.)

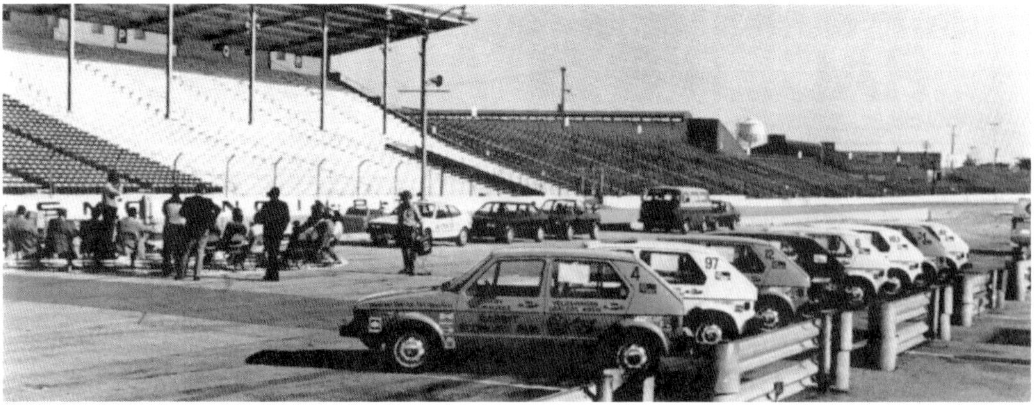

When Volkswagen introduced the Rabbit as a replacement for the Beetle, consumer acceptance was questionable. The Rabbit had to prove itself, and where better to experiment than at the State Fair Park speedway. The speedway was frequently used as a test track for everything from tires to fuel performance. In this late 1979 photograph, Milwaukee radio and television personalities were invited to race the Rabbits to showcase both performance and comfort. (JS.)

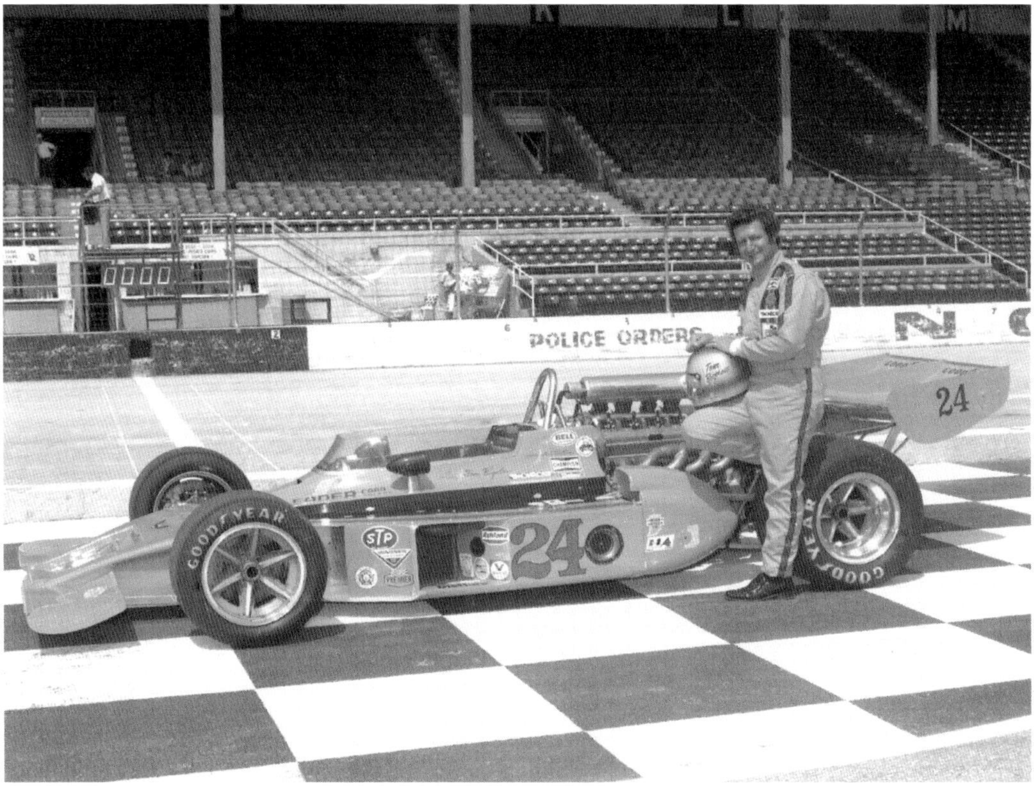

Tom Bigelow, originally from Whitewater, poses with the Indy car he drove for Milwaukee's Ralph Wilke prior to the Champ Car race on June 16, 1976. Bigelow competed in nine Indianapolis 500s and won the USAC sprint car championship in 1978 and the USAC midget championship in 1984. He is a member of both the National Sprint Car and National Midget Hall of Fame. (GGAK.)

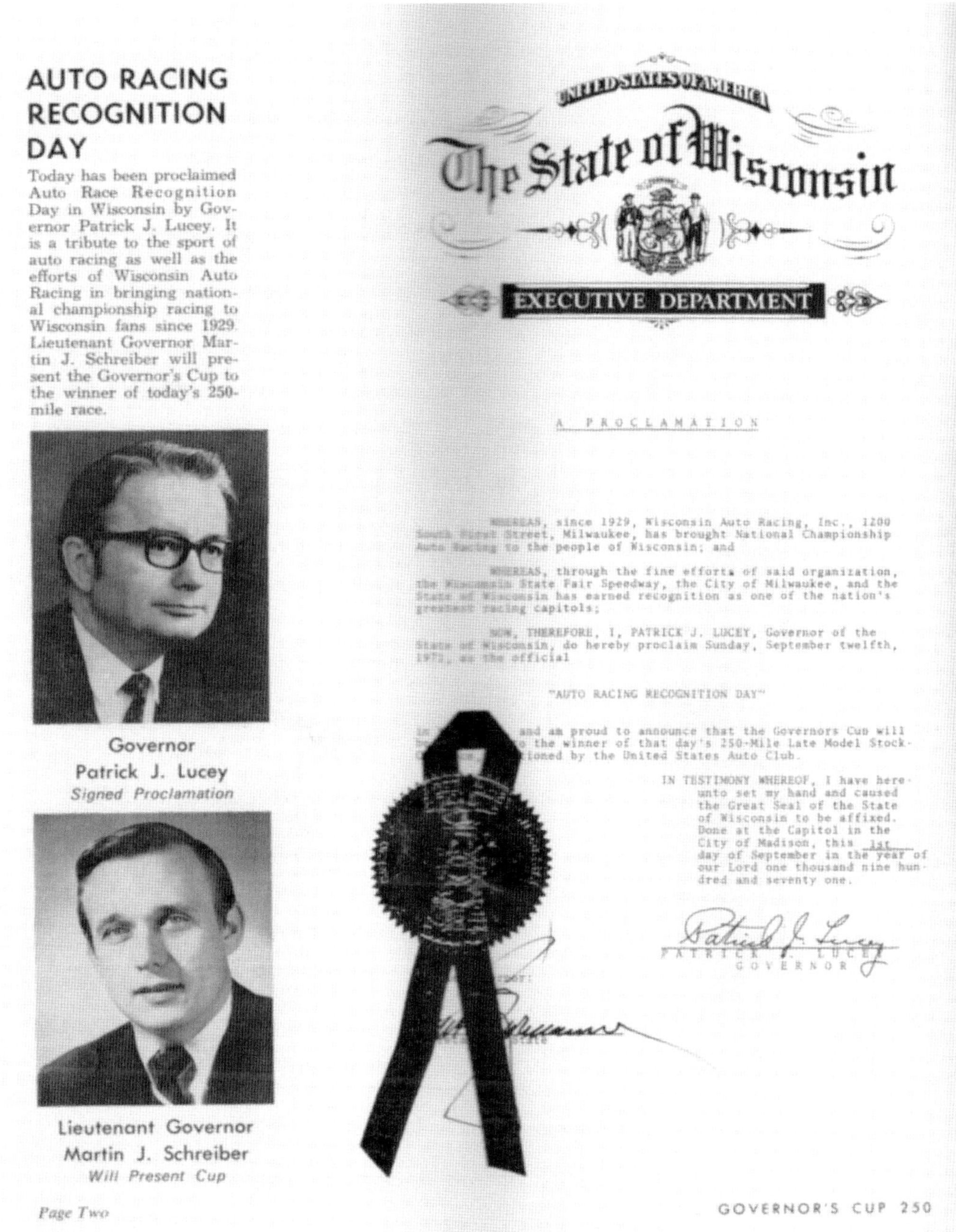

AUTO RACING RECOGNITION DAY

Today has been proclaimed Auto Race Recognition Day in Wisconsin by Governor Patrick J. Lucey. It is a tribute to the sport of auto racing as well as the efforts of Wisconsin Auto Racing in bringing national championship racing to Wisconsin fans since 1929. Lieutenant Governor Martin J. Schreiber will present the Governor's Cup to the winner of today's 250-mile race.

Governor
Patrick J. Lucey
Signed Proclamation

Lieutenant Governor
Martin J. Schreiber
Will Present Cup

UNITED STATES OF AMERICA

The State of Wisconsin

EXECUTIVE DEPARTMENT

A PROCLAMATION

WHEREAS, since 1929, Wisconsin Auto Racing, Inc., 1200 South First Street, Milwaukee, has brought National Championship Auto Racing to the people of Wisconsin; and

WHEREAS, through the fine efforts of said organization, the Wisconsin State Fair Speedway, the City of Milwaukee, and the State of Wisconsin has earned recognition as one of the nation's greatest racing capitols;

NOW, THEREFORE, I, PATRICK J. LUCEY, Governor of the State of Wisconsin, do hereby proclaim Sunday, September twelfth, 1971, as the official

"AUTO RACING RECOGNITION DAY"

in [illegible] and am proud to announce that the Governors Cup will b[illegible] to the winner of that day's 250-Mile Late Model Stock-C[illegible]ioned by the United States Auto Club.

IN TESTIMONY WHEREOF, I have hereunto set my hand and caused the Great Seal of the State of Wisconsin to be affixed. Done at the Capitol in the City of Madison, this 1st day of September in the year of our Lord one thousand nine hundred and seventy one.

PATRICK J. LUCEY
GOVERNOR

Page Two

GOVERNOR'S CUP 250

Taken from the September 12, 1971, Governor's Cup 250 program, this proclamation reinforces the importance of auto racing to Wisconsin. Gov. Patrick Lucey recognized the efforts of Wisconsin Auto Racing to bring national championship racing to Milwaukee for (at the time) 42 years. That day, Al Unser, driving his 1971 Ford Torino, earned the Governor's Cup, winning the USAC stock-car race. (GGAK.)

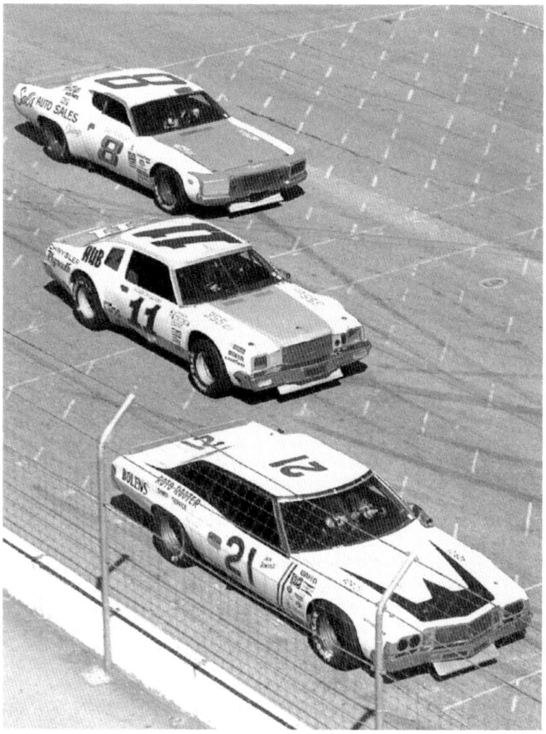

Jack Bowsher (No. 21) leads Roger McCluskey (No. 11) and Sal Tovella (No. 8) as the field completes the opening lap of the September 12, 1976 Governor's Cup 250 USAC stock-car race. McCluskey, driving a 1976 Volare, went on to win the event, while Tovella finished fifth. Bowsher blew the engine in his car and was credited with an 18th-place finish. (RL/MC.)

In this 1977 image, Carl Marchese sits in a car he drove in 1920s big car competitions. Standing at right is Carl's brother Tom Marchese, promoter of the races at the State Fair Park speedway from 1929 through 1967 (when he went into partnership with John Kaishian). Next to Tom is Dave Uihlein, who started the Harry Miller Meet, a vintage racing event held each July at the track. (RL/MC.)

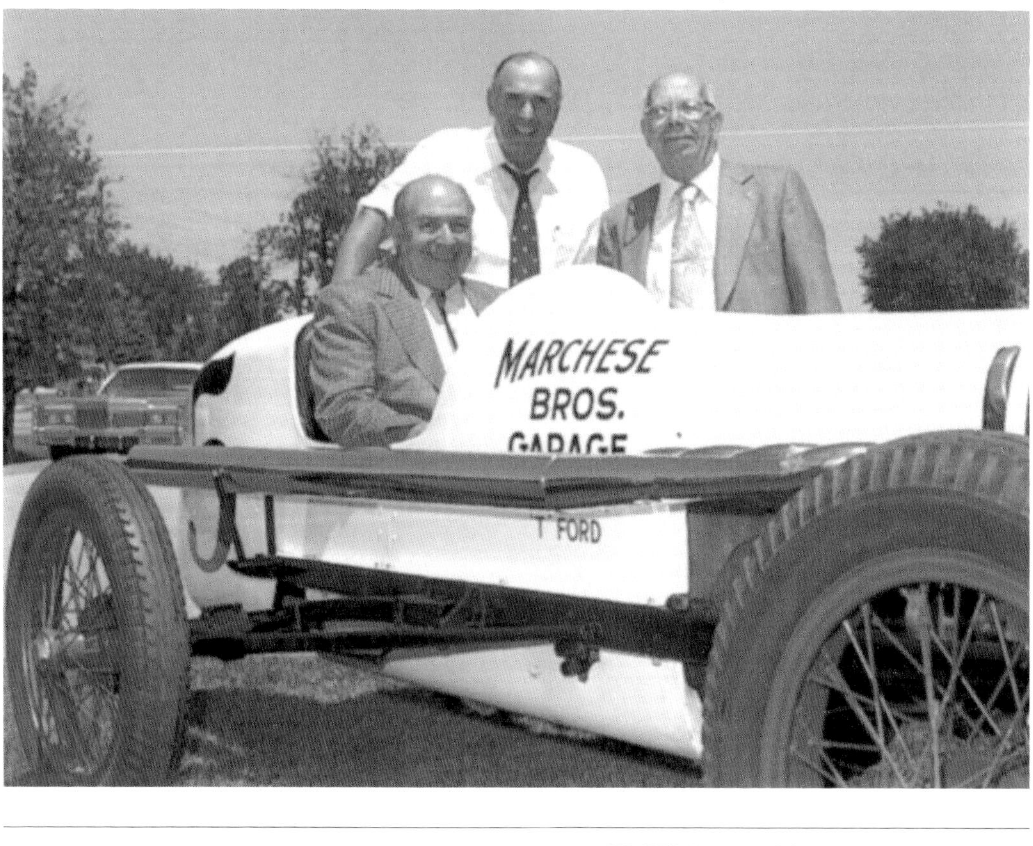

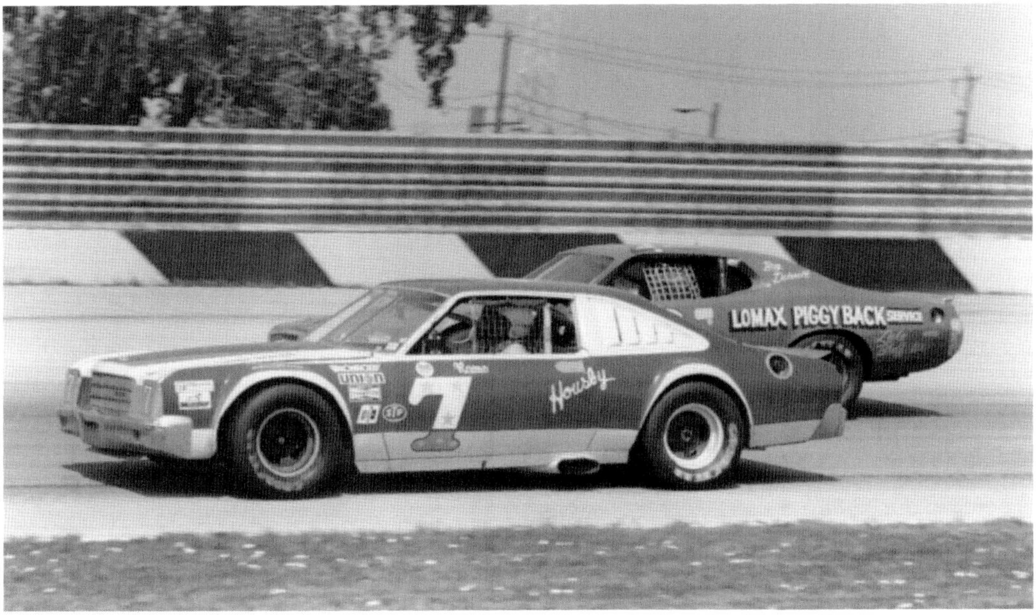

Pulling out of turn four is No. 7 Ramo Stott driving his 1977 Plymouth Volare. He is passing No. 12 Bay Darnell in his 1974 Dodge Charger during the July 1977 Miller 200. Both popular State Fair Park drivers gained champion status driving in ARCA, USAC, and NASCAR. Darnell has found success in USAC, NASCAR, and Indy Car races. Both drivers have children and grandchildren currently racing to carry on the family tradition. (GGAK.)

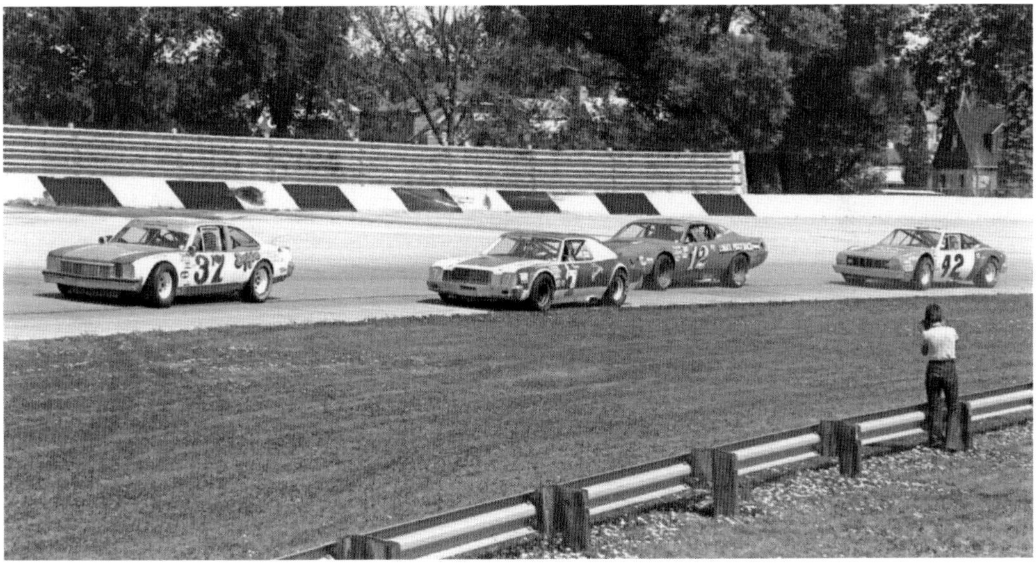

Eventual winner of the USAC Miller 200 stock-car race on July 10, 1977, Dave Watson (No. 37) leads several of the front-runners through turn three. Behind Watson are Ramo Stott (No. 7), Bay Darnell (No. 12), and Bobby Allison (No. 42). Allison, who was making his first appearance at the track, finished second, while Darnell finished fourth. Stott encountered mechanical problems and finished 11th, nine laps down. (RL/MC.)

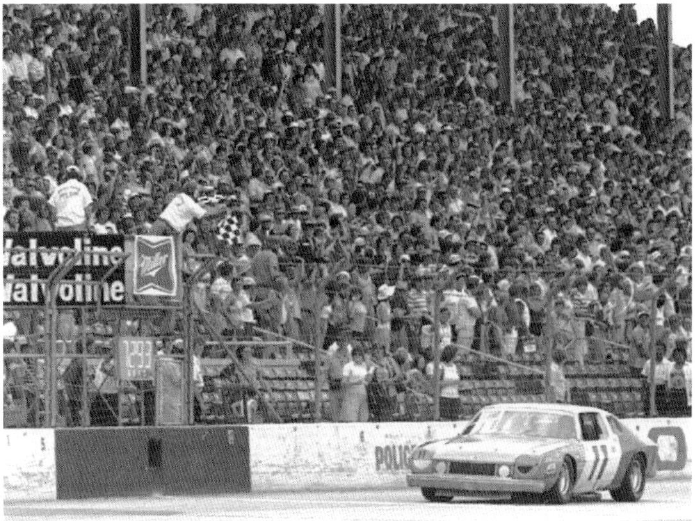

NASCAR star and Hall of Fame member Bobby Allison made a trip to the State Fair Park speedway on July 9, 1978, and won the USAC Miller 200 stock-car race. Allison drove a 1977 AMC Matador to victory in front of a packed grandstand. It was the first win for an AMC car at the track since Marshall Teague won a 200-mile stock-car race on September 12, 1954. (RL/MC.)

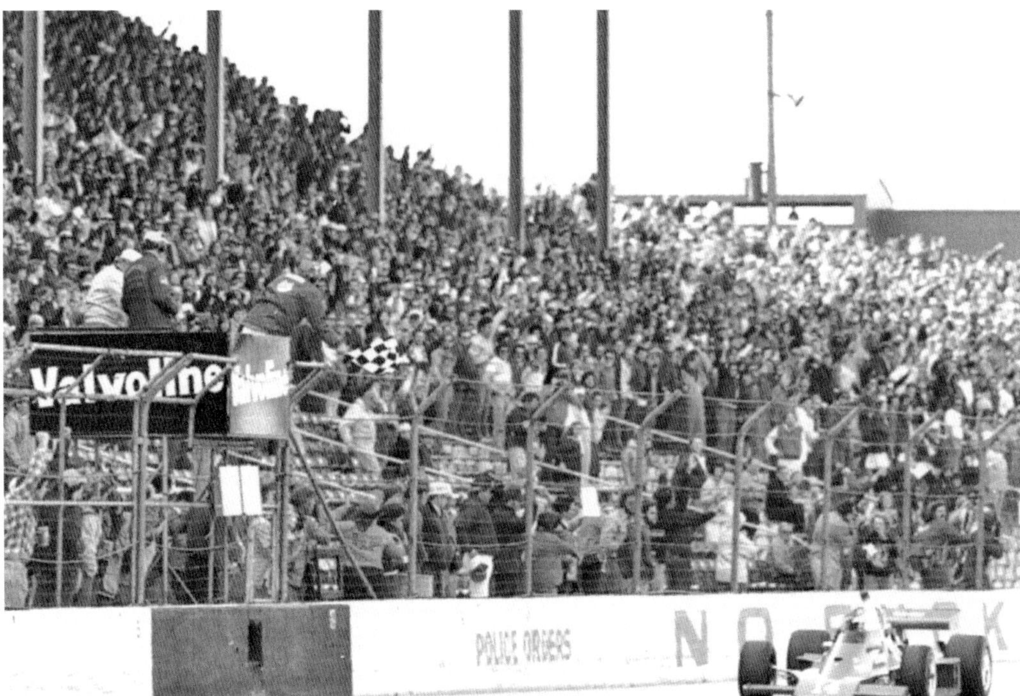

The crowd is on their feet as A.J. Foyt drives under the checkered flag to win the June 10, 1979, Rex Mays 150 Champ Car race. Foyt finished a half lap ahead of second place, Bill Vukovich, on a cold, windy day with the race start delayed 30 minutes by rain. It was Foyt's fourth career win in the Rex May Classic. (RL/MC.)

On May 4, 1980, Mark Martin took the checkered flag, winning the ASA Superamerica 150. At this point in his career, Martin was the defending two-time ASA champion. He went on to become one of NASCAR's top drivers for over three decades. Other well-known drivers in the race were Butch Miller, Ted Musgrave, Dick Trickle, and 1992 NASCAR Winston Cup champion Alan Kulwicki (No. 32). (RL/MC.)

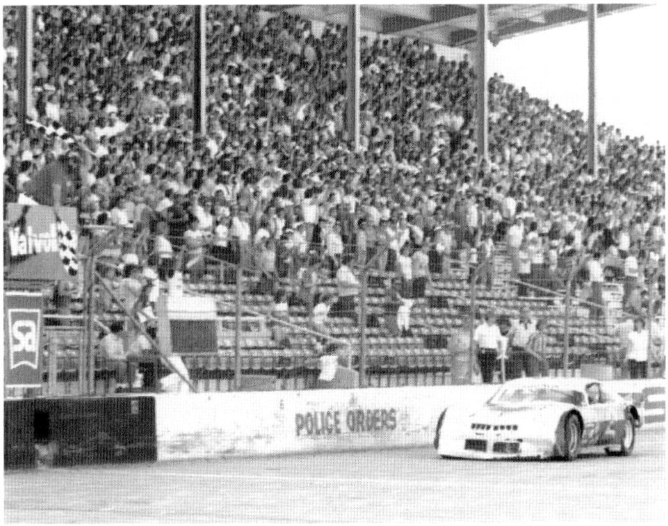

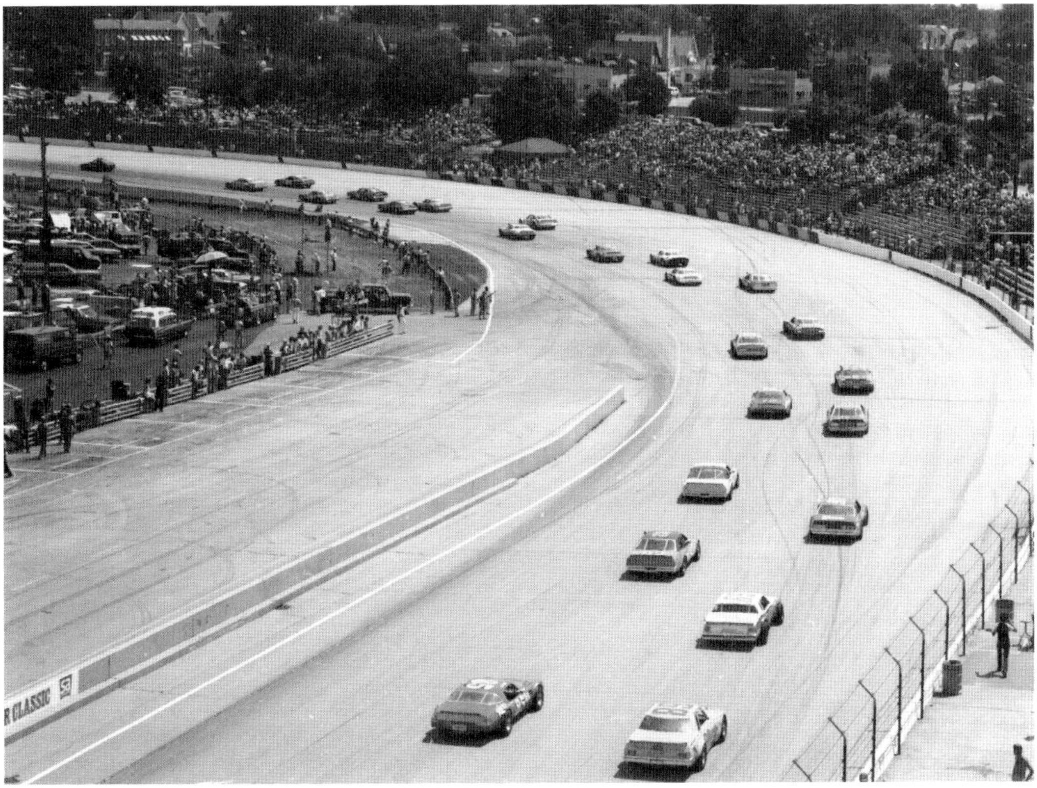

As seen from the grandstand roof, the 32-car field for the July 13, 1980, USAC stock car Miller 200 makes its way through the first turn on the pace lap. The field is well aligned, with Joe Ruttman and Rusty Wallace making up the front row. Wallace won the race, his second victory at the track, while Ruttman finished third. (RL/MC.)

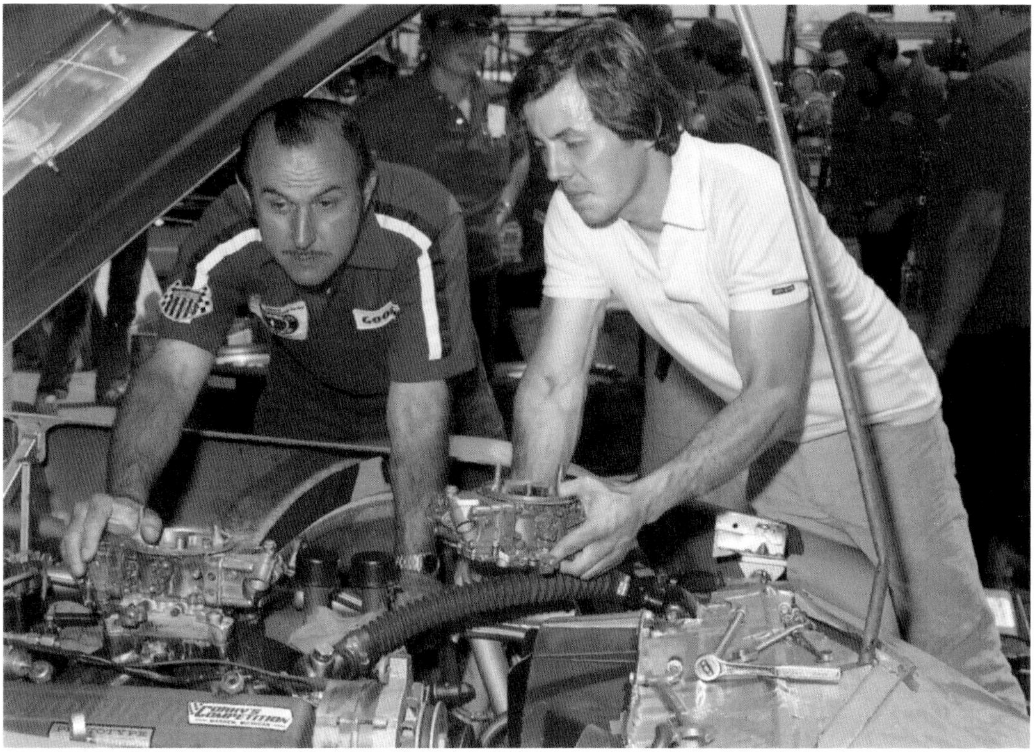

Greendale's Alan Kulwicki (right) and his father, Gerry, work on their car together on August 3, 1980. Gerry, a well-known builder of stock-car engines, worked with championship driver Norm Nelson. Alan won a number of short-track races in the area and an ASA race at the Mile on July 10, 1983, before moving south and achieving the ultimate in stock-car racing success: winning the 1992 NASCAR Winston Cup championship. (RL/MC.)

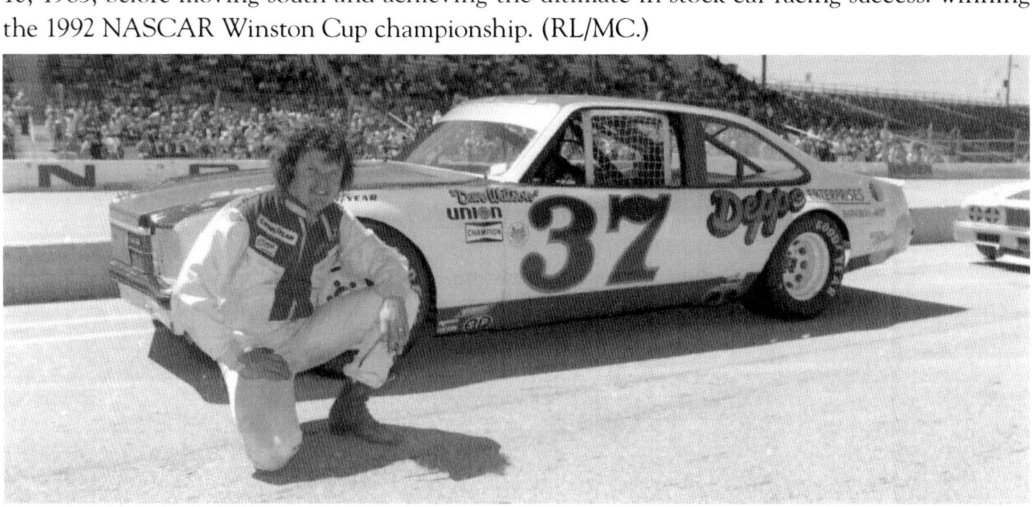

Dave Watson, from Milton, Wisconsin, is all smiles as he poses before the Miller High Life 200 with his 1977 Buick Skylark. He must have had a premonition, because he won that race. Driving for car owner Dave Deppe, Watson finished the race in 2 hours and 17 minutes. The year 1977 proved to be good for Watson, who ended the year as the USAC Rookie of the Year. (JS.)

6

Decade of Firsts

1981–1990

The State Fair Park track was an essential part of the fairgrounds; in fact, it would be true to say that the fair was built around the track. Every summer, fans could count on auto racing during fair time—until 1981 that is, when the practice was discontinued (although races were held at other times during the season). CART continued to expand Indy car racing across the country, eliminating the Bettenhause 200 but retaining the Rex Mays Classic in June for the 1983 season.

The State Fair Park drew hundreds of national drivers, but it was the Wisconsin drivers who made their fans proud. Norm Nelson, Dick Trickle, Jim Sauter, Alan Kulwicki, and Dave Watson, just to name a few, could bring the crowds to their feet. The ASA circuit continued to grow, and Milwaukee fans witnessed victories by future NASCAR greats Rusty Wallace and Mark Martin. USAC's once popular stock-car series began to decline, and by 1981 was running only two events. It sanctioned its final Milwaukee event in 1983, terminating the division in 1984.

At the conclusion of the 1983 season, the track's promotional contract was up for bid. The park's board awarded the rights to Frank & Dominic Guiffre of GO Racing. The brothers, local businessmen as well as previous Indy car owners, promised to "bring fun back to the track." To accomplish that, they brought in Tom Sneva to support promotional events. Their first season as promoters featured the first ever appearance for the NASCAR Busch Late Model Sportsmen Series, as well as CART and ASA races.

Wins at the State Fair Park continued to help propel family racing dynasties for both the Andrettis and Unsers. Fan favorites Mario and Michael Andretti saw back-to-back victories, with Mario winning the Miller 200 in 1985, and Michael winning the same race in 1986. Al Unser Jr. added a win to his family's total (nine) by winning the Miller Genuine Draft 200 in 1987, as well as the 1990 CART race after Michael Andretti ran out of fuel.

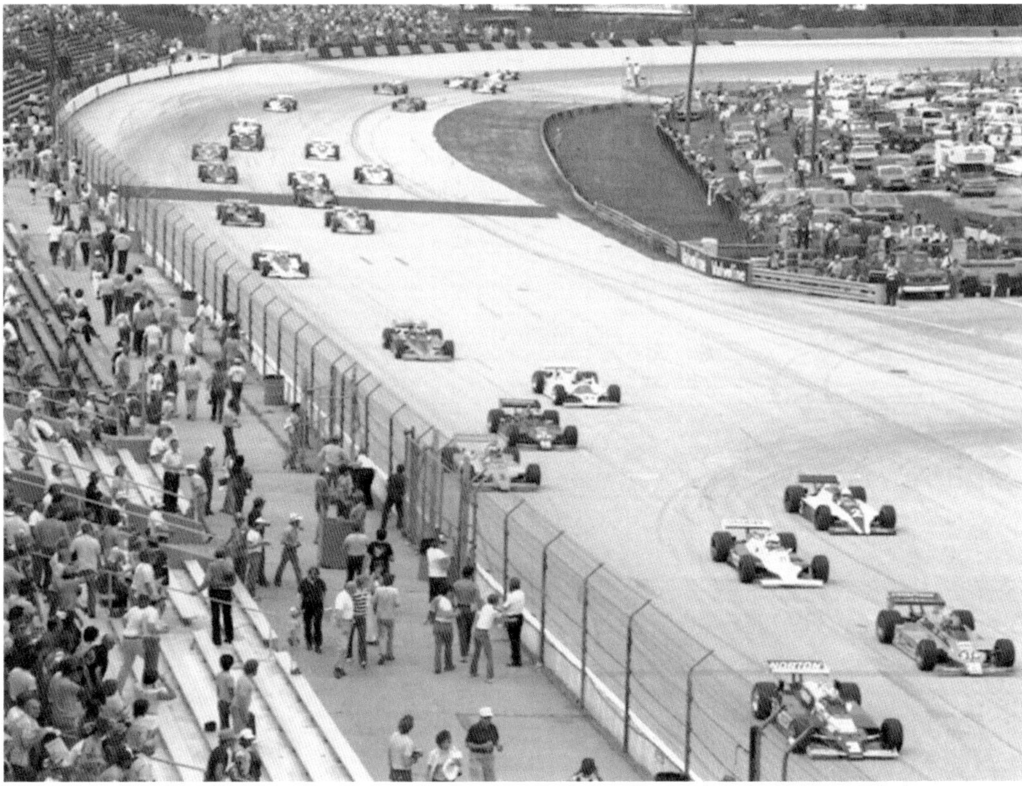

Pole-sitter Gordon Johncock (No. 20) and Bobby Unser (No. 3) comprise the front row as the field comes to the green flag for the start of the June 6, 1981, CART Indy Car World Series event. Mike Mosely, who started at the rear of the field because of engine problems in qualifying, went to the front and lapped the entire field en route to winning the event. Neither Johncock nor Unser finished the race. (RL/MC.)

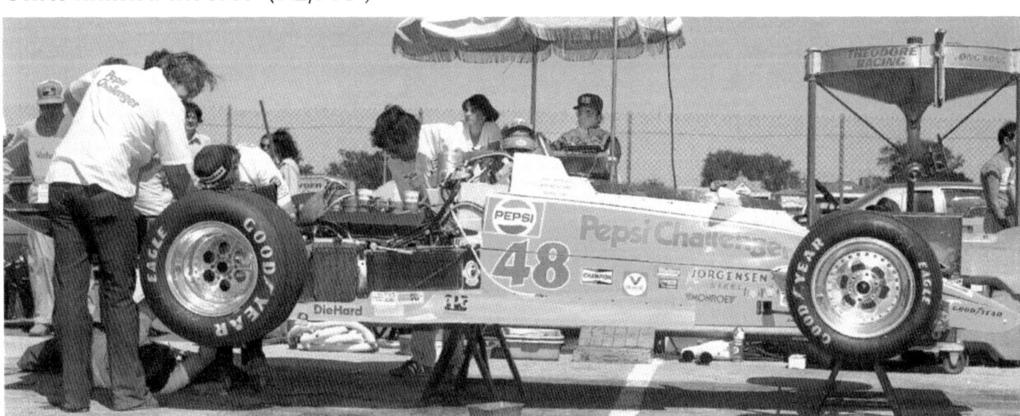

From the looks of it, Mike Mosely has it (almost) made in the shade. Taking it easy while his crew makes an engine exchange, Mosely takes advantage of some downtime. The pit crew does a fantastic job of mechanical repairs within minutes; their efficiency is necessary to get the driver back on the track. (RL/MC.)

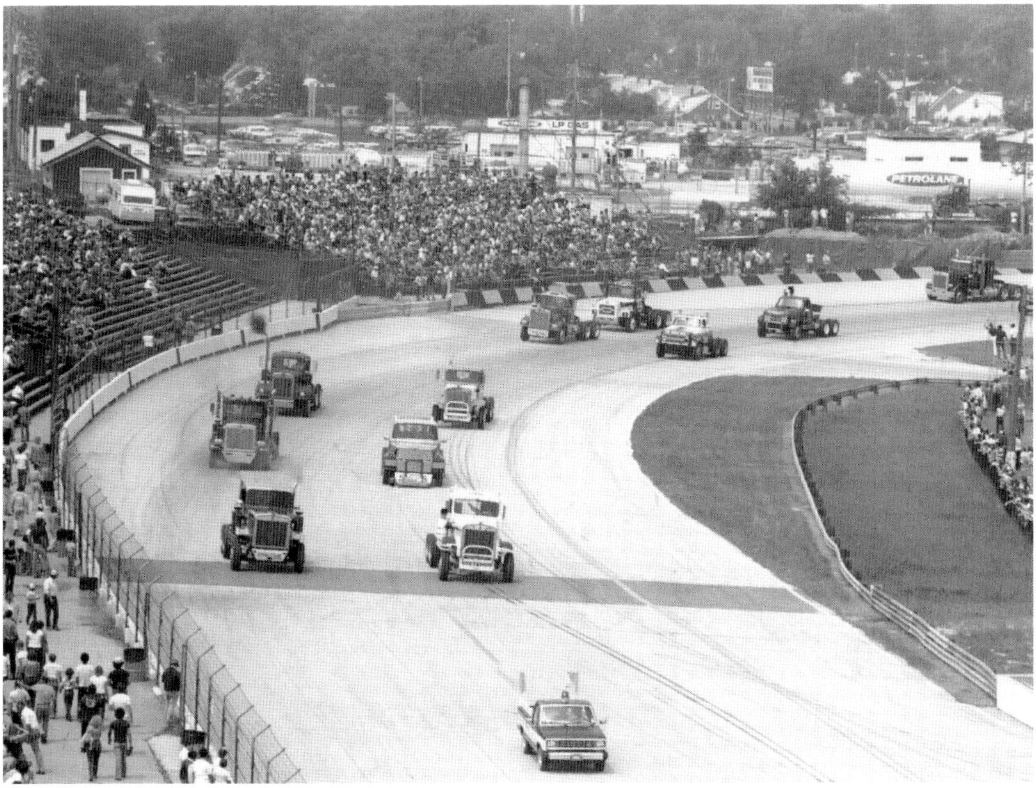

Luther Burton leads the field of the Great America Truck (GATR) Bobtail trucks on the pace lap before the start of a 100-lap event on June 27, 1982. Burton also won the event. The series also ran at the track in 1984 but was dissolved shortly thereafter as the trucks were found to be too heavy for track surfaces, causing tracks to break up. (RL/MC.)

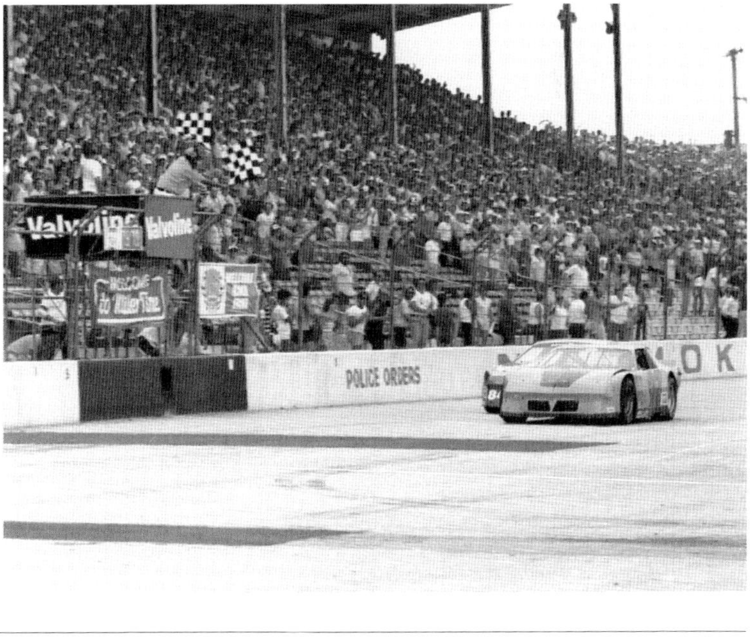

Alan Kulwicki (No. 97) just edges Bob Senneker (No. 84) in front of a full grandstand to win the ASA Miller High Life 200 on July 10, 1883. The win was lucky No. 13, as it was Kulwicki's first victory in 13 starts at the track. It turned out to be Kulwicki's only victory at his hometown track. (RL/MC.)

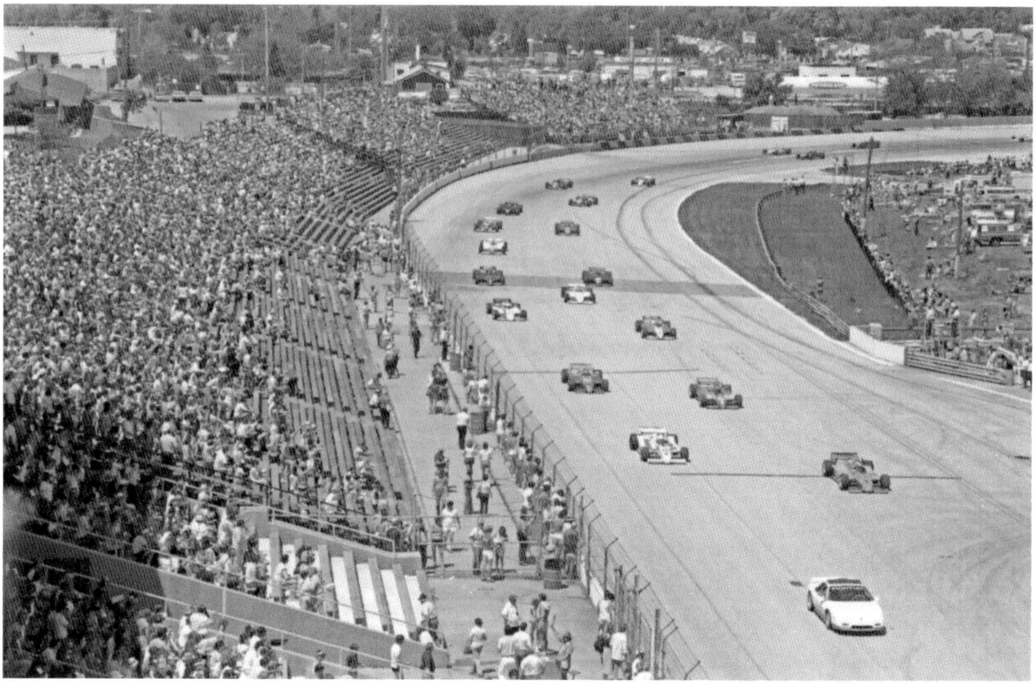

The grandstand roof was a great vantage point to see the pace lap of the June 3, 1984, Rex Mays CART Indy Car World Series event. The winner of the previous week's Indianapolis 500, Rick Mears, started on the pole, while Tom Sneva was on the outside of the front row. The pair reversed positions at the checkered flag, with Sneva just edging Mears for the win. (RL/MC.)

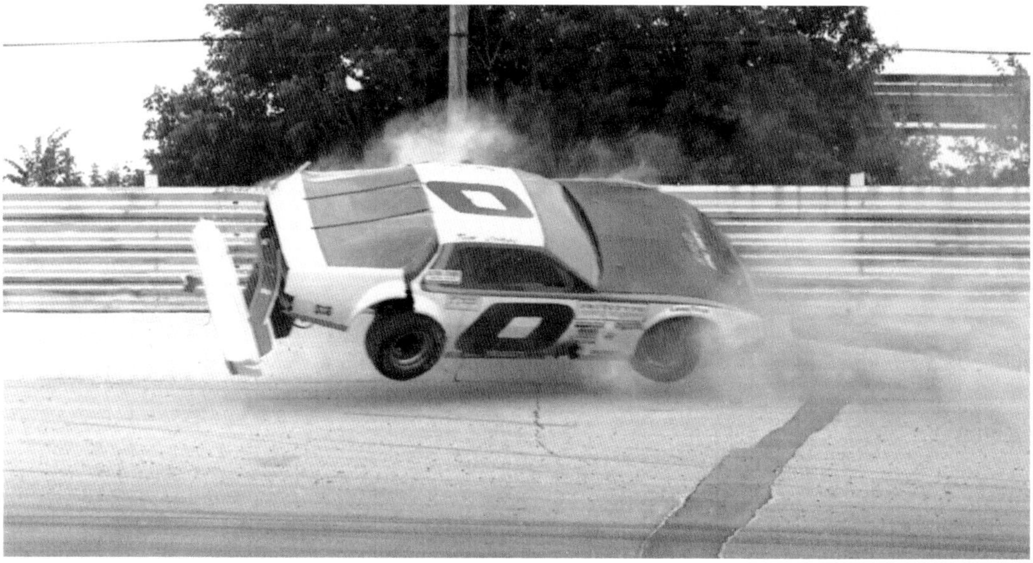

On July 8, 1984, Tom Jones crashes on the 173rd lap of the 200-lap ASA event. He spun backward after hitting the wall and got all four wheels off the track, scattering parts of his car on the third turn. He was credited with a 39th-place finish after starting in the same position in the 44-car field. (RL/MC.)

Rusty Wallace, who was the 1983 ASA champion and, by 1985, a regular on the NASCAR Winston Cup circuit, took a break from his NASCAR schedule to return to ASA and won the July 7, 1985, ASA Miller 200 stock-car race. Wallace, who started second, beat fast qualifier Dick Trickle to take the win. (RL/MC.)

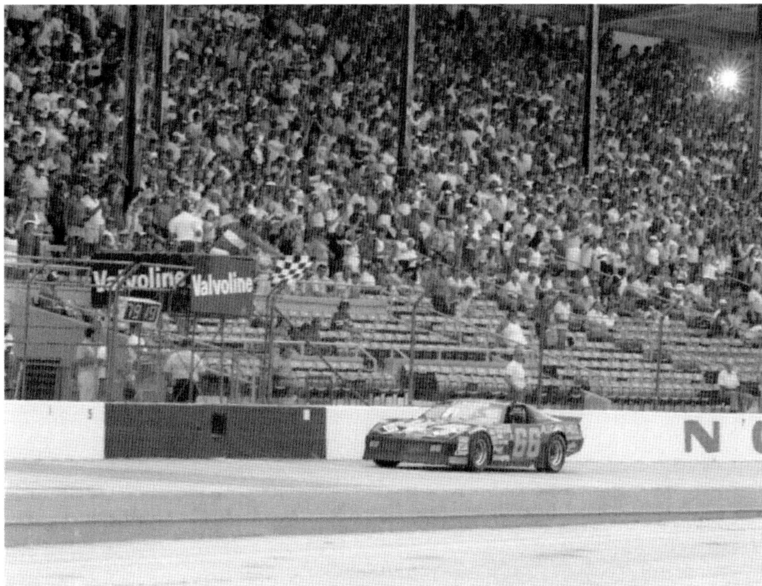

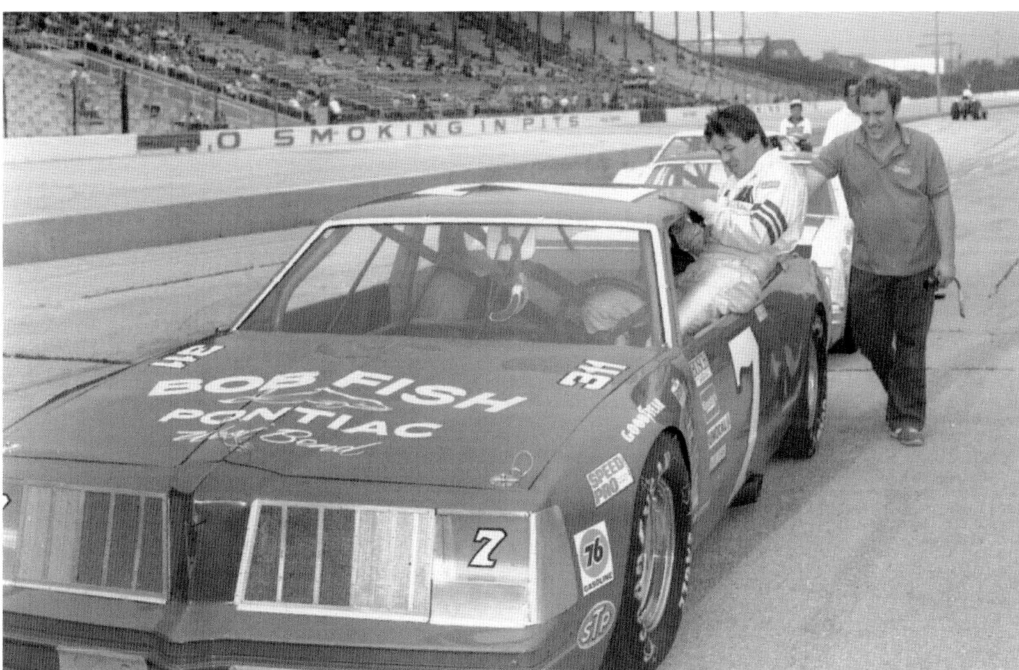

Alan Kulwicki climbed into his Bob Fish Pontiac-sponsored car before practice for the August 18, 1985, NASCAR Busch Late Model Sportsman (now Xfinity) Series 200-mile race. Kulwicki, the fastest qualifier, led the first 28 laps but finished 14th after his car suffered a blown engine. (RL/MC.)

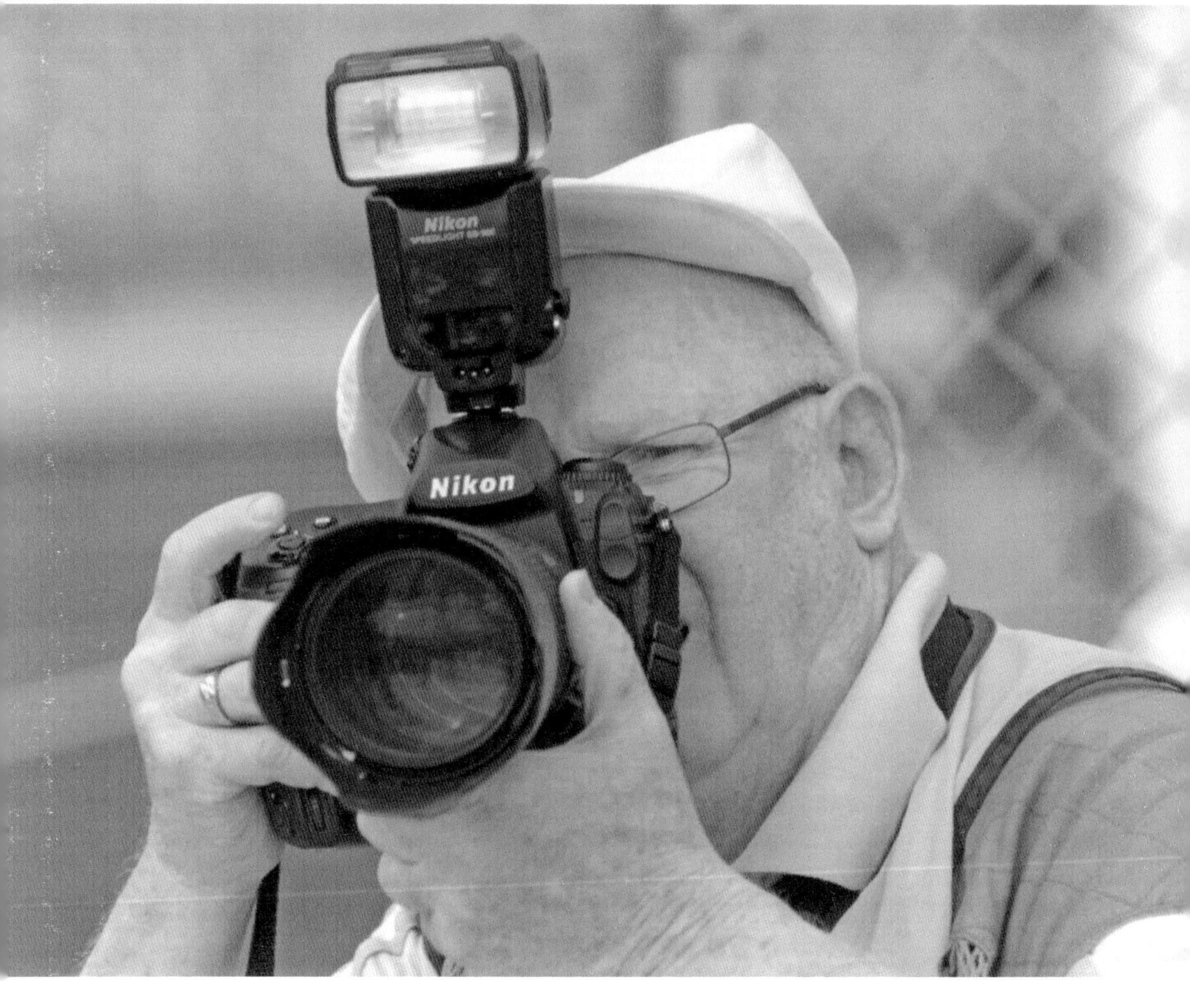

Many of the photographs in this book were taken by Russ Lake. Lake, pictured here at work, has been taking racing photographs since age 14, and 2015 marks his 65th year of photography. Through the years, his work has been featured in many racing books, magazines, and newspapers. He has become an institution at the Milwaukee Mile and has served as track photographer on a number of different occasions. (RL/MC.)

7

NASCAR and Indy Cars at the Mile

1991–2010

In 1991, the Andretti family dominated the CART event at the Mile when Mario, Michael, and cousin John made it a triple-podium day. The threat of losing the 1992 CART race influenced the State Fair Park board's decision to seek a new promoter. Tapped for the position was Carl Haas. Haas, as driver and co-owner of the Newman/Haas Racing team, knew racing personally and possessed the business sense to succeed. He immediately renamed and promoted the track as "the Milwaukee Mile."

New renovations, improved promoting, and resurfacing of the track seemed to be enough to draw NASCAR back to Milwaukee. The NASCAR Busch Grand National Series returned in 1993, and fans could not have been happier. Two years later, the NASCAR Craftsman Truck series made a stop at the Mile. Both the Busch National and the Craftsman Truck series appeared annually until 2009.

The new century brought upgrades and improvements in time to celebrate the Mile's 100th anniversary in 2003. These included a center grandstand addition, repaving and widening of the infield road course, and improved sightlines. 2003 featured the first ever Champ Car World Series night race, and NASCAR's first nighttime doubleheader. The Mile has made and witnessed many legends in its time, none more revered than A.J. Foyt. To celebrate Foyt's 50 years of Indy racing, the Mile's victory lane was forever declared "A.J. Foyt Victory Lane" in 2006.

Racing fans filled the stadium to see IndyCar and NASCAR races in 2007 and 2008, but sadly, it was not enough, and again the Mile experienced multiple challenges, giving Wisconsin's Joint Legislative Audit Committee reason to suggest sale of the property for redevelopment. This additional threat, and the loss of another promoter, left the State Fair Park board with unwanted track responsibilities. Honoring 2009 obligations, NASCAR completed the season's commitments. Saddled with the burden of the track and unable to commit to future NASCAR or IndyCar race dates, the board stood by as it lost major races to competitive tracks.

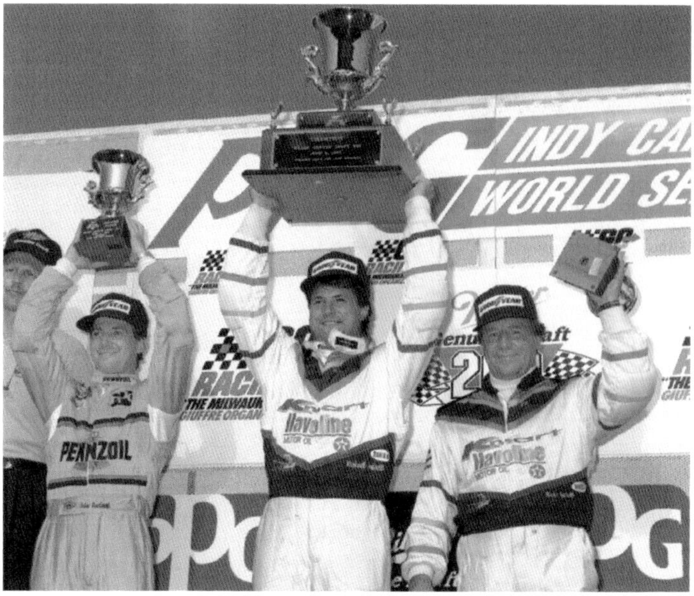

It was an Andretti family affair on the podium at the Milwaukee Mile on June 2, 1991, following the PPG Indy Car World Series race. Michael Andretti (center) won the event, while his cousin John (left) was second, and his father, Mario, rounded out the top three. Michael is now a successful car owner in the IndyCar series and the promoter of the IndyFest race weekend at the track. (RL/MC.)

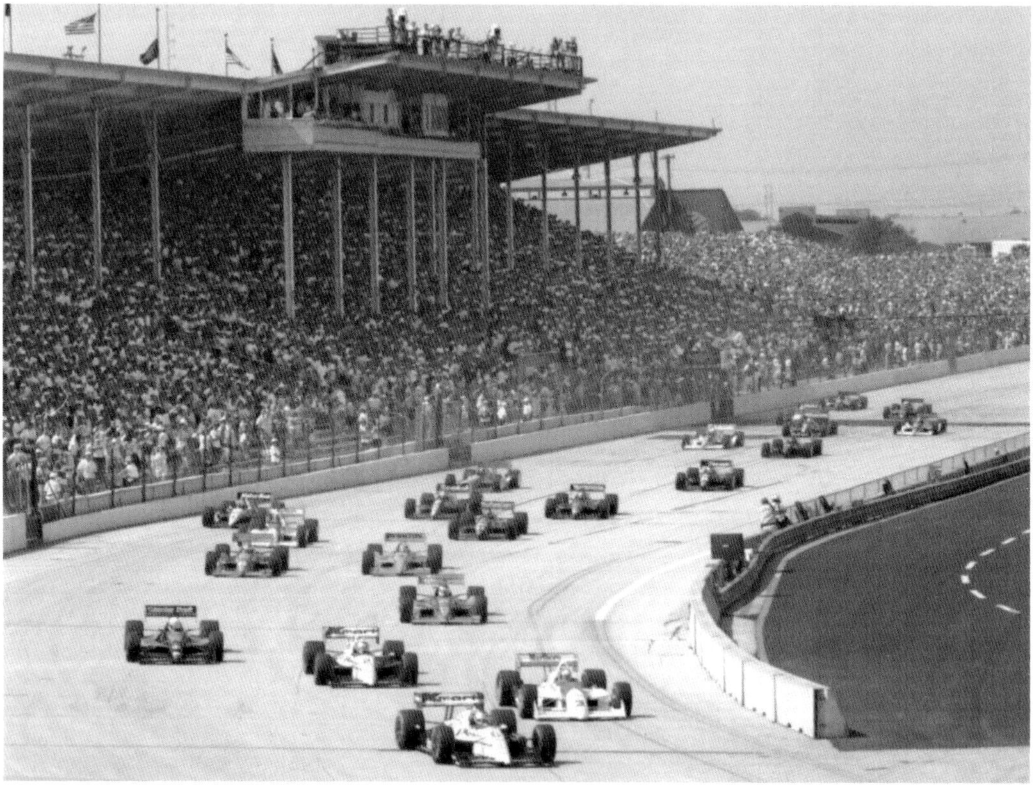

Mario Andretti (No. 6) jumps past pole-sitter Rick Mears (No. 3) to take the lead going into turn one at the start of the PPG Indy Car World Series Miller Genuine Draft 200 on June 2, 1991. The pair were trailed by Michael Andretti, Danny Sullivan (No. 20), and the rest of the Indy car field in front of a packed grandstand. (RL/MC.)

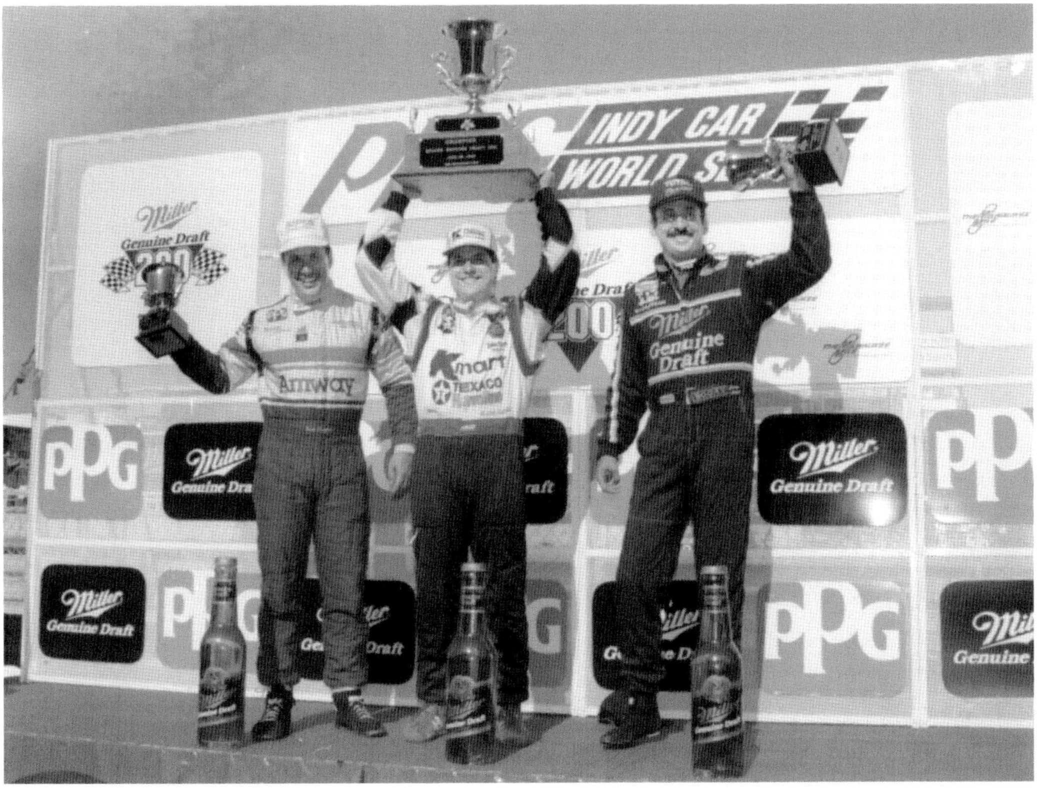

Holding the winner's trophy high overhead, Michael Andretti occupies the center of the victory podium after winning the PPG Indy Car World Series Miller Genuine Draft 200 on June 28, 1992. On the right is Bobby Rahal, who finished second, while third-place finisher Scott Brayton is on the left. (RL/MC.)

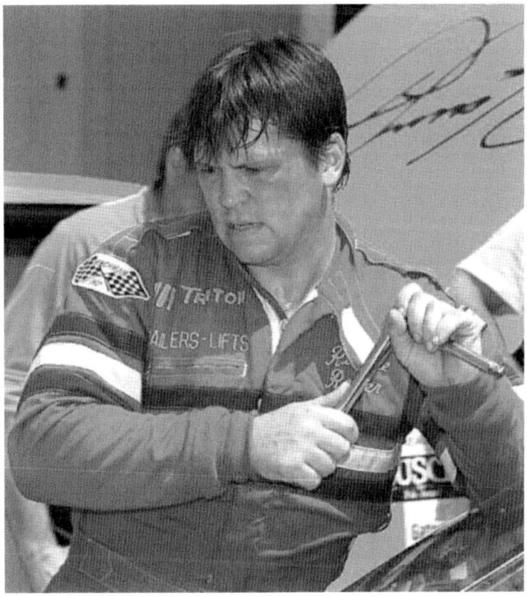

Robbie Reiser, originally from Allenton, Wisconsin, was working furiously on his NASCAR Busch (now Xfinity) Series car before the Havoline 250 on July 4, 1993. He qualified 17th and finished 21st in a true local effort, as Fish Pontiac-GMC of West Bend sponsored his car. Reiser came up through the NASCAR ranks and is now vice president of competition for Roush-Fenway Racing. (RL/MC.)

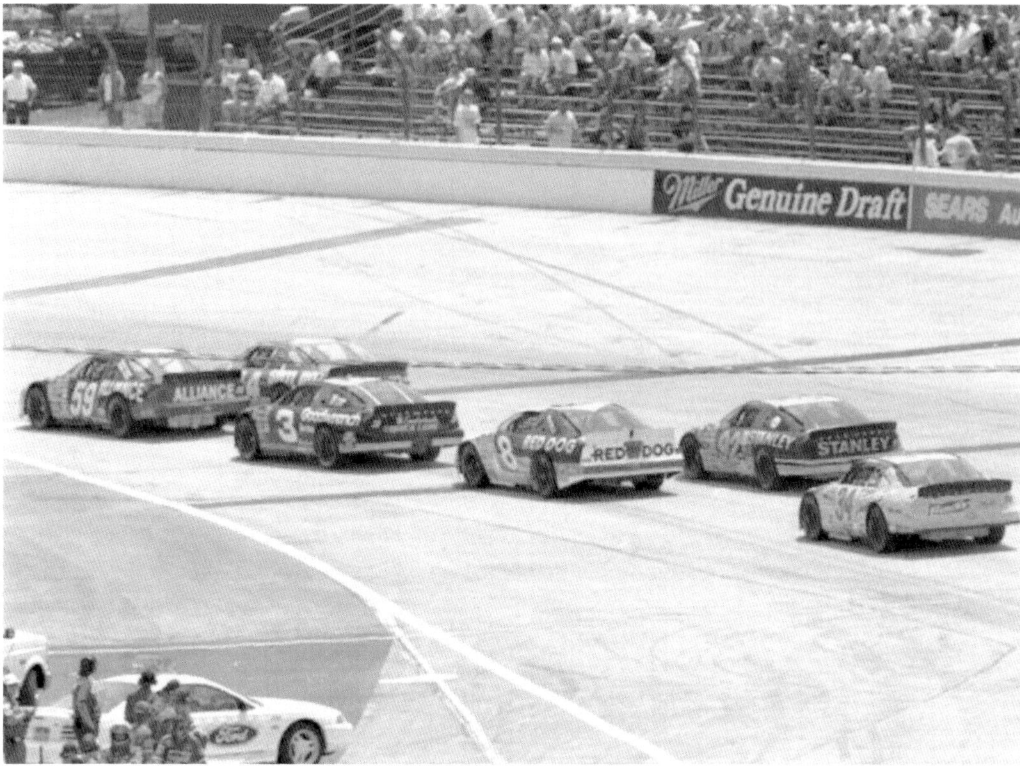

The lead cars are tightly bunched as they head into the first turn at the start of the July 2, 1995, Sears Auto Centers 250 Busch Grand National race. Pole-sitter Dennis Setzer (No. 59) leads a pack that includes David Green (No. 44), Jeff Green (No. 3), Kenny Wallace (No. 8), Larry Pearson (No. 92), and Mike McLaughlin (No. 34). Dale Jarrett (not pictured) won the event, while everyone pictured, except David Green, finished in the top 11. (RL/MC.)

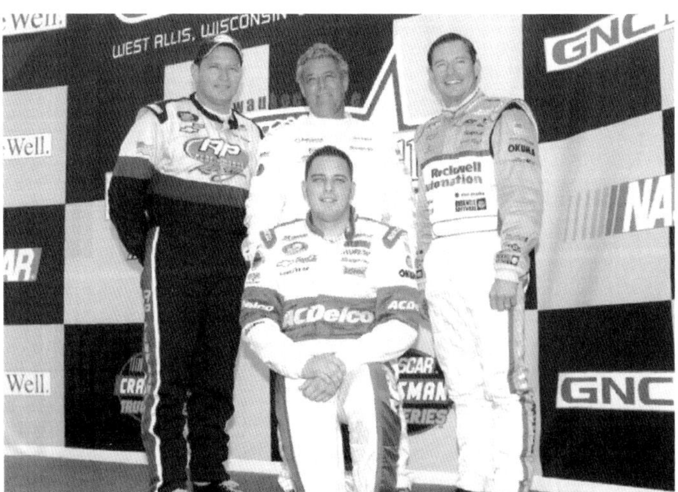

Four Sauter family members raced together for the last time at the June 28, 2002, NASCAR Nationwide (now Xfinity) Series at the Mile. Johnny is kneeling in front, and behind him stand, from left to right, Tim Sauter, patriarch Jim, and Jay. Tim races occasionally, Jay is retired, and Johnny competes in the NASCAR Camping World Truck Series. Unfortunately, Jim died on October 31, 2014. (RL/MC.)

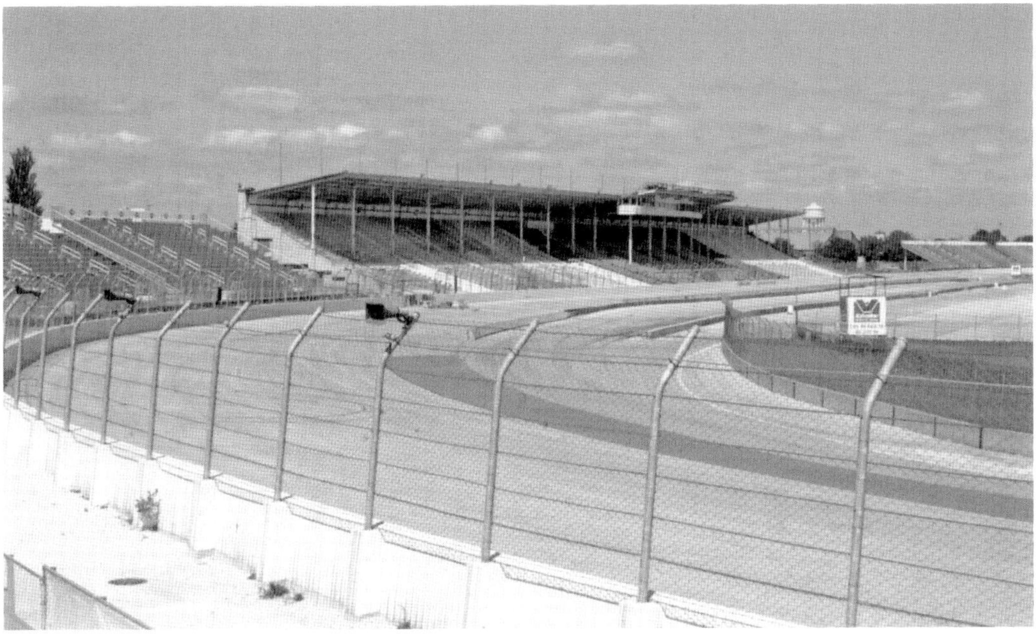

This photograph of the old Milwaukee Mile grandstand, taken August 29, 2002, marked the end of an era; the grandstand was demolished later in the fall of 2002 and replaced by the current structure for the 2003 season. The grandstand had been in place since the 1930s, constructed as a Works Progress Administration project during the Depression. (RL/MC.)

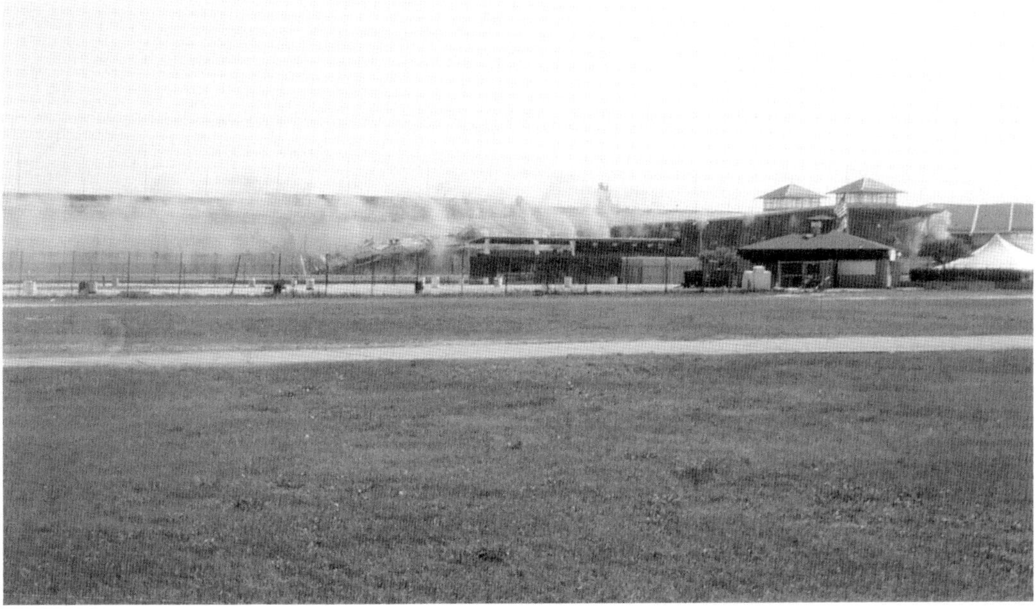

Bigger and better things were expected with the demolition of the stadium, and to help it along, National Midget Auto Racing Hall of Fame member Frank Burany triggered the implosion. Burany began his career in 1935, and it was only fitting that a longtime friend make the first strike. (GGAK.)

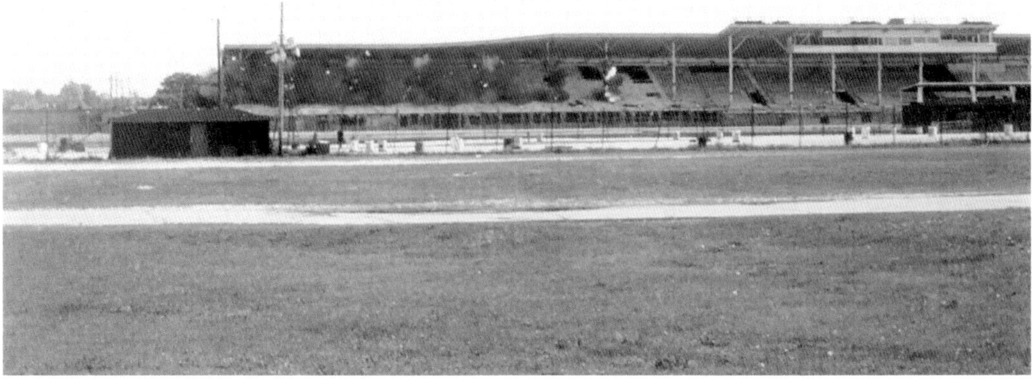

The new century brought an additional facelift to the facility. In June 2002, the grandstand was imploded to make way for a new and better experience for race enthusiasts. Added were a new main grandstand with enough seating for 25,000 fans, new aluminum seating for the north and south terraces, and additional restrooms and concession area. (TP.)

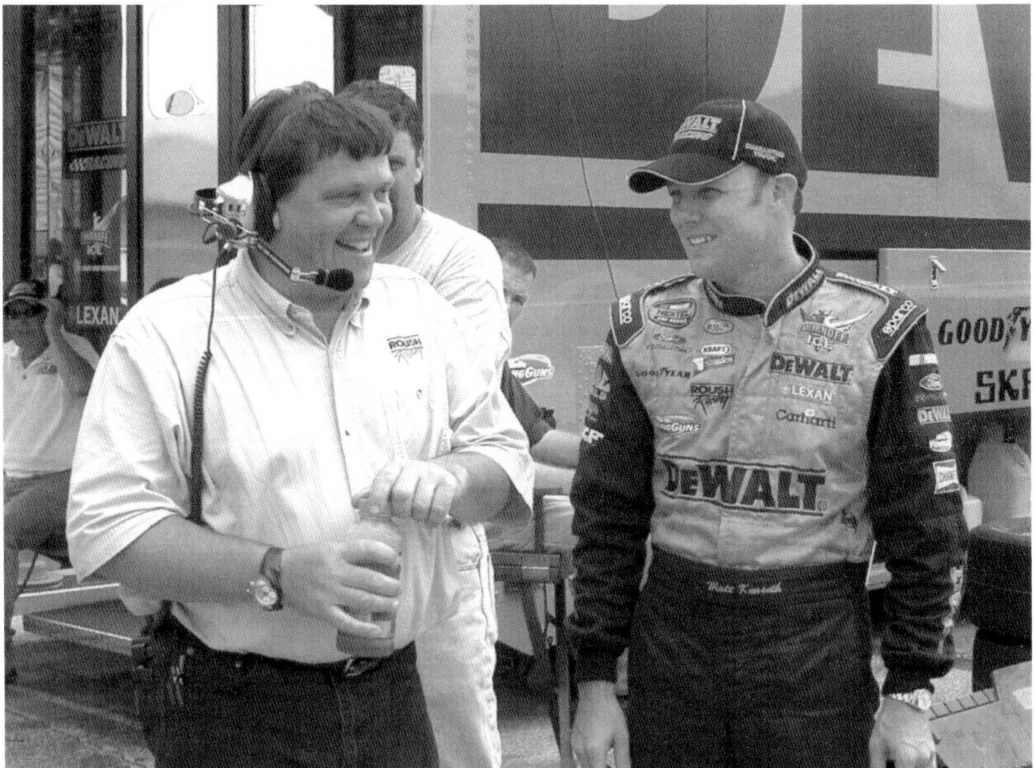

In a NASCAR test session at the track on July 13, 2004, driver Matt Kenseth, from Cambridge, and crew chief Robbie Reiser, from Allenton, are both smiling during some downtime. The pair had won the 2003 NASCAR Winston Cup (now Sprint Cup) championship at Roush Racing. Reiser is now vice president of competition for Roush-Fenway Racing, while Kenseth currently drives for Joe Gibbs Racing. (RL/MC.)

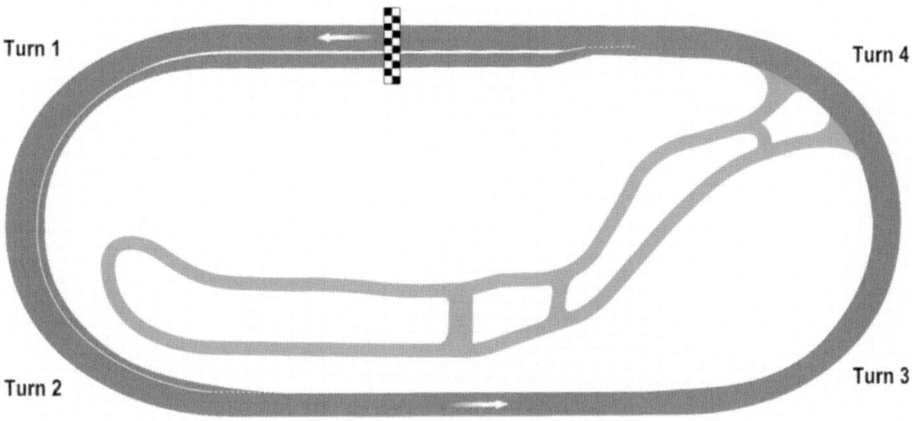

In 2004, the present track at the Milwaukee Mile experienced some changes. The road course was widened and resurfaced, with more crossovers added. The road course and oval have been used for various programs besides Indy car racing, including Rusty Wallace Racing Experience, Team Velocause, and other clubs. The Harry Miller Club and corporate functions bring a new energy to the track. Marketing the Mile takes a solid team, and that is the job at Andretti Sports Marketing. (NTRC.)

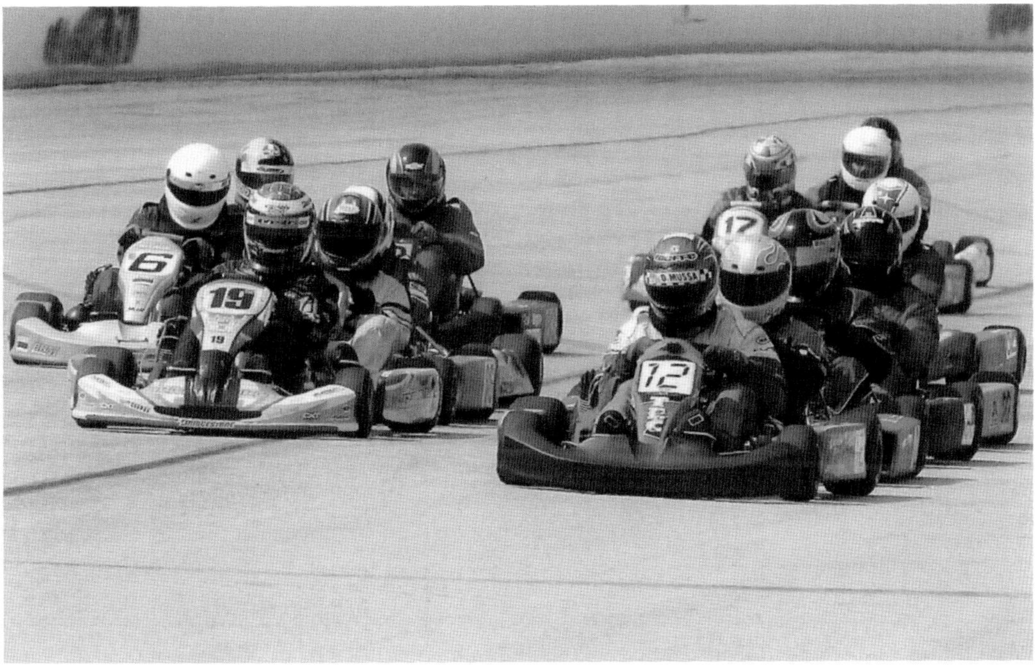

Kart racing at the Milwaukee Mile has been sanctioned by various organizations, including Badger Kart Club, sporadically over the years. This image from 2004 features drivers drafting on the oval. Kart racing offers the same excitement and challenges as other auto sports. Drivers as young as five can gain valuable experience in competitive racing, either on the oval or the infield course. Often, karting has served as the catalyst for today's IndyCar and NASCAR drivers. (TTa.)

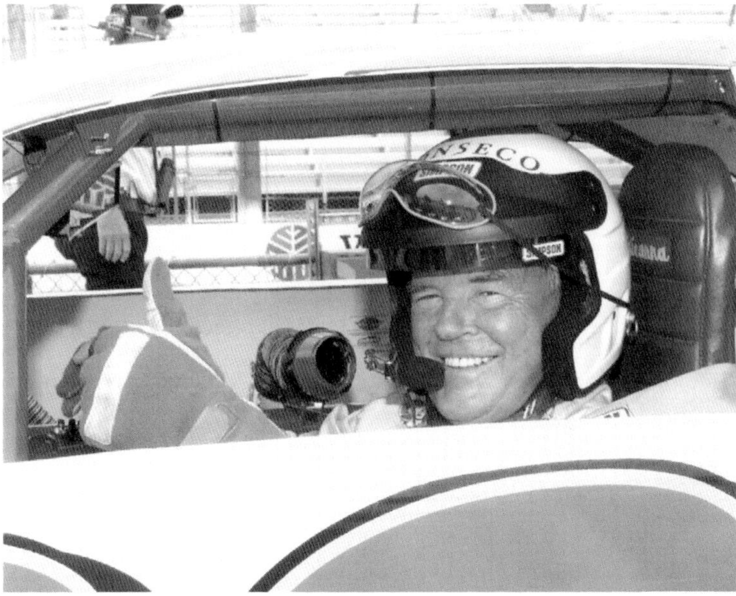

Dick Trickle presents a big smile and a thumbs-up as he prepares to hit the track for practice on August 26, 2005, in preparation for the Governor's Cup MARS Super Late Model 50, which was held on August 28. The race was at the twilight of Trickle's legendary short-track racing career, in which he won more than 1,000 races. (RL/MC.)

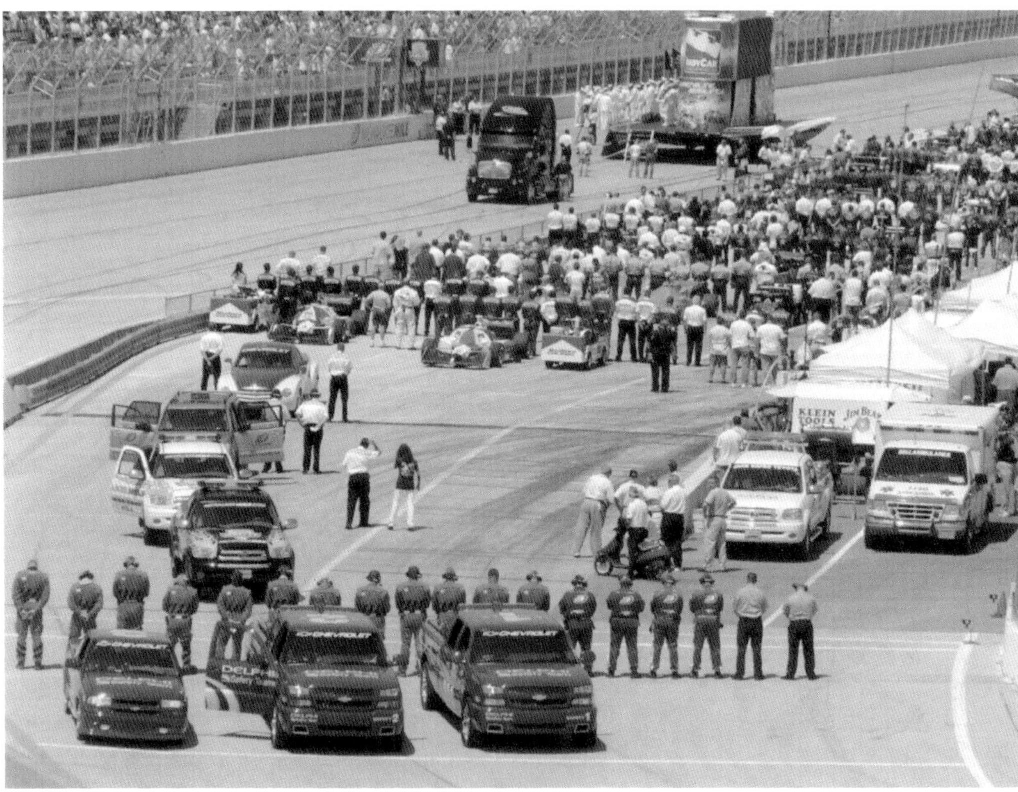

All crews, officials, and track personnel lined up to show respect during pre-race ceremonies, especially during the playing of the national anthem, prior to the start of the July 24, 2005, ABC Supply Co./A.J. Foyt 255 at the Milwaukee Mile Indy Racing League event, which was won by Sam Hornish Jr. (RL./MC.)

8

Saving the Mile

2010–Present

The loss of major races, coupled with legislative threats, rallied race fans, local businesses, and neighbors to "Save the Mile." Disappointed in the loss of the IndyCar race, fans held out a glimmer of hope when NASCAR announced a possible 2010 date for its Truck Series event. The year 2010 also brought two ASA Late Model Series stock-car races to the track for July and August. Seduced by the track's legend, IndyCar returned again in 2011; unfortunately, poor attendance cancelled any plans to return in 2012, or so it was thought.

The story of this legendary oval is not over yet; as with most stories, a champion comes to the rescue. In this case, it happened to be Michael Andretti. Intimately familiar with the Mile and part of its history, Michael Andretti knew he had to step in. Promoted by Andretti Sports Marketing, in partnership with Verizon for the Verizon IndyCar series, and sponsored in Milwaukee by ABC Supply and the Metro Milwaukee Honda Dealers, the Milwaukee Mile was offered another chance to win big. There may be no better way to promote a race than with a party, and that is exactly what IndyFest and Indy Lights are about: exciting, fun, family entertainment. The three-day event features music, food, driver meet and greets, and the best Indy car racing.

Outside of racing, the track is active from spring to fall hosting Sports Car Club of America (SCCA), ARCA Fest, Millers at Milwaukee vintage Indy car event, Young America on Wheels, the Rusty Wallace Racing Experience, and corporate celebrations. Bicycle racers have returned to the track in the form of Team VeloCause, featuring cycle enthusiasts with a passion for civic responsibility and a desire to contribute to their community and children at risk.

Positive and consistent events, featuring family-friendly programming, are what the Mile needs to save it from extinction. The legend will live on.

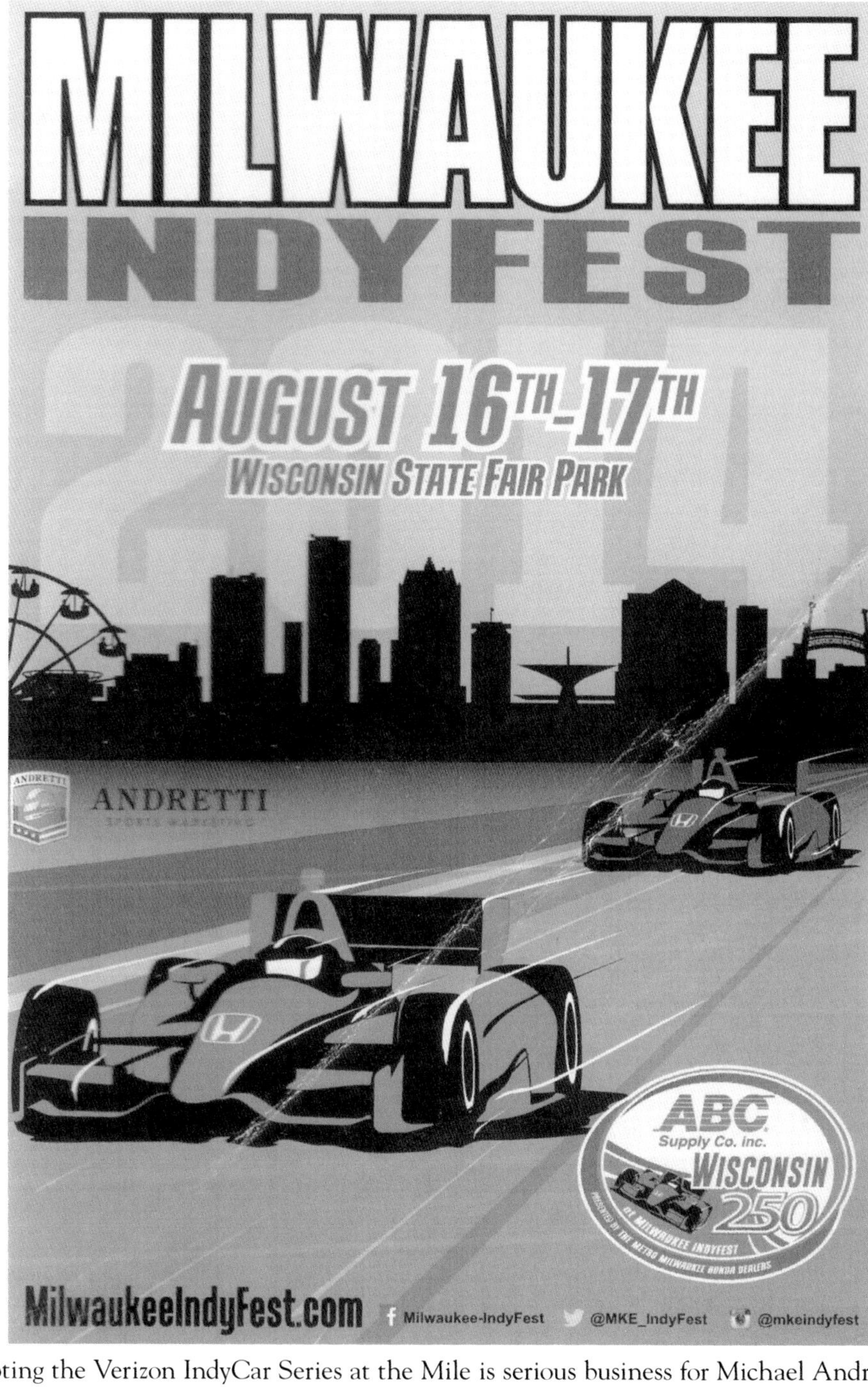

Promoting the Verizon IndyCar Series at the Mile is serious business for Michael Andretti and Andretti Sports Marketing. Two days of music, race cars, and drivers, plus wicked speeds, makes for one heck of a good time. Thanks to title sponsor ABC Supply Co. and David Hobbs Honda, race fans can again experience every emotion an Indy-style race can bring, right in their own backyard. (AC.)

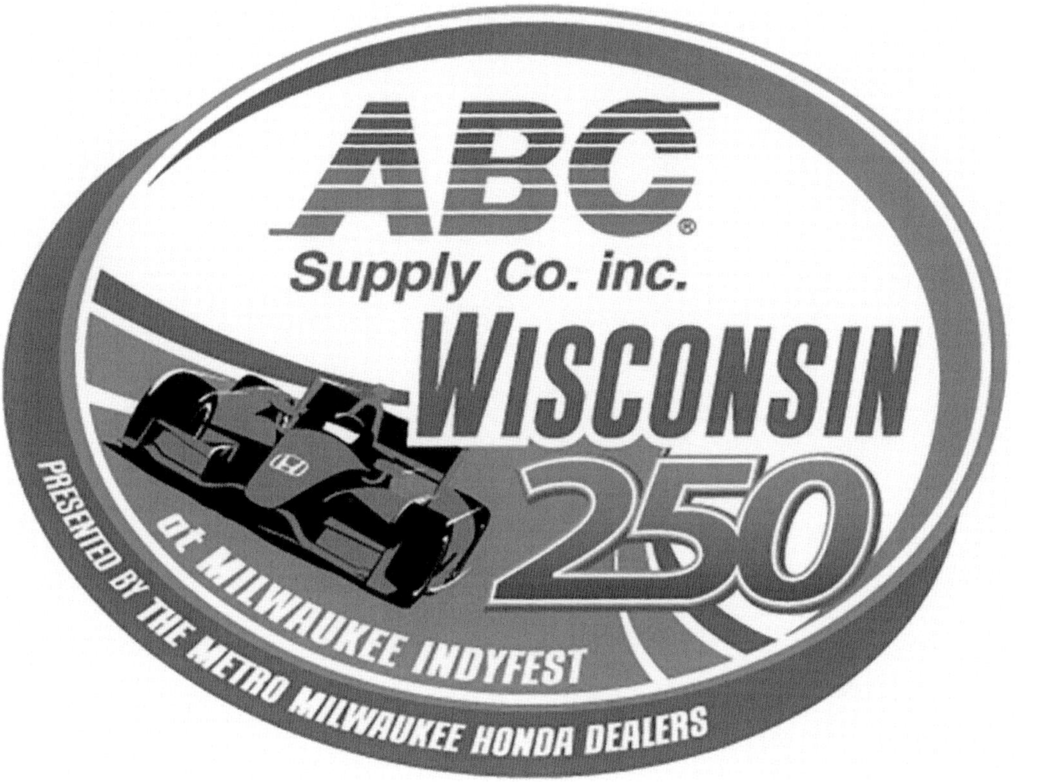

ABC Supply Co. Inc. was the title sponsor of the IndyCar series at the Mile for the 2014 and 2015 races. ABC Supply is the nation's largest wholesale distributor of exterior building products, tools, and related supplies. IndyFest is also presented by the Metro Milwaukee Honda dealers. (AC.)

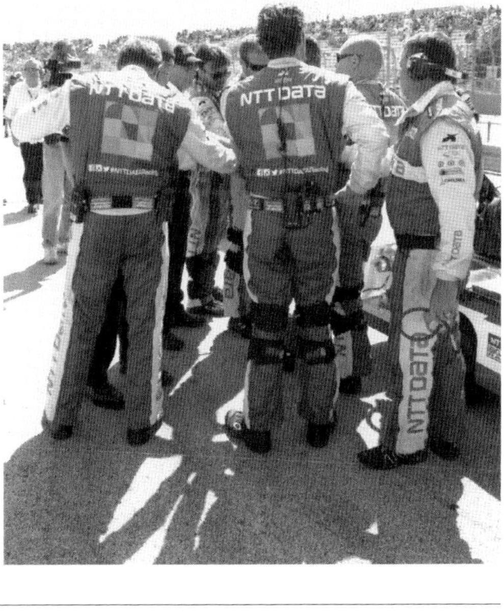

Huddled for briefing, Team NTT DATA's pit crew appears at the 2014 IndyFest sponsoring the Chip Ganassi Racing team. Driving for the team was No. 8 Ryan Briscoe. NTT DATA, a subsidiary of NTT Group, Nippon, is a Japanese telecommunication company. Given the broadcast potential IndyFest offers, large, small, and global businesses sponsor cars and drivers for the exposure. (DKM.)

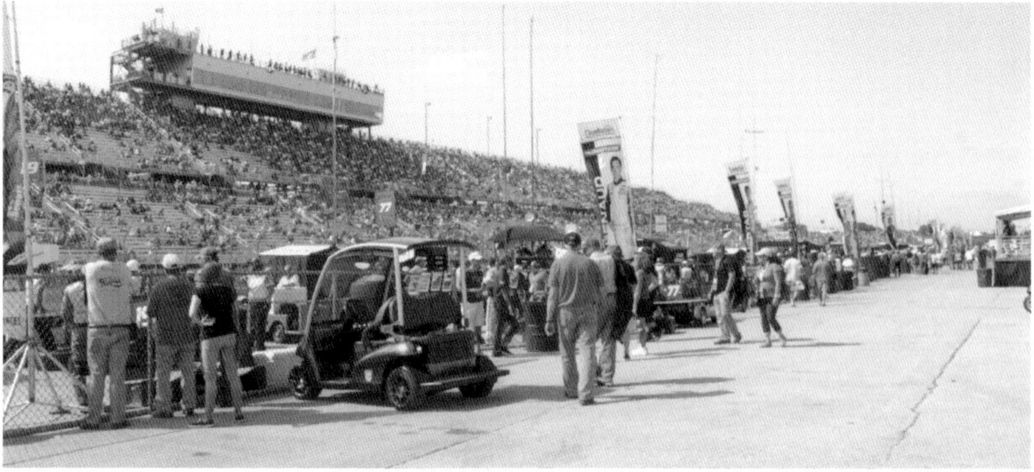

Fans fill the bleachers for an exciting day at the races. The 2014 IndyFest was a perfect blend of fun, fans, and great racing. With plenty of opportunity for fans to meet their favorite driver, check out the onsite garages, learn about the latest race technology, and experience great family fun, IndyFest is staged to draw fans to Milwaukee. (DKM.)

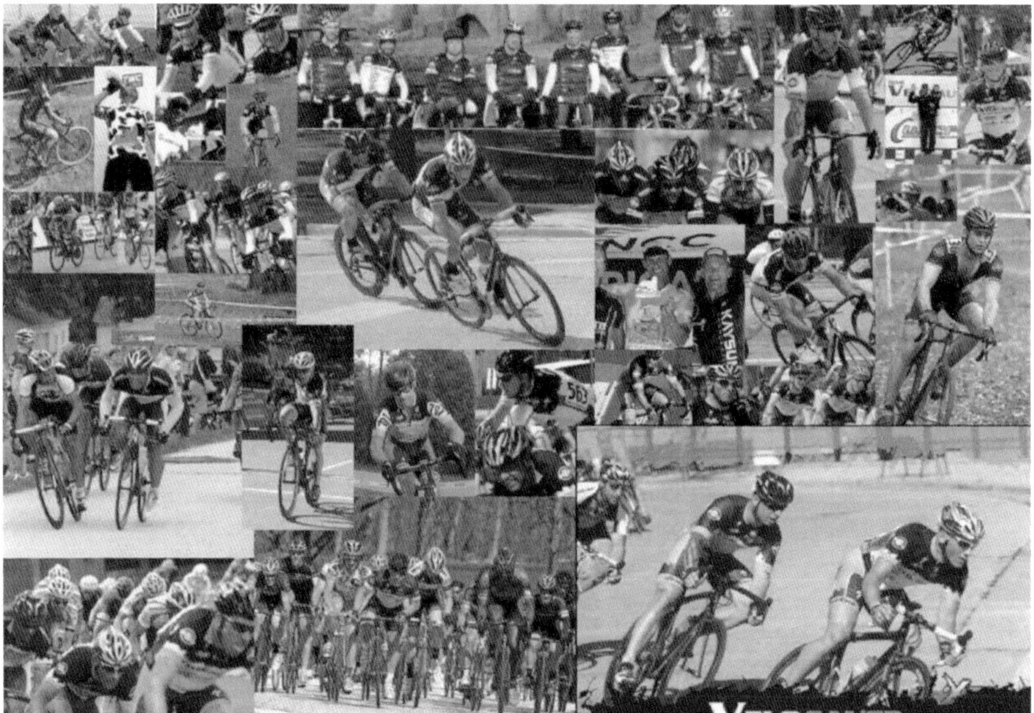

Team VeloCause has a mission declaration that reads, "Racing to Give!" And that is what they do. Teams of socially conscious master bicycle racers with a deep passion for civic responsibility use their competition winnings to enhance nonprofit organizations that support a better life for children. They race in sanctioned events across the Midwest and Wisconsin, including race dates at the Milwaukee Mile. (TV.)

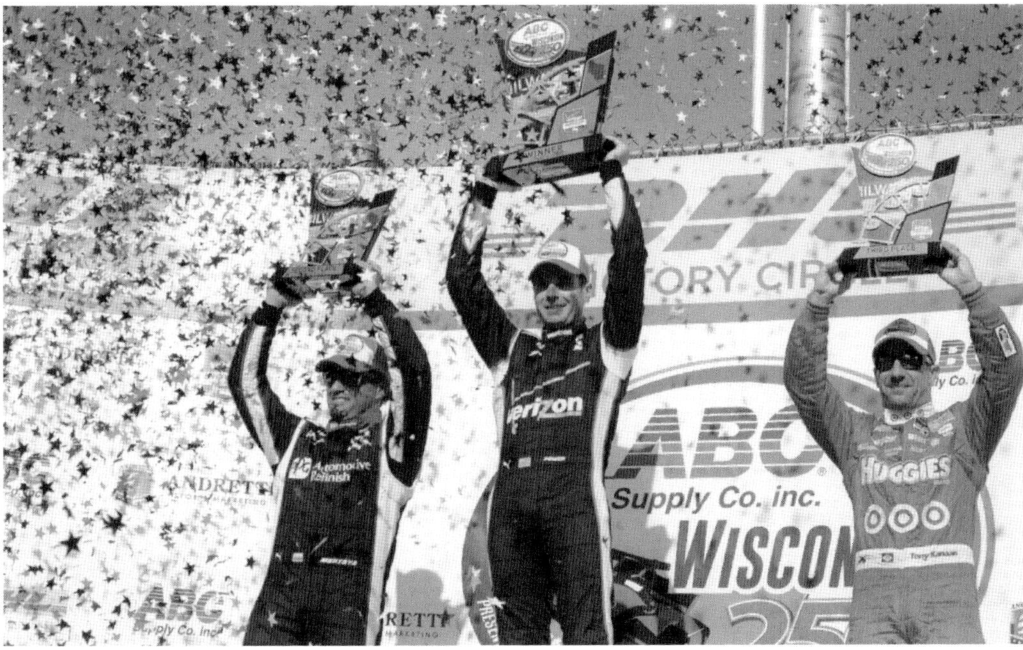

Will Power wins the 2014 ABC Supply Wisconsin 250 on his way to becoming the 2014 Verizon IndyCar champion. Joining him on the podium are Team Penske teammate Juan Pablo Montoya, who finished second, and Tony Kanaan with Chip Ganassi Racing, who finished third. (MB.)

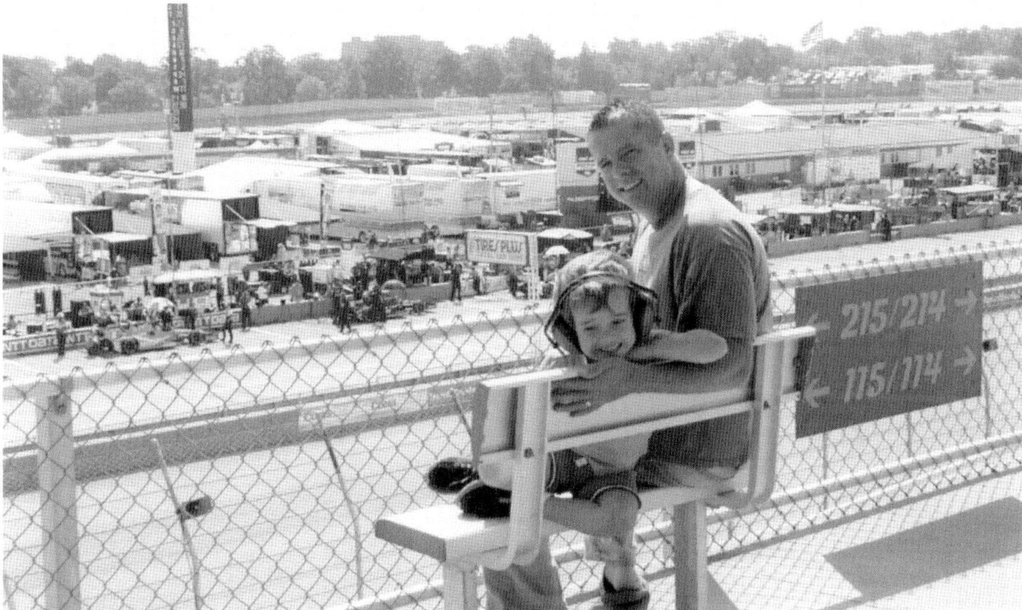

From the early days of racing, fans young and old were drawn by the excitement. Quality, thrilling programming kept the stands full. Drivers and promoters realized the importance of making race day an event that creates memories to cherish. It is about the future, and fans like Noah and his dad, Andrew Rich, of Oconomowoc, Wisconsin, cannot wait to share in the memories. (AC.)

THE MEN WHO RACE FOR THE CHECKERED FLAG

By: Neil Bonnett

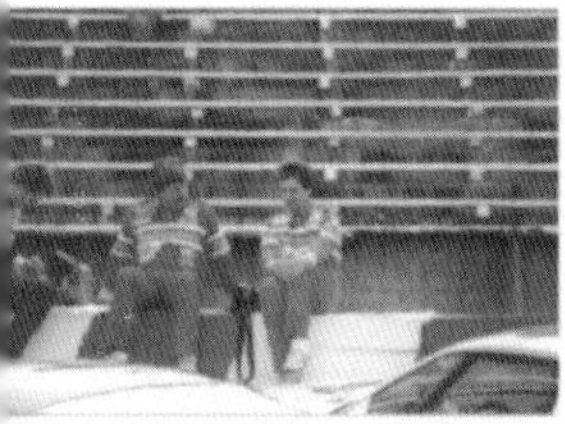

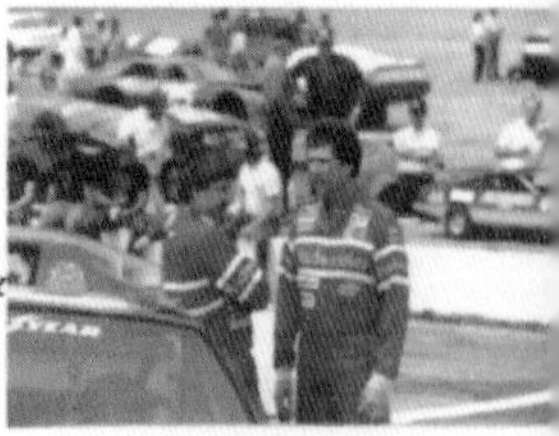

VERSE ONE

THERE'S A SPECIAL BREED OF MEN, WHO LOVE TO TAKE A CHANCE

OCTANE AND FAST TRACKS ARE THEIR NUMBER ONE ROMANCE

YOU'LL FIND THEM AT THE STOCK CAR TRACKS AROUND THE USA

FROM THE SMALLEST OF THE DIRT TRACKS TO THE SUPER SPEEDWAY

CHORUS

THAT'S THE MEN WHO RACE FOR THE CHECKERED FLAG

A FLYING MASS OF METAL AS THEY MASH UPON THE PETAL

THEY TOOK A CHANCE WITH DEATH AND LIVED TO BRAG

THAT'S THE MEN WHO RACE FOR THE CHECKERED FLAG

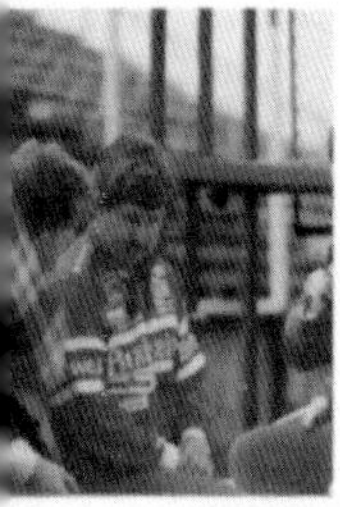

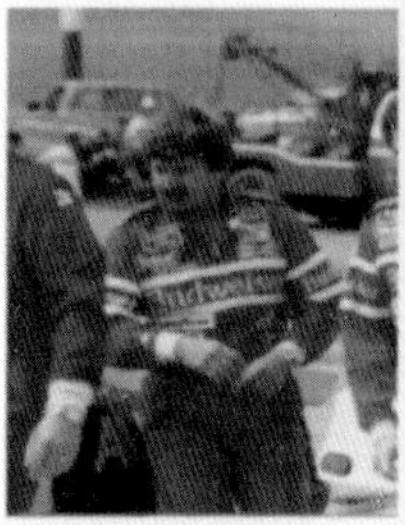

VERSE TWO

THEY SPEND THEIR HARD EARNED MONEY, AS THEY GO FROM TRACK TO TRACK

DON'T MATTER IF THEY WIN OR LOSE, YOU CAN BET THEY'LL BE BACK

FOR THE MIGHTY ROAR OF AN ENGINE, IS ALL THEY CAN HEAR

AND TO GET THAT CHECKERED FLAG IS THE THING THEY HOLD DEAR

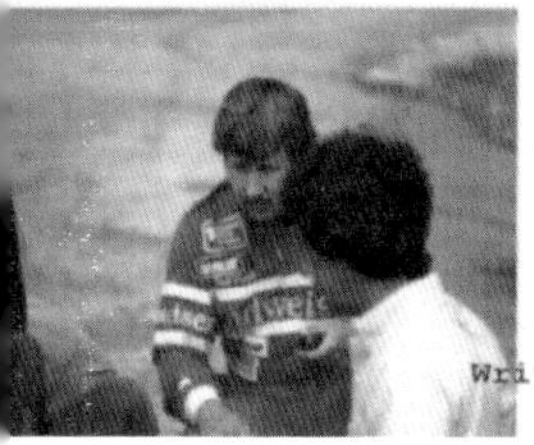

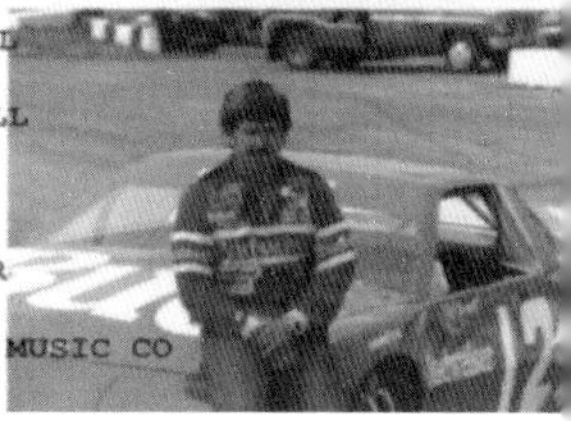

VERSE THREE

YOU'VE NEVER HEARD THEIR NAMES AND YOU PROBABLY NEVER WILL

IT'S A MIGHTY DANGEROUS CLIMB TO THE TOP OF RACE TRACK HILL

FOR EVERY PETTY AND ALLISON WHO BECOMES A SUPER STAR

THERE'S MANY A THOUSAND DRIVERS WHO'LL NEVER GET THAT FAR

Written by: George Wells and Billy Stone

There are record books, box scores, and stories about race drivers, but none tell a driver's tale better than the song "The Men Who Race for the Checkered Flag." Sung by Neil Bonnett and written by George Wells and Billy Stone of FTH Music Company (BMI), the lyrics speak of the bravery and dedication that drivers hold in their hearts. The song can be heard on the Facebook page of the same name. (GW.)

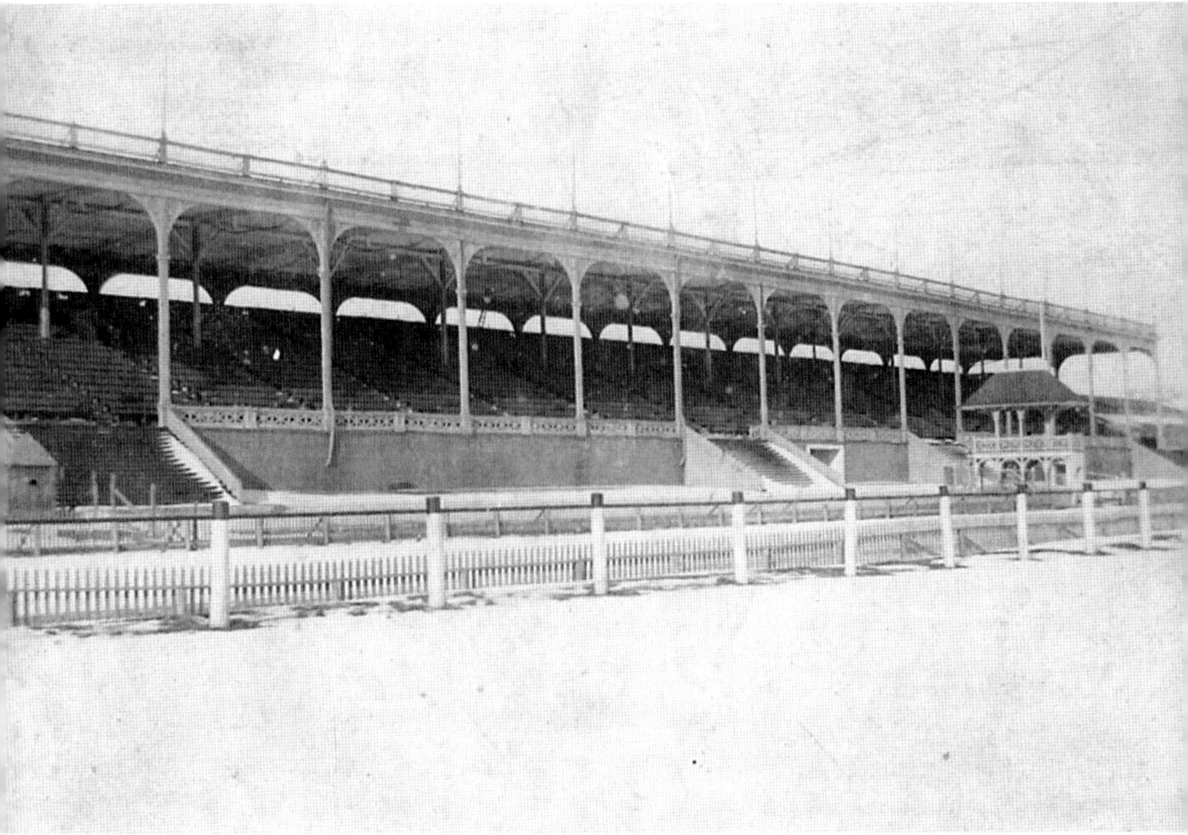

The State Fair Park stadium, pictured around 1910, sits frozen in time, as do the memories that have been told and retold over the past 130-plus years. From the beginning, the track served one purpose: speed. From the first hoof to hit the dirt to today's Indy cars, it has been one heck of a ride. (TMS.)